250th Summer Exhibition Illustrated 2018

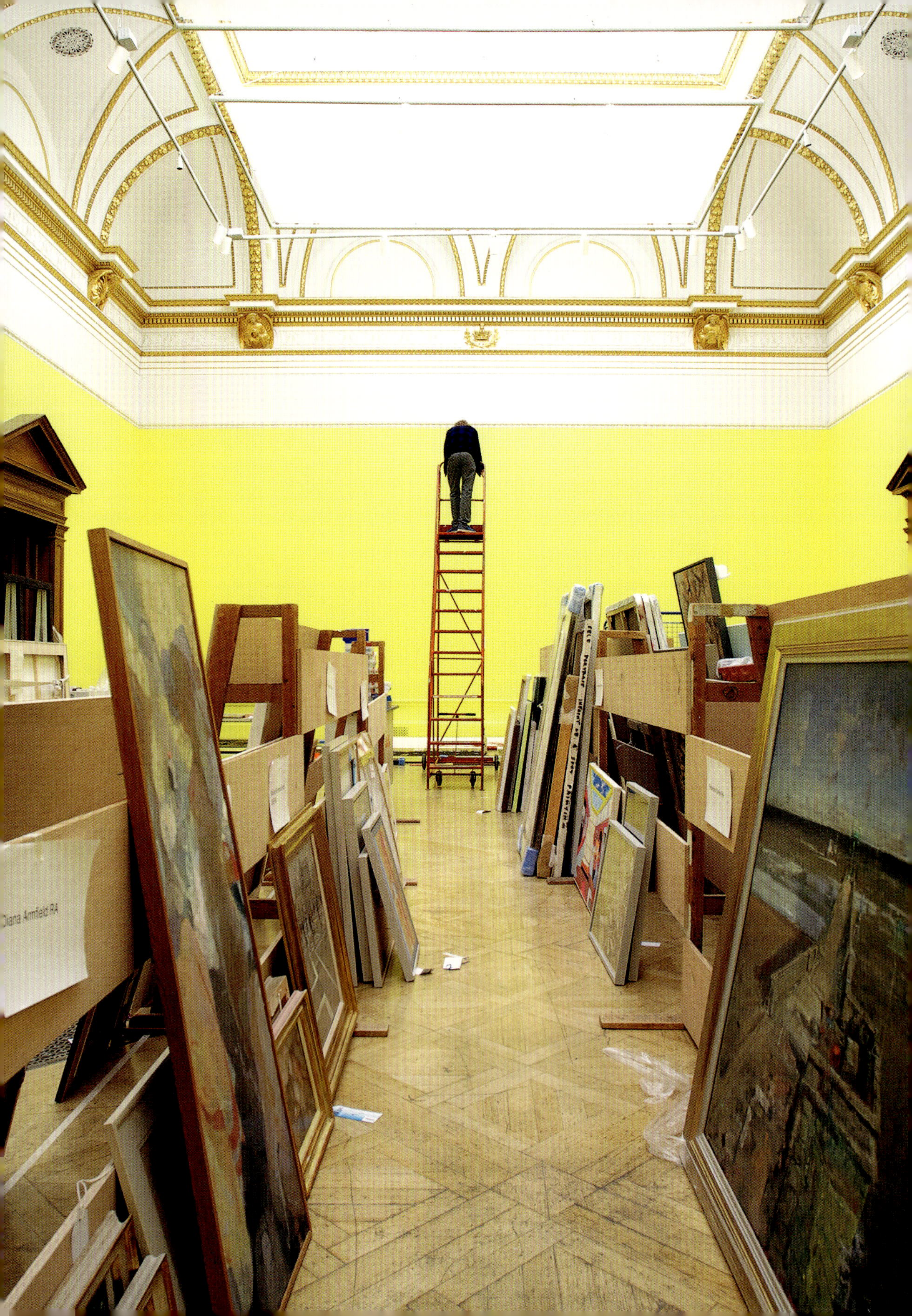
Diana Armfield RA

A Selection from the 250th Summer Exhibition
Edited by Grayson Perry CBE RA

250th Summer Exhibition Illustrated 2018

Sponsored by

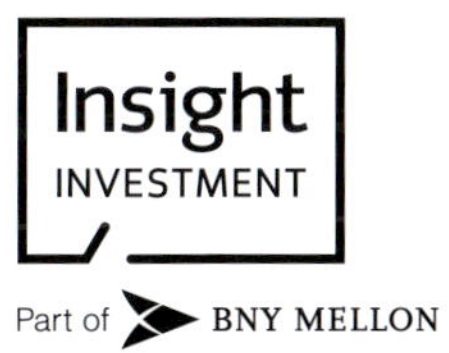

Royal Academy of Arts

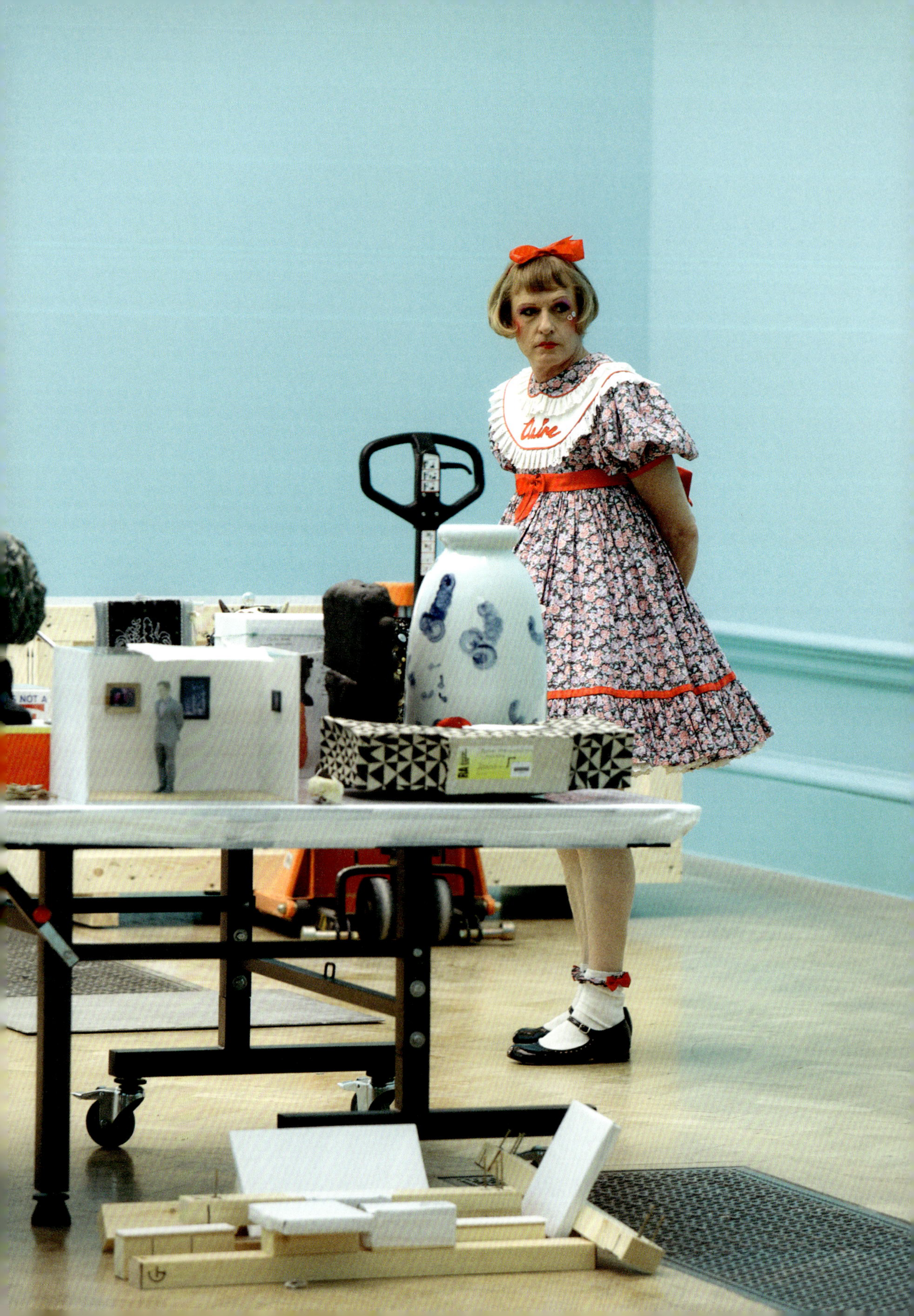
Claire
NOT A

Contents

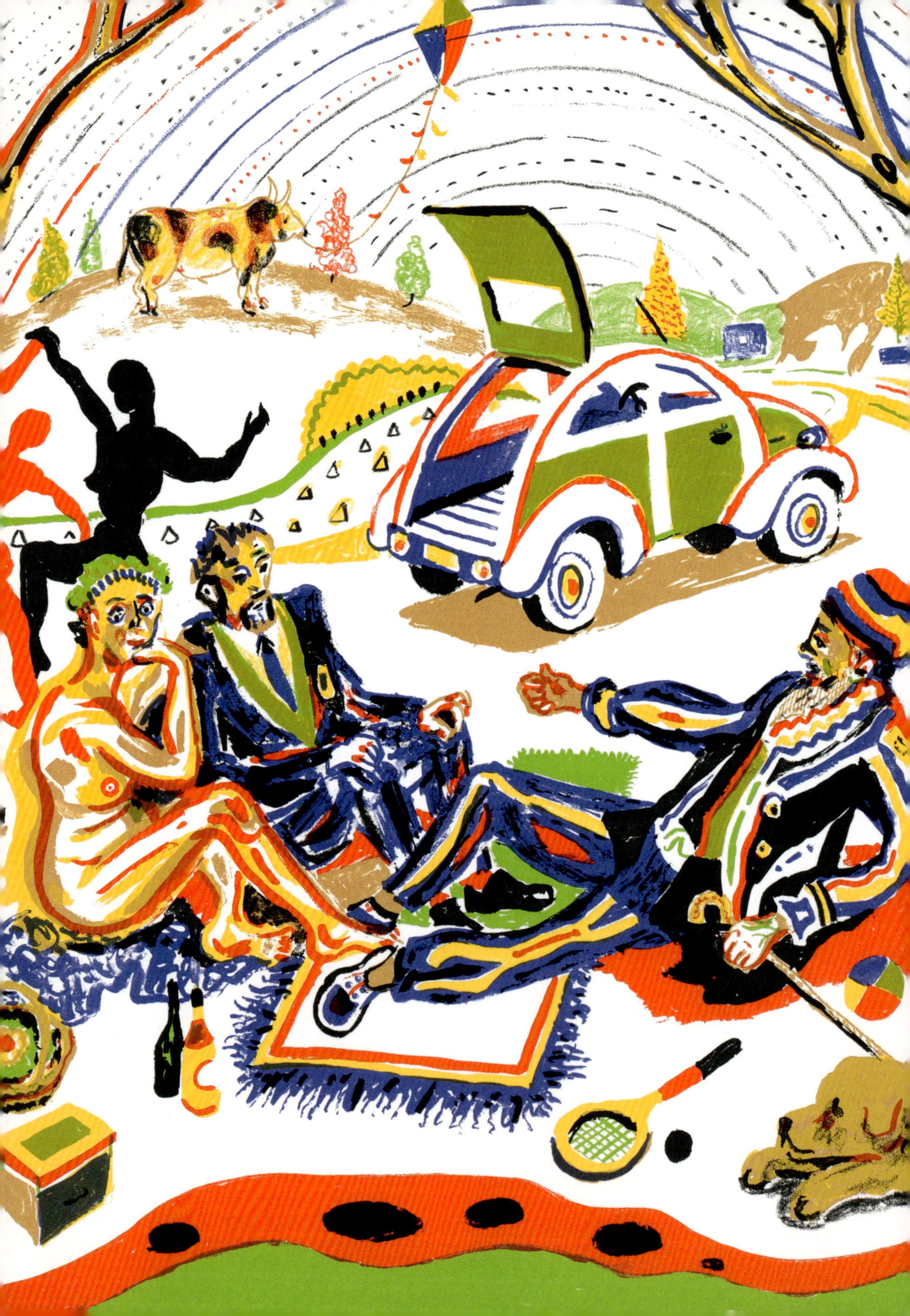

President's Foreword

Christopher Le Brun PRA

2018 is an historic year for the Royal Academy, as we celebrate the 250th anniversary of our foundation. Shortly before the opening of the Summer Exhibition, we were delighted to inaugurate the New RA, linking Burlington Gardens and Burlington House. The completion of this project has effectively doubled the Academy's size, providing us with a wonderful new lecture theatre and gallery spaces as well as putting a spotlight on the vital activity of the RA Schools.

One of the primary objectives of the founders of the Royal Academy was to establish a fine-art school and to fund it from the proceeds of an annual exhibition of recent work by Royal Academicians and other artists and architects. This year, therefore, also marks the Summer Exhibition's 250th year. The exhibition has run every year without exception for the entirety of the Academy's existence and continues to uphold the principles upon which the Academy was founded. We are particularly proud that the funds generated by the Summer Exhibition still allow our Schools to provide each student with the benefit of a free art education.

Council began to ruminate early on which of our Academicians might be best suited to the challenge of coordinating the Summer Exhibition in this celebratory year. Quite quickly, we decided to ask Grayson Perry. His refreshingly broad and open-minded interests in the fine and applied arts, coupled with his fascination with the notion of taste in art – not least the changing tastes over the many decades of the Exhibition – marked him out as the obvious choice.

Within this celebration we are sad to mark the passing of two painter Royal Academicians: Gillian Ayres and Bernard Dunstan. Memorial displays for both can be found in the Exhibition. Just as the hang was commencing we were saddened to learn of the deaths of the architect Will Alsop and the Danish painter and sculptor Per Kirkeby. A memorial display of their work will be arranged for next year's Exhibition.

On behalf of the Royal Academy and Council, I would like to thank and congratulate Grayson Perry for the wit and enthusiasm he has brought to the coordinator's role. Also very deserving of our thanks are the members of this year's Summer Exhibition Committee, who have supported and worked with Grayson throughout the year: Phyllida Barlow, Piers Gough, Allen Jones, David Mach, Humphrey Ocean, Chris Orr, Cornelia Parker, Tom Phillips, Conrad Shawcross and Emma Stibbon.

Our thanks go to Insight Investment, for whose unstinting support we remain extremely grateful.

Sponsor's Preface

For 250 years, the Royal Academy of Arts Summer Exhibition has set the stage for both established and emerging artists to contribute to this wonderfully unique, challenging and uplifting showcase of contemporary art.

Our association with the Exhibition has spanned more than a decade and we are honoured to play a role in its enduring success. As the world's largest open-submission exhibition, it provides such a unique opportunity for artists from all walks of life to be associated with this world-leading cultural spectacle.

In this remarkable anniversary year, the founding principles of the Summer Exhibition remain clear to see. Visitors to the Exhibition will experience an extraordinary array of works, which, under the curatorial stewardship of Grayson Perry, reaches the furthest corners of the RA's galleries and spreads further still onto the streets of London's West End in a fitting celebration of 'art made now'.

We hope everyone who experiences this year's selection of works will share our enthusiasm for this truly unique display of artistic endeavour.

Abdallah Nauphal
Chief Executive Officer

Sponsored by

Insight
INVESTMENT

Part of BNY MELLON

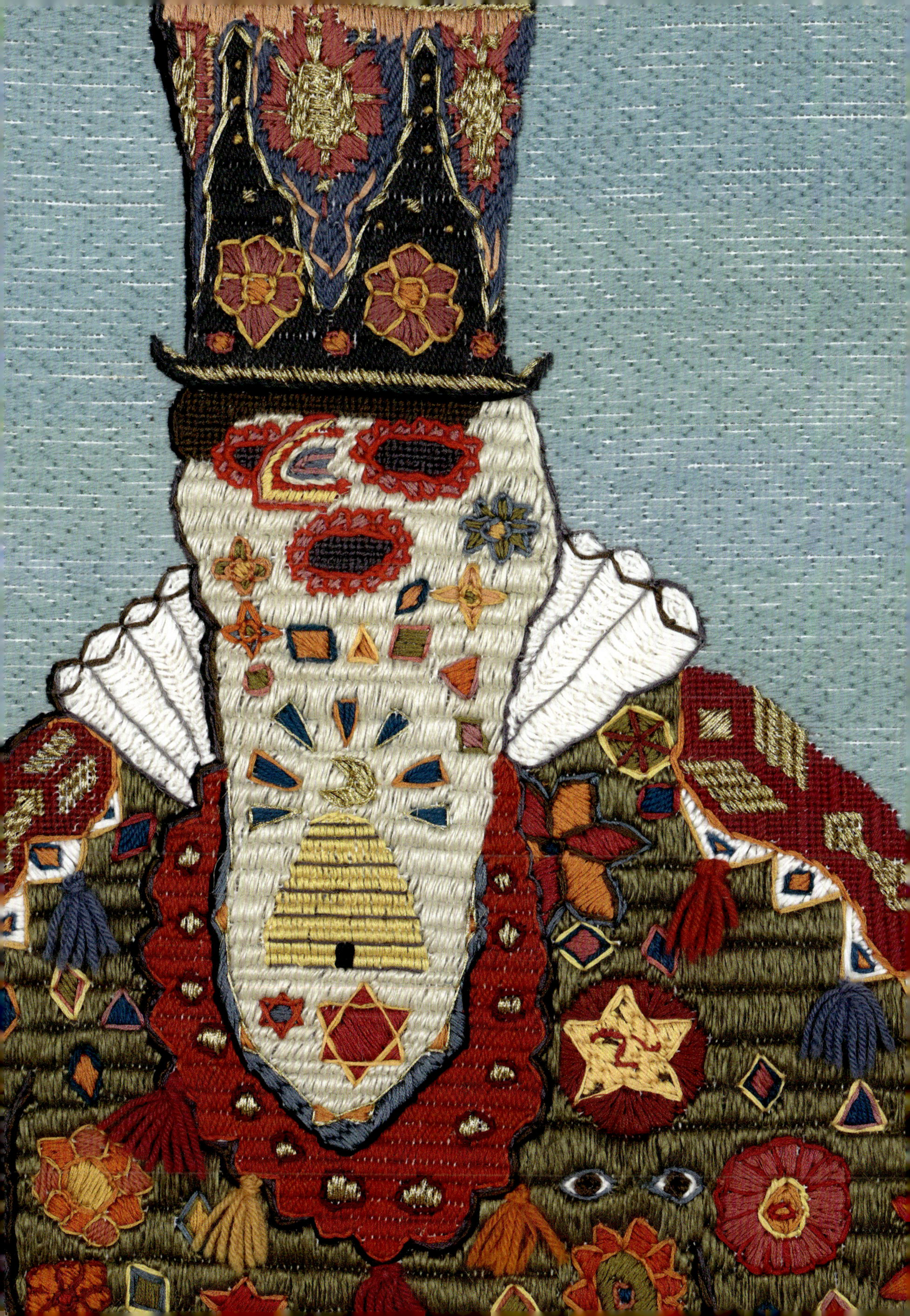

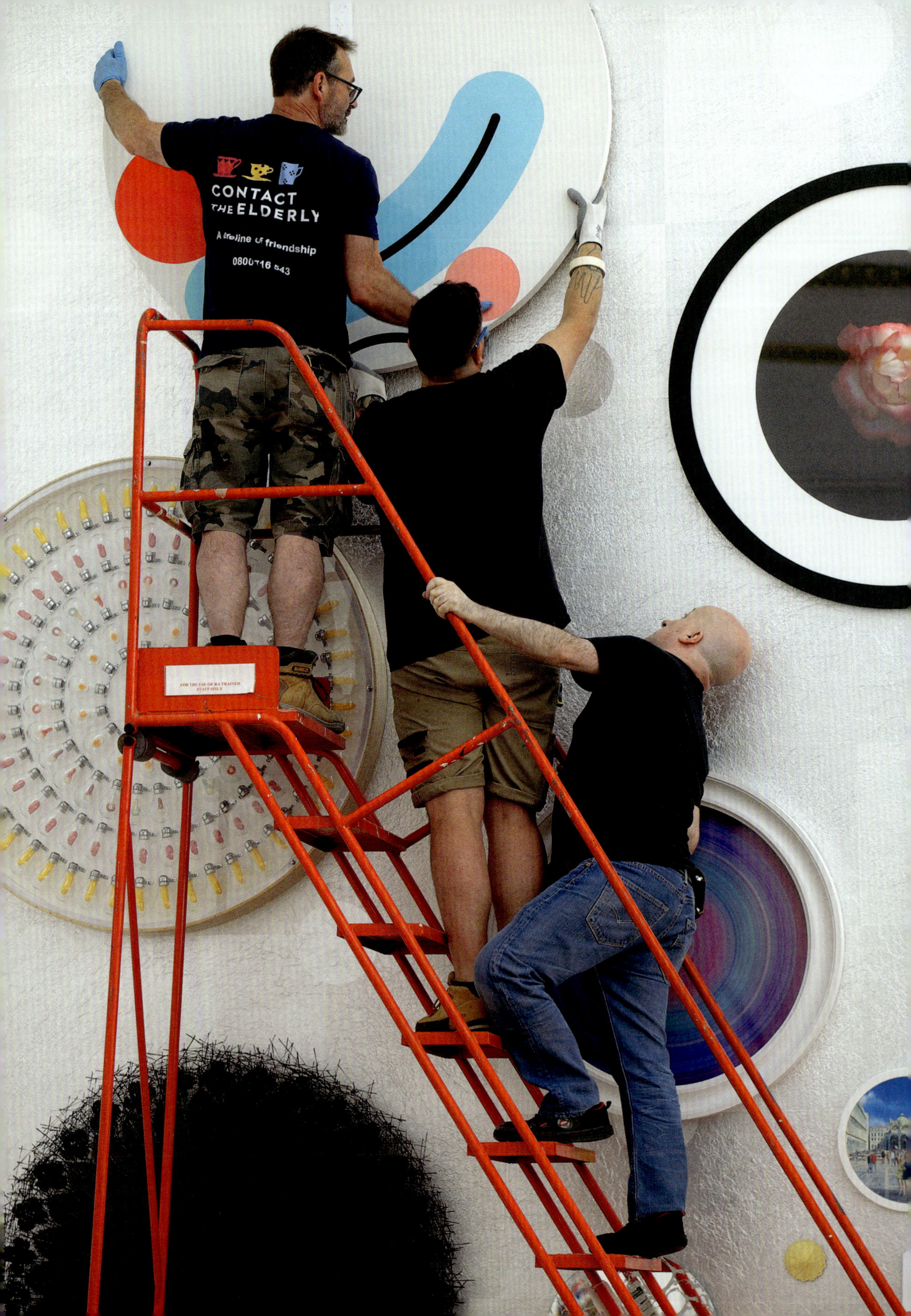
CONTACT THE ELDERLY
0800 716 543

The 250th Summer Exhibition

Grayson Perry CBE RA

This essay, like everything to do with the Royal Academy Summer Exhibition, was put together in a hurry with little time for reflection or revision. I think this very necessary spontaneity is a good thing. The art world often suffers from overthinking things. I record here my immediate responses to my experience of being the coordinator at a time when we are midway through the hanging process.

I truly believe the Summer Exhibition is one of the great glories of the Royal Academy, a chaotic swirling anachronism in a contemporary art world often characterised these days by a prim intellectual orderliness. Well over a thousand artworks packed into some of the world's grandest galleries, half of them sent in by the general public and half the work of members of a 250-year-old artists' trade union. It's a village-hall art show on a gigantic scale mashed up with an eccentric survey of the current output of a couple of hundred established professionals.

The Summer Exhibition is unique. Nowhere else will you find this mixture, where blue-chip artists and architects like Anselm Kiefer, David Adjaye, Tracey Emin, David Hockney and Marina Abramović hang cheek by jowl with Joe and Joanna Bloggs from Bridlington who have plugged away in their studios for decades and never made the big time. It's huge and baggy, loved and loathed, serious and farcical. I find myself increasingly addicted to this odd mix of tradition, high status, democracy and pandemonium. Unlike the famous beef tea that they traditionally serve the hanging committee…

The most shocking aspect that struck me as I took on the role of coordinator for this year's show was how fast it all happens. A high-profile exhibition of this magnitude and duration would normally be at least three years in the planning. Themes and theories would be agonised over, loans delicately negotiated, curators would pore over doll's-house-sized gallery models, artists would be flattered and coaxed into contributing. Of course the Summer Exhibition has all of that, but it is compressed into a tenth of the time. There is no time to hone an argument and make it material, no time to tinker with the exquisite. The Summer Exhibition is a juggernaut careening towards a week of annual rituals and parties at the beginning of June. It will not be stopped and I have felt barely in control, and that is how it should be.

As I crossed the courtyard at the beginning of March on my way to begin the week-long selection process for the send-in artworks, I had the sobering

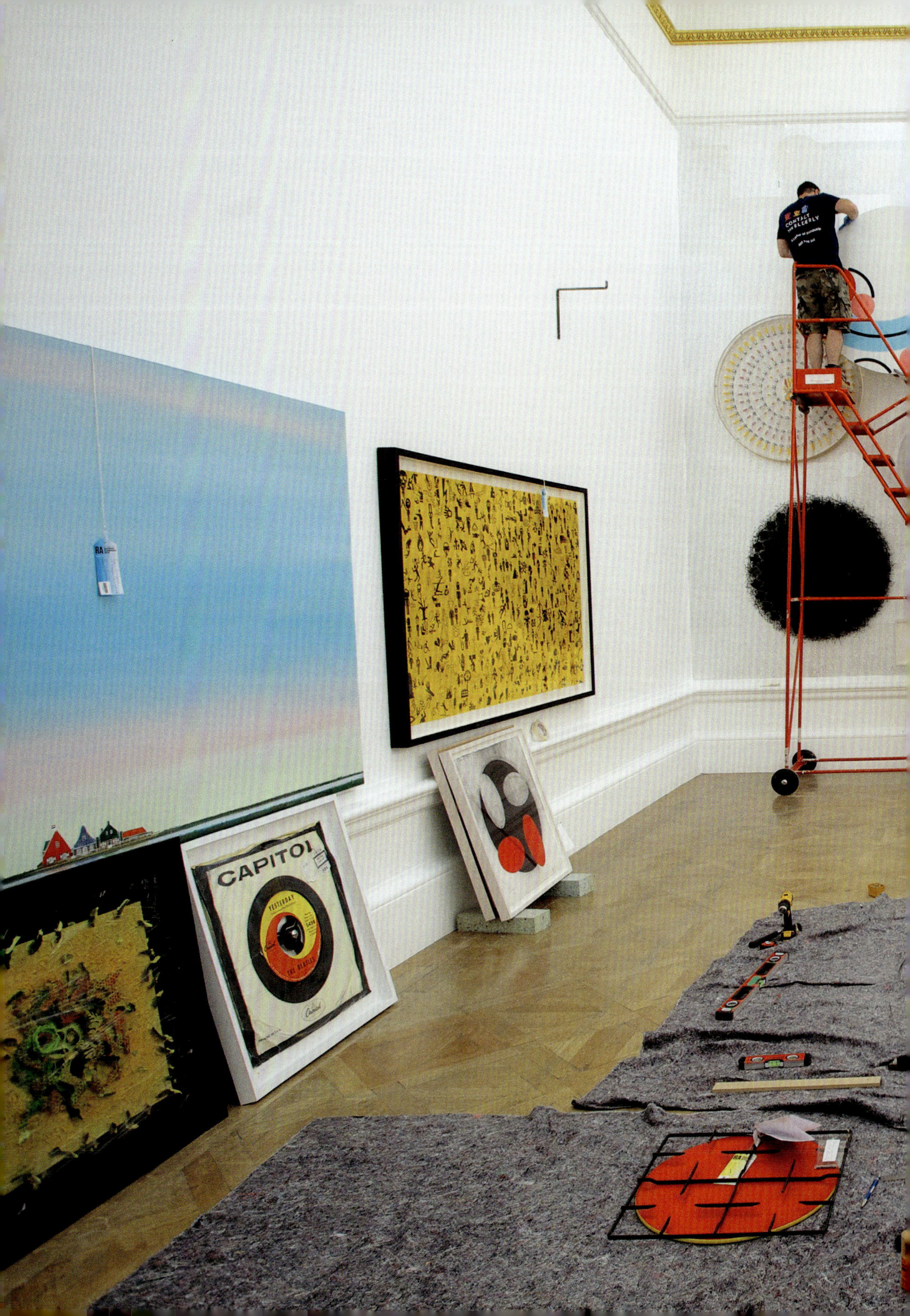
CAPITOL
YESTERDAY
THE BEATLES

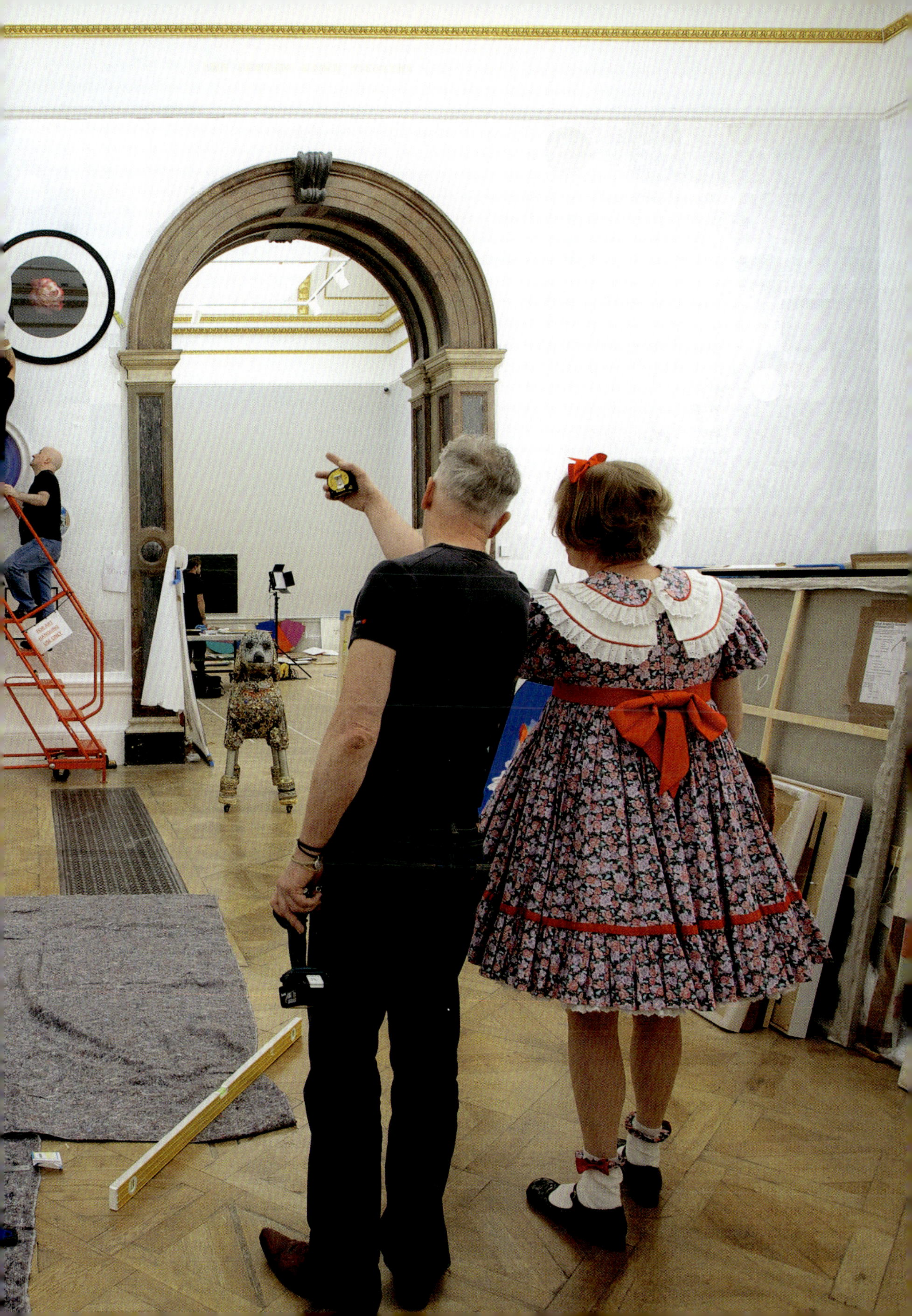

thought that I had not seen a single work, either by members of the Academy or members of the public. Yet, in three months' time, the whole exhibition would be hung and signed off. Standing in the freezing slush beneath the statue of Joshua Reynolds, I fell to my knees and gave silent prayer that I would cope (no I didn't). I thought of the glitzy preview party where colourfully dressed celebrities would cross the red carpet in front of the paparazzi in the summer sunshine, on this very spot! In three months!

My first task was to assemble the committee. Some were there as of right, by rotation, but others I could select. I tried to put together a diverse chorus of voices, diverse not just demographically but artistically too. Being the RA, many of my choices were just too busy on their own projects to commit to the task. The committee that assembled for our first meeting consisted of the President, Christopher Le Brun, who is the chairman, Cornelia Parker, Conrad Shawcross, Tom Phillips, Allen Jones, Phyllida Barlow, Piers Gough, Chris Orr, Emma Stibbon, David Mach and Humphrey Ocean. I was delighted with the group because they all fulfilled the most important criteria, they would be fun to be around and they would hopefully be *fairly* easygoing, qualities that are paramount during the give and take of selecting and hanging a whole heap of art.

When I was first approached about becoming the coordinator on this our 250th birthday year, I was flattered but also daunted. I was tempted by the offer not only of heading up this glittering facet of 'the season' in such an auspicious year, but also by the promise of a much expanded venue. The plan was to have the Summer Exhibition occupy the entire campus: the grand galleries in Burlington House, the gilded splendour of the Fine Rooms and the refurbished newly top-lit Sackler Galleries, plus the newly completed spaces across David Chipperfield's bridge in Burlington Gardens. My head was turned by visions of an almost Biennale-sized exhibition, a rambling souk of varied spaces each given character by an RA. I recruited my Summer Exhibition committee with this vision in mind, including artists like Phyllida Barlow who I knew could handle a grand gesture.

Then, bit by bit, my fantasy of a gargantuan sprawling art experience was reined in. First came an exhibition called 'The Great Spectacle' about the history of the Summer Show that would occupy the Fine Rooms and two of the galleries normally used. Then I was told Tacita Dean was to mount a show

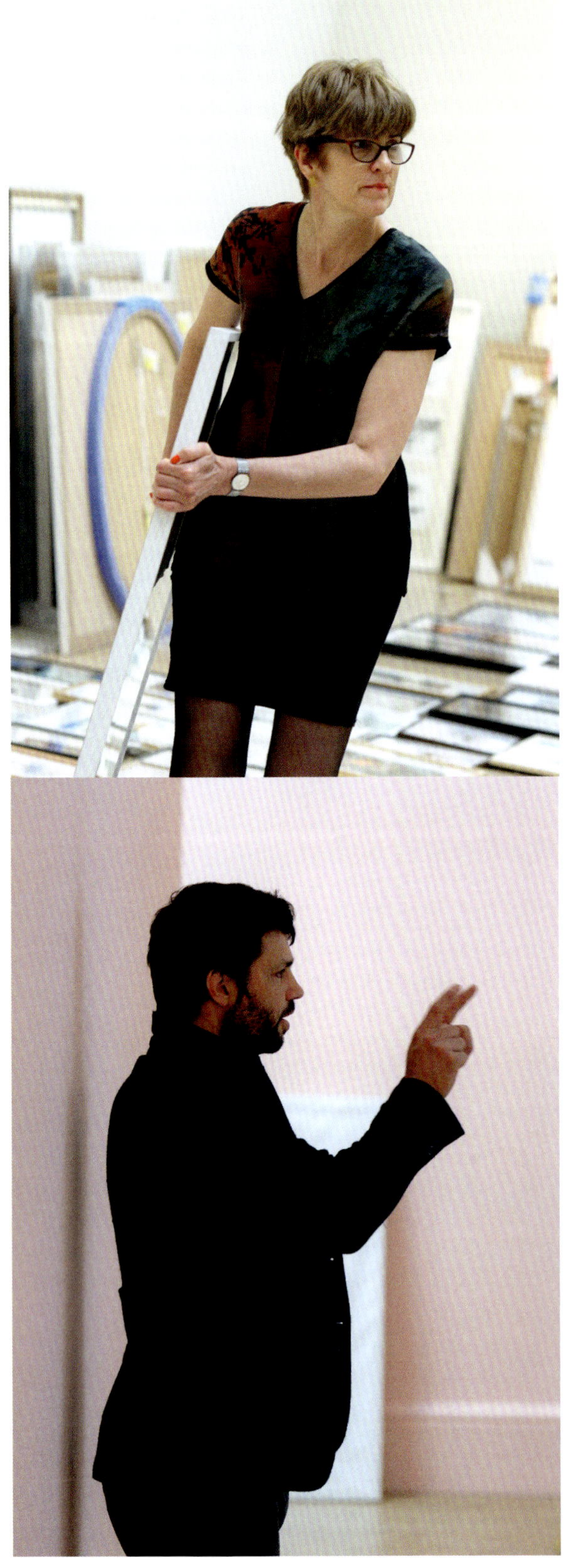

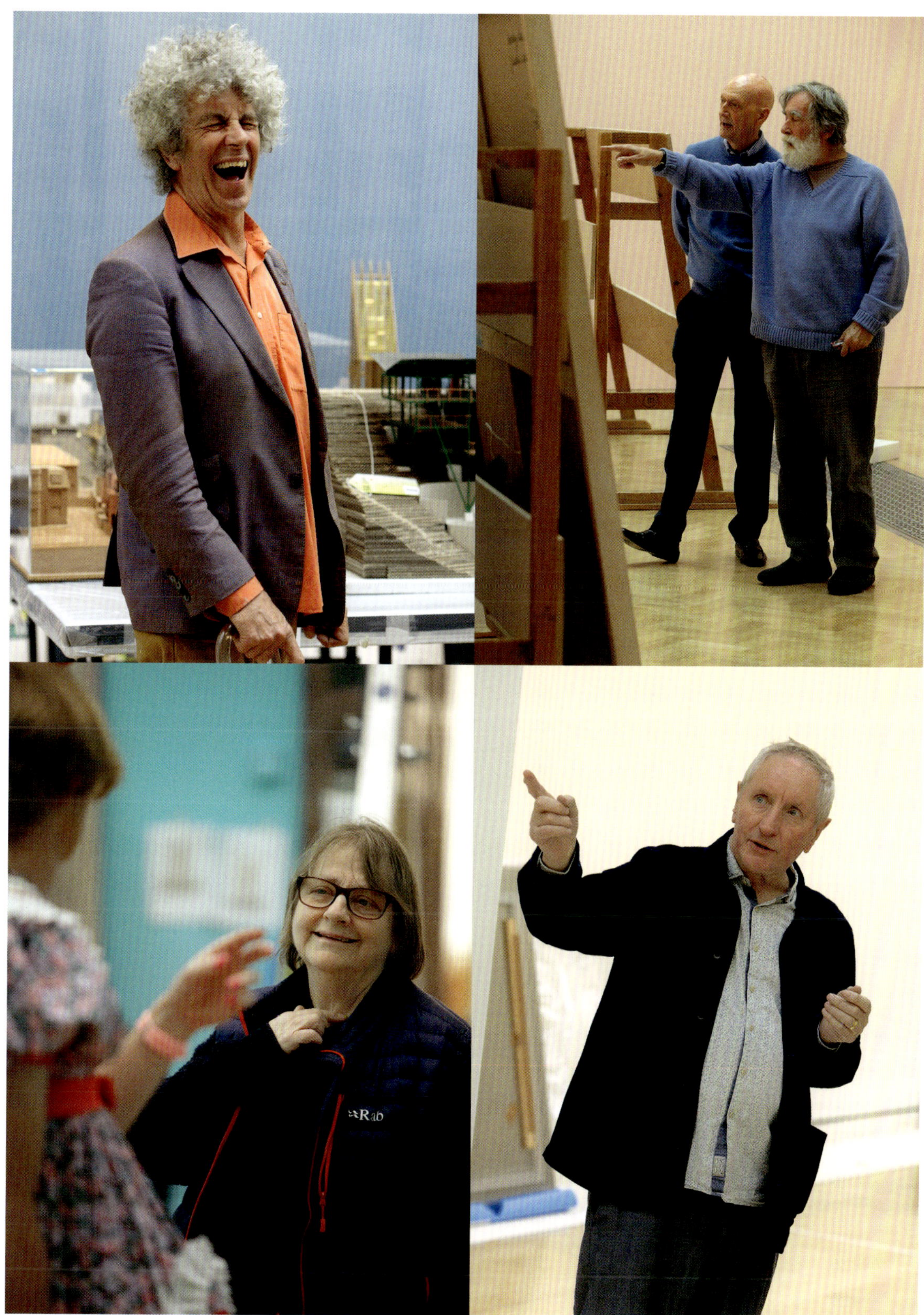
Rab

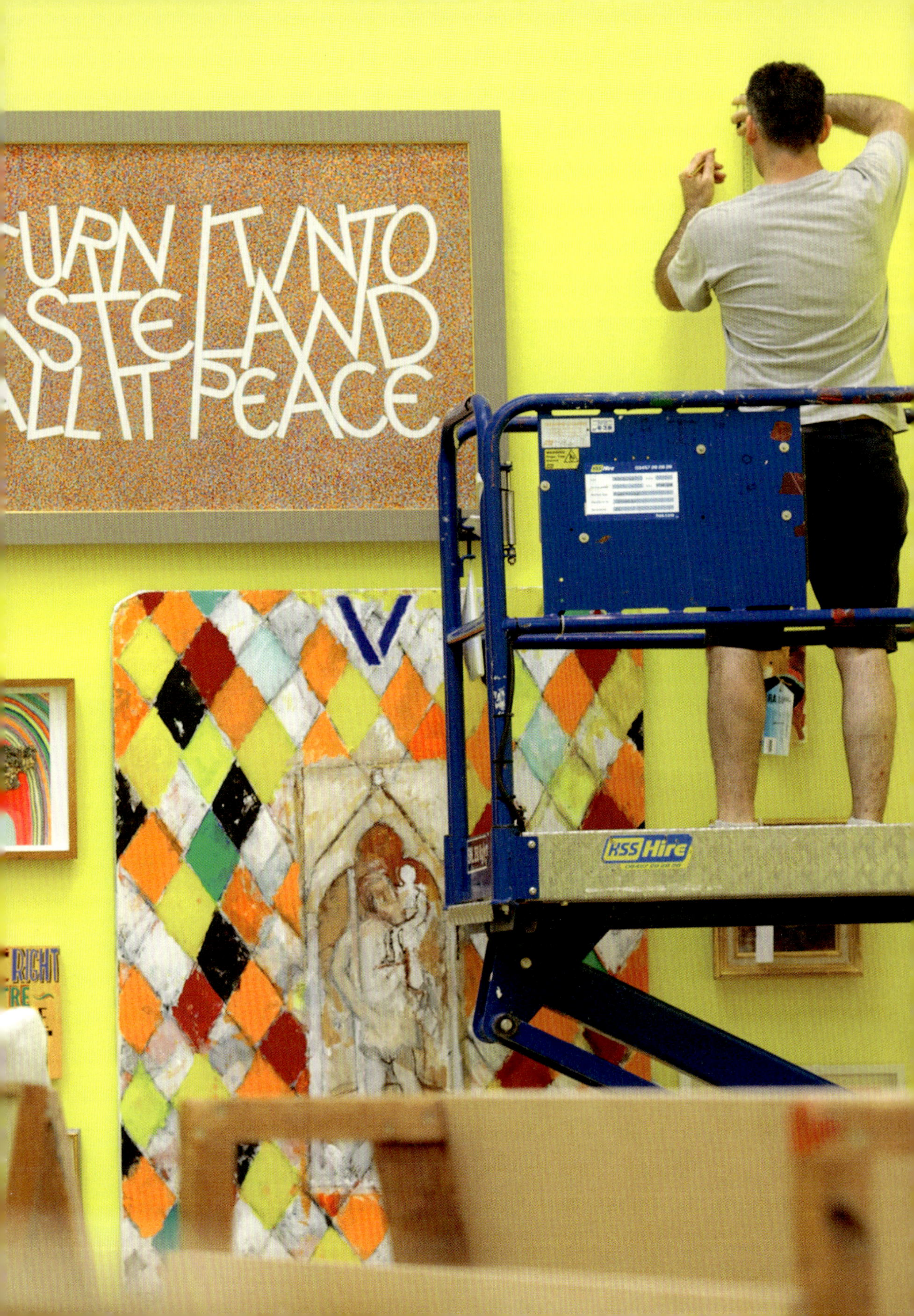
URN IT INTO
STELAND
ALL IT PEACE
HSS Hire
RIGHT

in the two largest spaces in the Burlington Gardens building and finally I was informed that the prosaic need for a room to cook in meant Gallery X would be unavailable to me. Hey ho, and so I was left with pretty much the same amount of space as usual but broken up over two floors and two buildings. This situation somewhat deflated me.

But, dear reader, even though I had to change plans with little time before the off, I was not daunted. I struggled on! I met with the brilliant curator Edith Devaney to rejig my masterplan. 'Well I suppose I should treat it as just another contemporary art exhibition,' I moped. 'We don't call the Summer Show contemporary art,' whispered Edith. 'We call it *art made now*.' When I had finished giggling I was struck by a bolt of inspiration. Art Made Now, that would be my theme. The Summer Exhibition has always been about art that is being made at the time – it's just that most of it probably would not qualify as cutting-edge contemporary art. Art Made Now sounds like one of those generic titles given to contemporary art exhibitions but in our case it's just honest. The Summer Show is a vaguely representative sample of all the different sorts of things made in the name of art at the moment. It is a slice cut through the artist demographic, a taster visit to all the thousands of studios from international superstars through professional artists at all stages and price points in their careers, to art-school graduates and enthusiastic amateurs. This year I also include a selection of artists variously described as self-taught, folk or outsider, as well as work by people who have been patients in psychiatric wards and inmates in prisons. I wanted to embrace the wider idea of Art Made Now that the Summer Exhibition has always represented. Some of the members would probably describe the RA itself as a kind of psychiatric hospital! Ha ha ha.

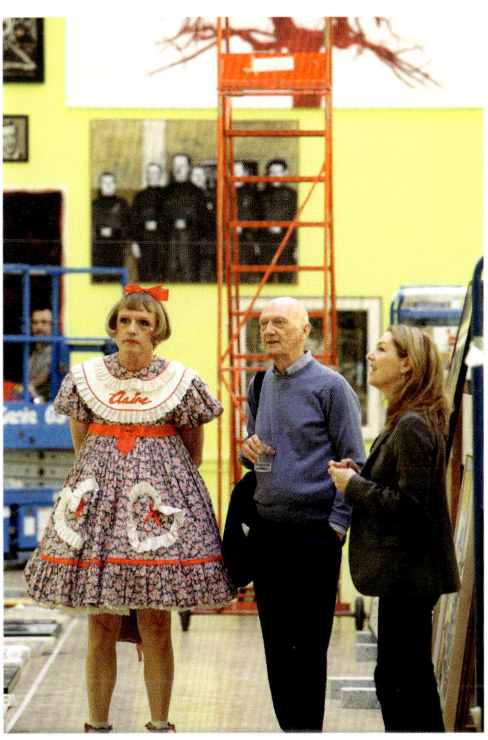

And so, once my merry band of co-conspirators had recovered from the heartbreak of not being able to express their curatorial exuberance in a campus-wide carnival of artists at play, we applied ourselves to the job in hand. As the unstoppable behemoth that is the Summer Exhibition hove into view, across the committee table I felt like we were but a tiny flock of seagulls flapping our wings vainly trying to change the course of the *Titanic*. I need not have felt so anxious. Despite its size and speed this annual extravaganza is unlikely to hit an iceberg. Over the years the RA has developed such a formidably skilful crew of curators, art handlers, administrators, party planners, painters

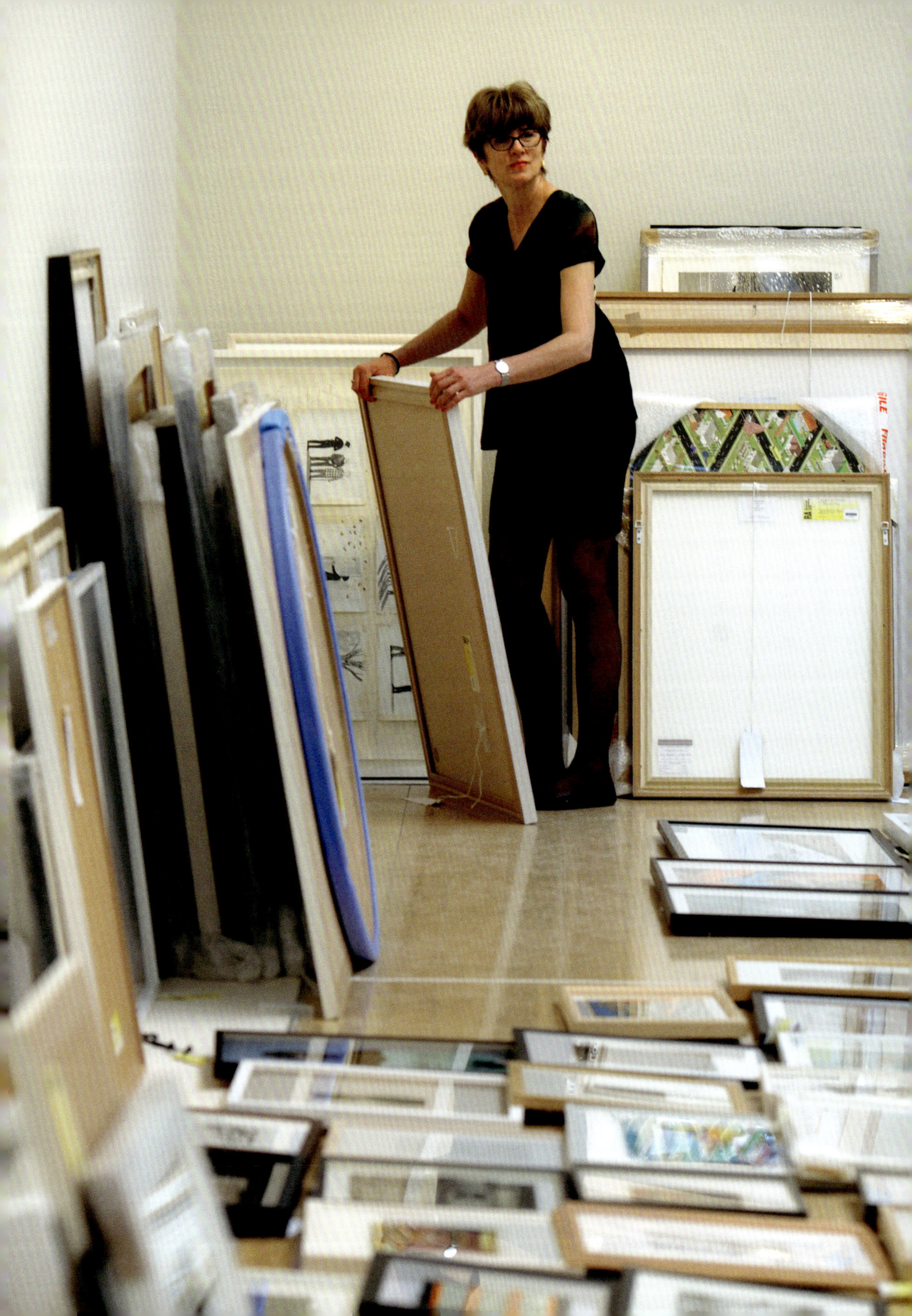

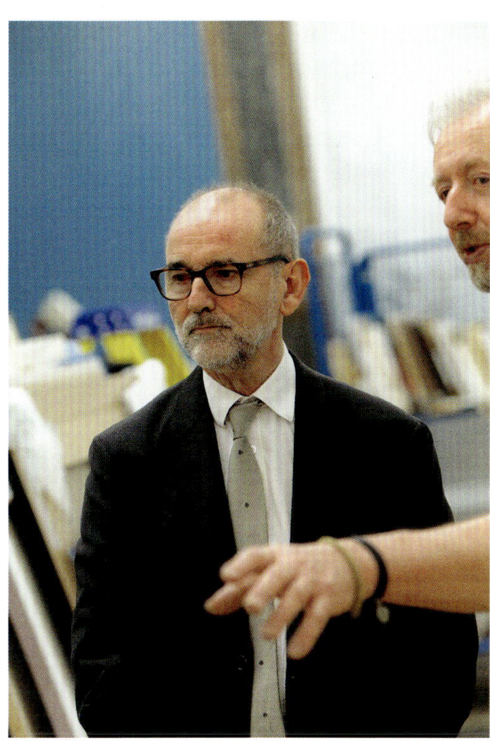

and technicians that the good ship Art Made Now is unlikely to meet with complete disaster.

The first endurance test our Summer Exhibition committee had to face was selecting the send-ins, the artworks entered by anyone willing to risk the £35 fee. The President thought that as it was our 250th year we should expand the entry. Normally the send-ins are capped at around 12,000. This year we looked at 19,800 works. In a week. Do the maths.

Applicants no longer need to lug the actual works to the RA for our judgement. We sit in a darkened room and survey the art on a screen. Next to each image is the silhouette of a little grey figure we dubbed Toilet Man. He is there to indicate the scale of the artwork, which is shown as a grey rectangle next to him. Toilet Man expressed no personal taste, but is obviously an agent of the patriarchy.

Due to the logistics I was unable to view the architecture or print send-ins, but I spent six days looking at painting, sculpture, mixed media, photography and video. Looking at more than 15,000 works in such a short time had a profound effect on me. Spending so many hours constantly in judgement with little time for debate called on a strange mix of intuition and stamina. Good things (of which there were many) sailed through and the awful were easily dismissed. Curiously it was the middle ground that took up our time. 'Is this so bad it's good?', 'Am I mad to like this?', 'Am I missing something here?' were the kind of utterances that would start a short often jocular debate. Only one of us had to like a work for it to go through.

To see so many artworks is maybe to glimpse the collective unconscious of a tranche of our society. Sometimes we squealed in delight, at others recoiled in horror. After a thousand or so images the border between art and life would begin to blur. When I popped out for a comfort break I would venture into the public spaces of the RA and the crowds climbing the staircase struck me as the subjects and creators of the stream of images I had just left behind. Had I just seen that respectable Home Counties lady naked on a cane chair with a parrot? Did that earnest man with a beard make that loopy abstract sculpture I had just seen photographed on a suburban lawn? After a few days my mind swam queasily with starey-eyed cows and moons glimpsed through silver birches. I dreamt of mafia families

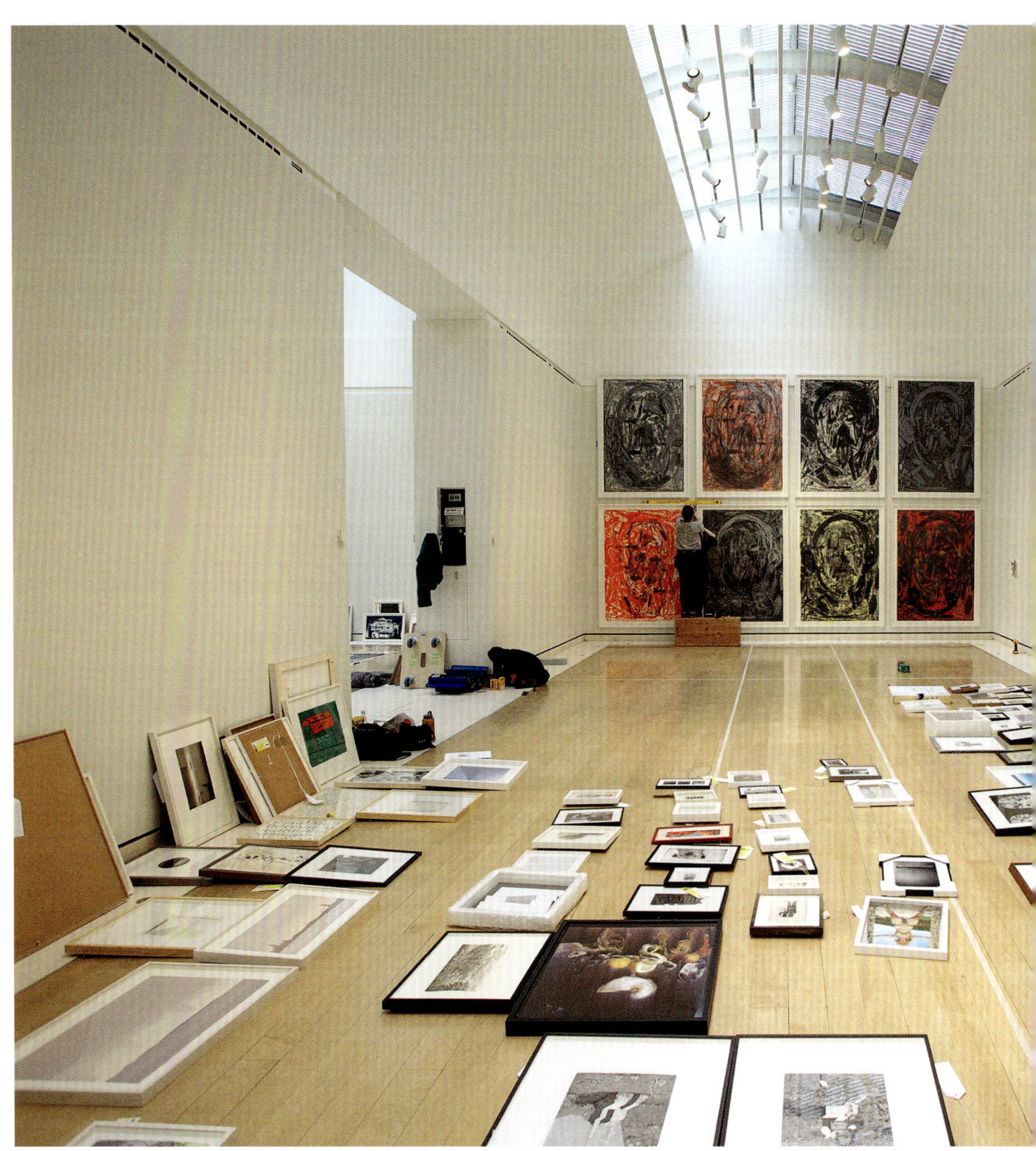

warring over who got the most work into the show. After a week I had trouble even choosing which colour t-shirt to put on in the morning.

Perhaps the most troubling symptom of prolonged exposure to large amounts of art of varying quality was seeing aspects of my own work reflected in works that I thoroughly disliked. Other members of the committee reported the same experience. I would spot certain colour combinations, stylistic habits, subjects and textures that I love to use, but they were now associated with art we had rejected. It took me at least a week to recover my enthusiasm for art-making and some tropes I may *never* use again.

At the end of the selection process I had made a list. It consisted of sorts of artwork that seemed to crop up again and again and again. I hesitate to list these subsets as it might appear cruel and also might put off about half the applicants! What mystified me about these works was where the inspiration for them had come from. They seemed to relate to nothing that had gone on in contemporary art for at least fifty years. I can understand people not liking contemporary art – there is very little of it I truly love myself – but I am an artist working now so I look at, acknowledge and react to the art being made around me. One of the committee commented that 'it was like walking through the art department of John Lewis'. Maybe not an entirely accurate description but in spirit it captured the lack of engagement with the art of our age that characterised a lot of the works sent in.

As a case in point, both the works I have submitted myself to this exhibition are inspired by a strong current that is flowing through contemporary art at the moment. Art has always been political, but at present politics seems particularly implicit in a lot of work – like, for instance, this year's Turner Prize shortlist. Though I agree with most of the typically liberal and progressive sentiments invoked by artists, I am not so keen when the issues seem to sideline, or even be a replacement for, aesthetic pleasure. Maybe I am old-fashioned but I go to art galleries and

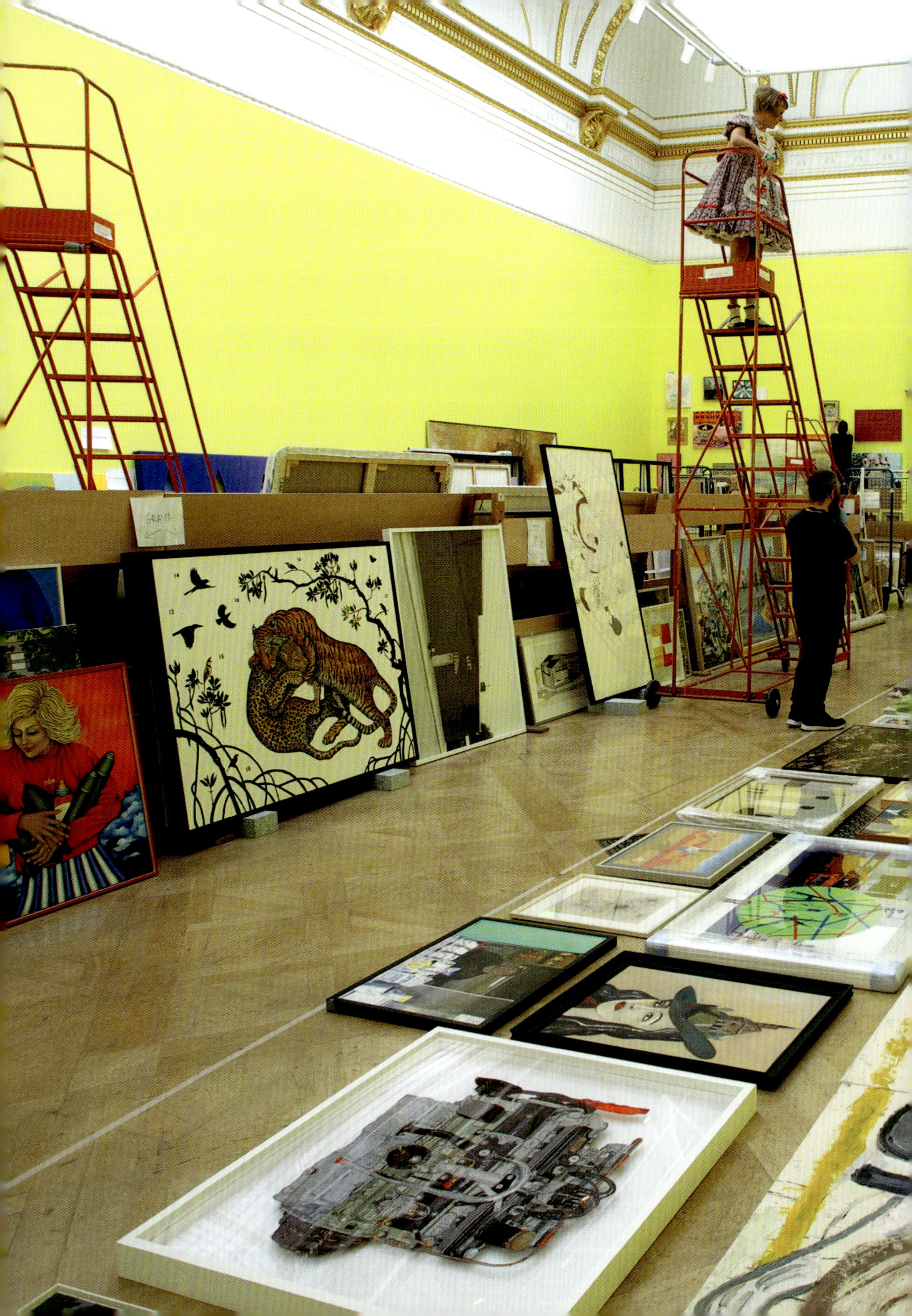

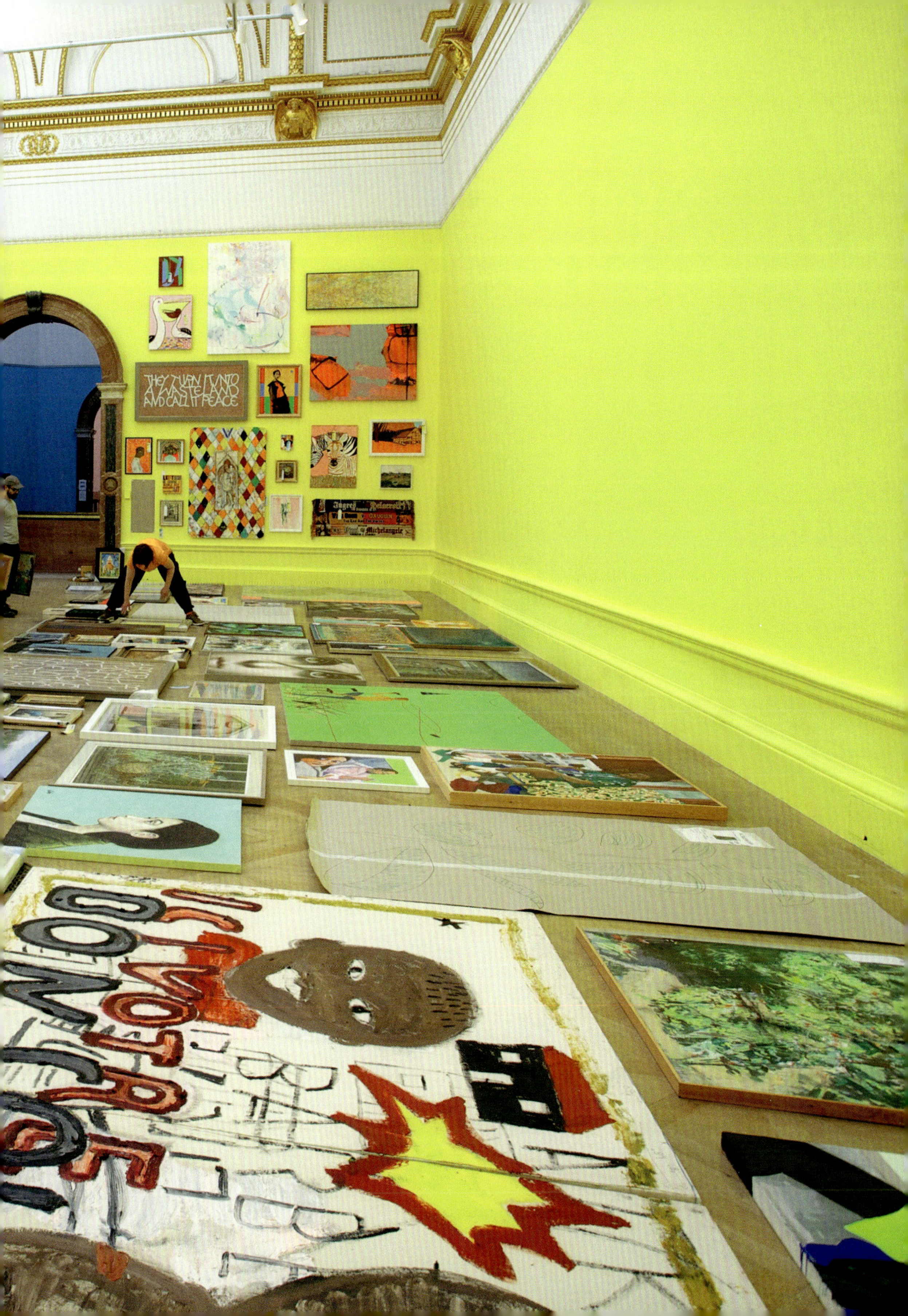
THEY TURN IT INTO
A WASTELAND
AND CALL IT PEACE

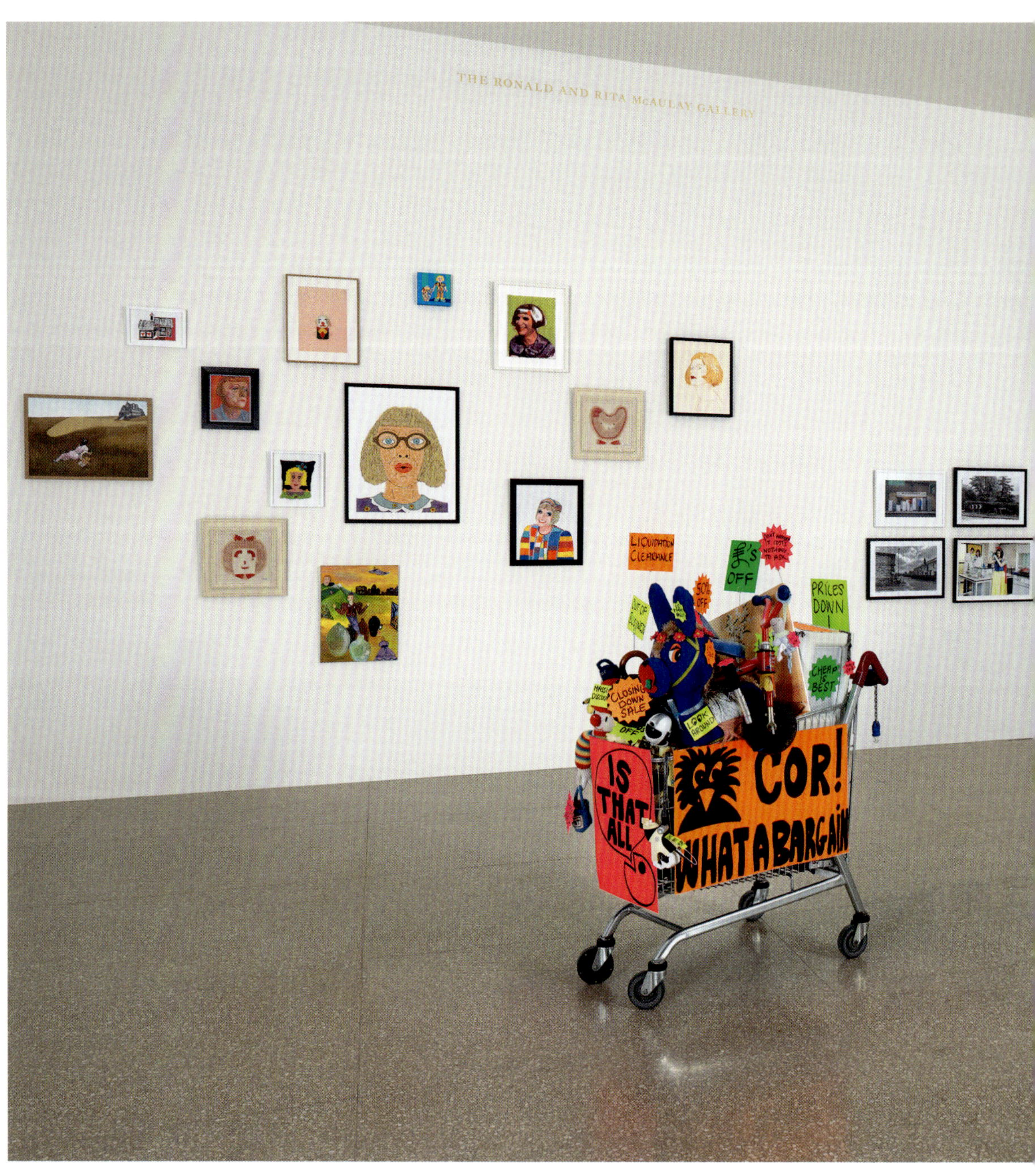
THE RONALD AND RITA McAULAY GALLERY
LIQUIDATION CLEARANCE
PRICES DOWN !
CHEAP IS BEST
CLOSING DOWN SALE
LOOK AROUND
IS THAT ALL
COR!
WHAT A BARGAIN

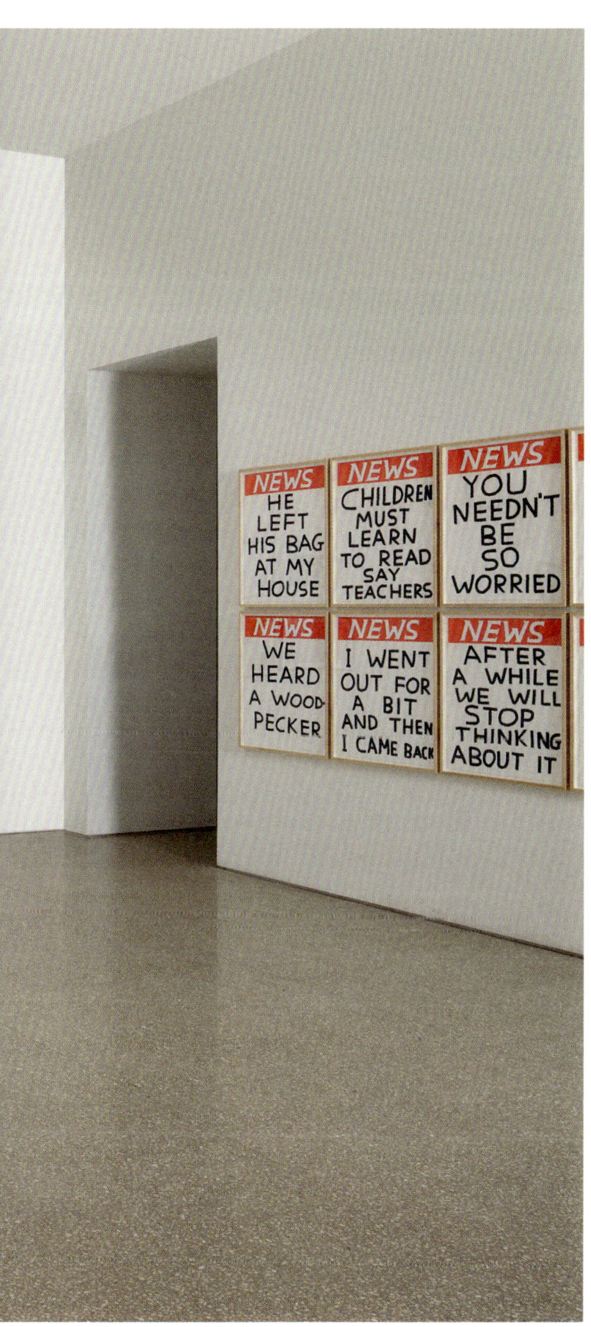

museums to enjoy myself. Too often I feel lectured at about subjects where I already agree with the artist. Oh wow, I never realised global warming/plastic waste/inequality/war/racism/sexism/homophobia etc was a bad thing, thank you artist fella for pointing it out to me! I feel I am left with little sensual reward – as I have been reminding curators for years, most people go to exhibitions on their day off!

If this Summer Show is to reflect my lead, there are two uplifting themes that I hope will be apparent, particularly in the vast Gallery III: humour and strong colour. Humour in art can be, as the young say nowadays, 'problematic'. It needs to catch you out. If I call an exhibit funny I have already lessened its chances of eliciting laughter. Nevertheless I have also taken the foolhardy step of dedicating the McAulay Gallery to being as my Room of Fun. At first I thought I would only select works for it that genuinely made me laugh intentionally, so works by David Shrigley, Magda Archer, Martin Parr and Michael Landy were no-brainers. Then, during the send-in selection, when I found myself guffawing at the failed ambition of many of the works, I was sorely tempted to make a rogues' gallery of the worst crimes against art but I'm not sure the artists would share my joke. I'm uncertain as to whether the artists who sent in the many portraits of yours truly were trying to make me laugh, but I have included a selection of the best (funniest, oddest…). As I hung Gallery III I found myself poaching works I had reserved for the Room of Fun in order to leaven the mixture. The temptation to juxtapose works for comic or cod-political effect is just too tempting for me. Who can resist hanging a four-metre wiggly Pink Panther next to a staid portrait of Nigel Farage over where the President and dignitaries sit at the very grand white tie Annual Dinner? Not me!

I think my enjoyment of bright colours is a reaction to the dampening blanket of muted 'tastefulness' that sags over our material culture. It is easy to find yourself sitting in a Tube carriage where everyone is wearing black or in a house that is all white, grey, black and beige. People seem to get the words subtle and dull confused, they seem afraid of strong colours. Maybe it is fear of getting it wrong, setting up clashing shades. Maybe it is fear of standing out and making a statement. To me the Summer Exhibition has always been a raucous celebration of chromophilia. In 2015 Michael Craig-Martin was the coordinator and he painted Gallery III an overpowering pink. I loved it. It taught me that you can hang art on any colour, so I have chosen a radiant lemon yellow for Gallery III, a rich grey–blue for the Central Hall and a fleshy pink for the Lecture Room.

We needed to choose the colours of the walls before we knew what we were going to hang on them, always a risk. But then, the Summer Show is all risk, we do not know what will be sent in or entered by the RAs and we HAVE to work fast with what we are given. We WILL upset some people who feel their work is not displayed to its best advantage. We will NOT be able to please both the traditionalists and the trendies. Someone will be offended by something or other. Some people are upset by the Exhibition's mere existence. Humphrey Ocean describes the Summer Show as 'The Most Dangerous Exhibition in the World'.

After the extended pain of viewing and choosing the send-in work, the reward is seeing all the things we have chosen and the joy of hanging them. I am particularly grateful for the exuberance and irreverence of many of the send-in artworks, particularly when I am able to hang them next to the muddier output of some of the members whose works I would christen the 'fatbergs', as they blocked the process of hanging a fresh and uplifting show. My tactic, one used I'm sure by many past coordinators, was to treat the fatbergs as blessed relief between the uproarious outpourings of the popular imagination.

Another trend that I became aware of during the process was that the bigger and more expensive the artworks the bigger and more brittle the egos of the members. The committee and the staff spend more emotional energy on a few touchy prima donnas than they do on the rest of the members and send-ins put together. My message to these 'household names' is: if you don't want to participate in the democratic rough and tumble of the Summer Show then don't submit works. What got me most angry was when large artworks arrived very late. Hanging a wall trying to accommodate a vast acreage of artistic manspreading

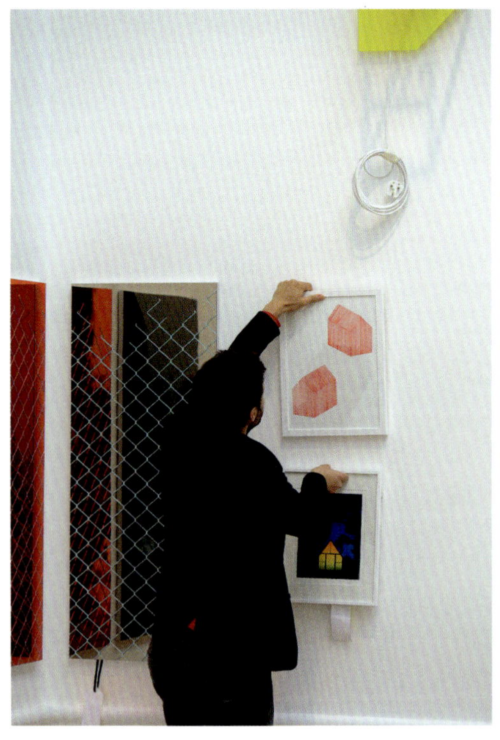

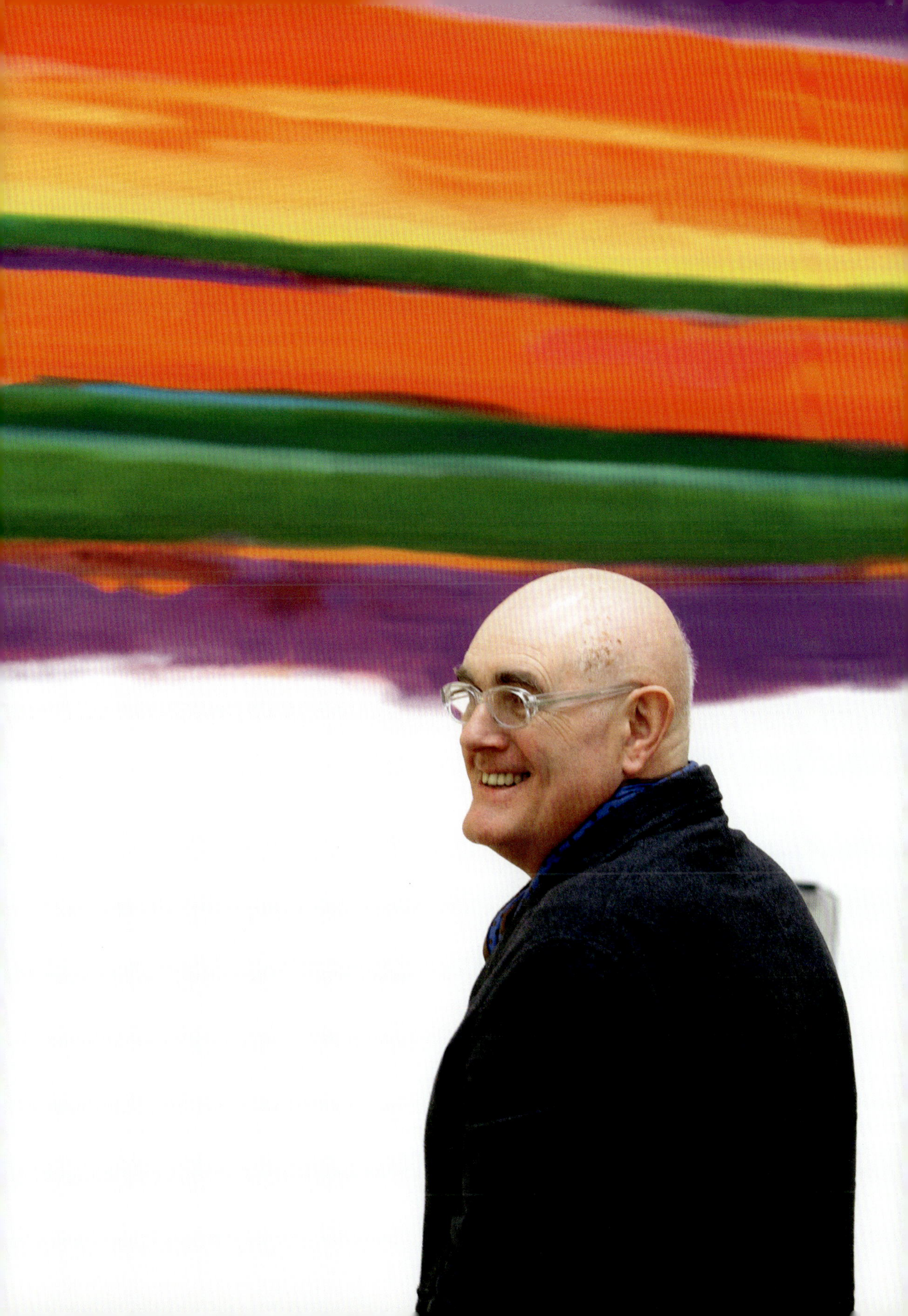

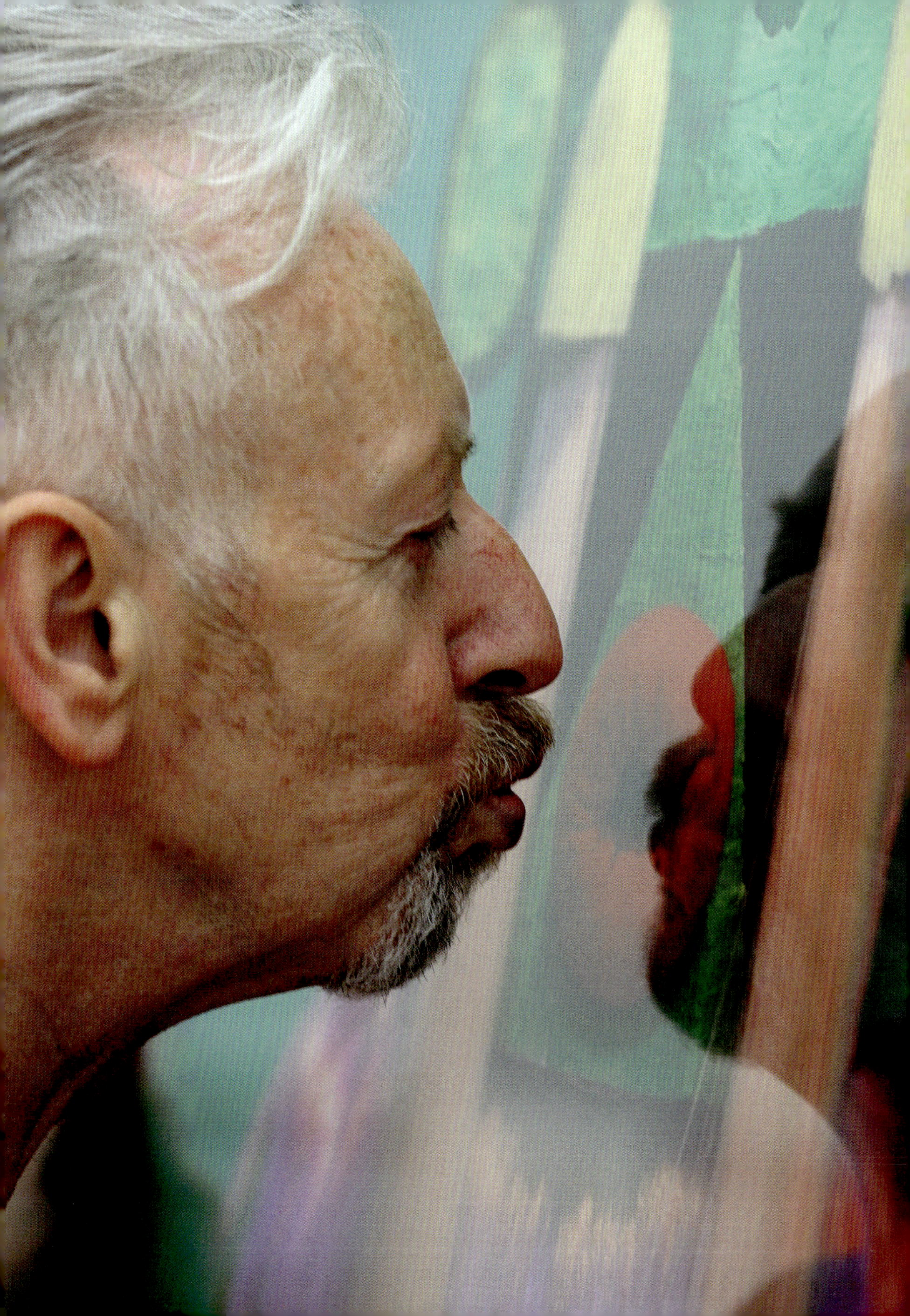

that is only there as a ghostly beige template is very difficult. It's not like the Summer Show crept up on them. The clue is in the title! It's been running for 250 years for Pete's sake!

Petty power-plays aside, hanging the show has been one of the most artistically rewarding experiences of my varied career. One of the most joyful moments is seeing all the send-in work arrive. Art we have selected appears before us in the flesh for the first time. Much of it looks even better than we hoped and thoughts of not having enough splendid art to make the expected overwhelming Salon-style hang soon evaporate. Watching the final display gradually come into focus out of the haze of endless submissions, seeing the selected works stacked up on racks, laying them out on the floor and finally seeing them on the walls in all their splendour is to witness a joyous human spring. Standing atop a five-metre ladder directing the art handlers, composing the walls, was to have the best toy box at my disposal, full of beauties, provocations, charms and mischief. A super-rich collage laid out on which to inflict my whim of iron was pure pleasure. Pat O'Connor, one of the art handlers, gave me the loveliest compliment. She said not only was I the fastest and most decisive hanger of Gallery III, my real achievement was doing it without making anyone cry. Not until my fellow members see it, that is!

The Royal Academy can easily be seen as a pillar of the Establishment, a cabal of the Liberal Metropolitan Elite, and of course it is, yet we preside over one of the least elitist of annual cultural events. There is no scientific method for putting together such a show. Our choices, collective or individual, are unapologetically subjective. All I need to say is that the committee have all dedicated their own lives to making art and we choose the works we genuinely love. No one is forced to view or exhibit. The Summer Show is a festival of the joy of making art, a mosh pit of aesthetics where all the works have to rub along together. It's 250 years old and it changes just a bit every year. It is full of Art Made Now. As we say at the RA: 'Honour and Glory to the next Exhibition!'

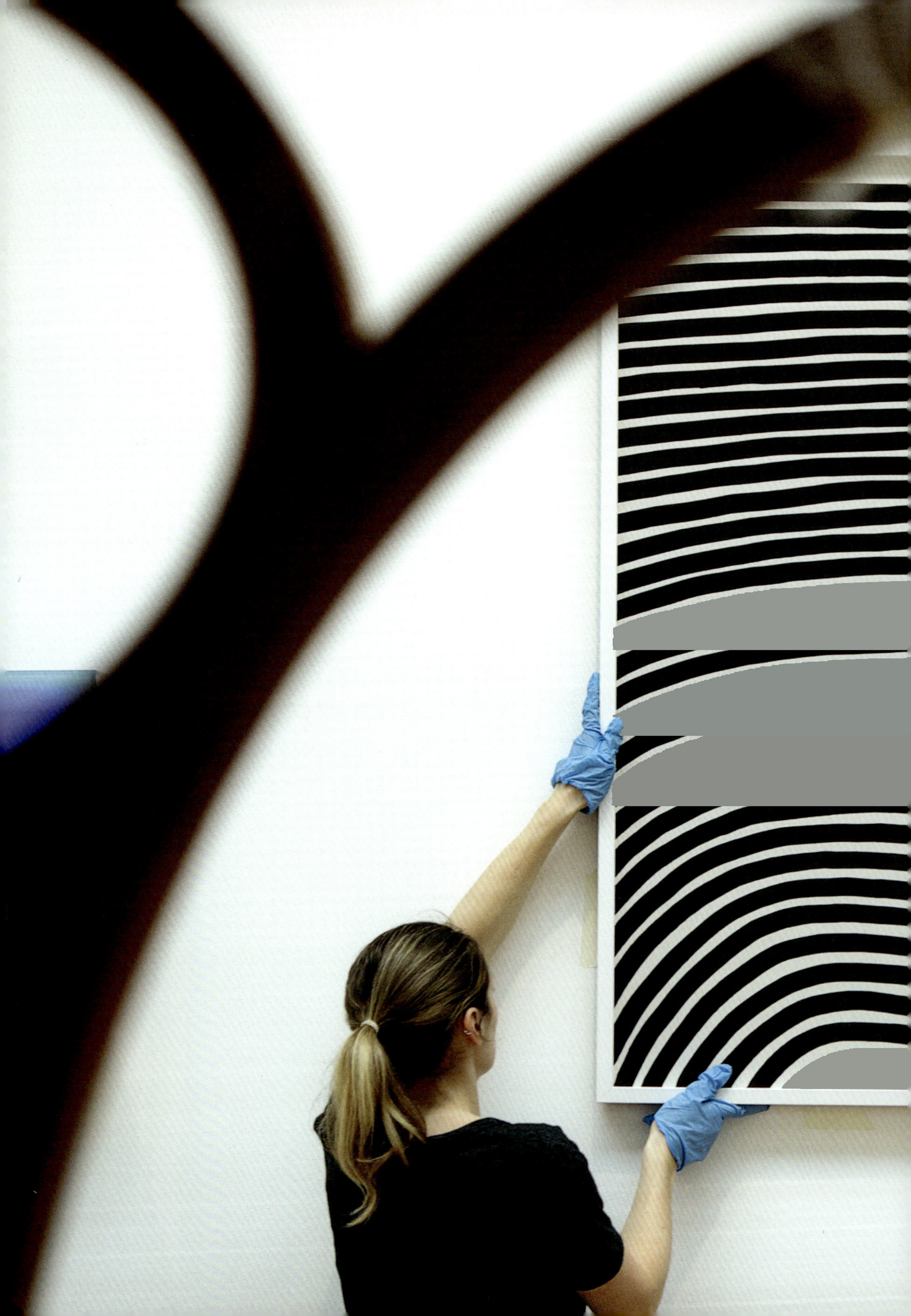

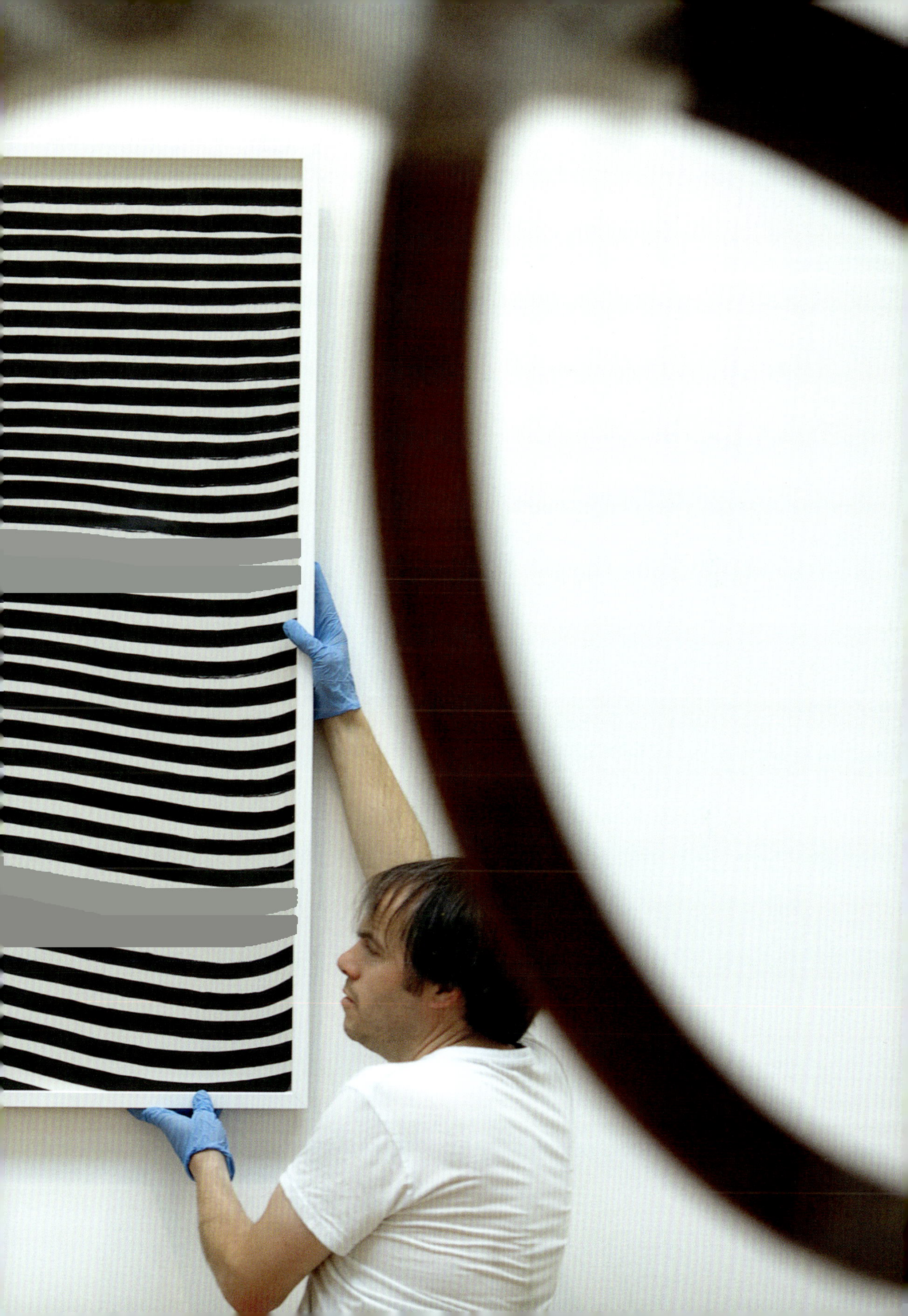

Tributes

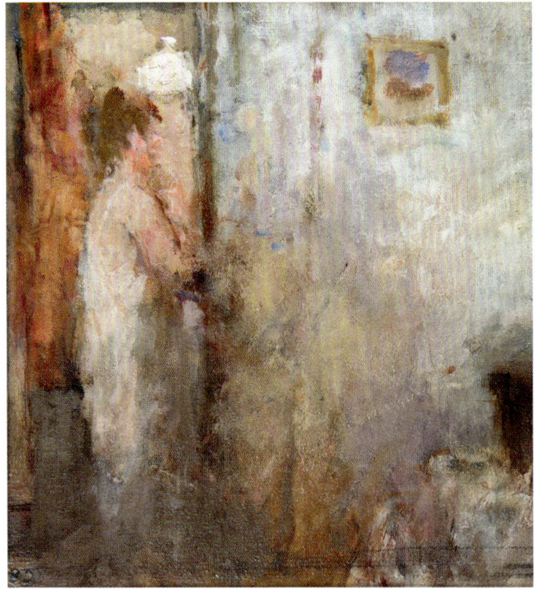

Above: The late Bernard Dunstan RA
Door to the Bathroom, Llwynhir
Oil
25 × 22 cm

Opposite: The late Gillian Ayres CBE RA
Maritsa
Oil
191 × 305 cm

Bernard Dunstan RA (1920–2017)

Bernard Dunstan first exhibited at the Summer Show in 1946 – a lifetime ago. He was elected to the Academy in 1968 (having been an associate member since 1959) and at the time of his death was its longest-serving member. He first took part in the Summer Exhibition when Alfred Munnings wore the President's medal and showed his work successfully every year since. I first got to know him in 1983 when I started editing RA Magazine. Bernard introduced me to an Academy quite different to the one we see today. It seemed to be filled with big, clubbable personalities like Ruskin Spear and Robert Buhler, both members of the group memorialised in Rodrigo Moynihan's portrait of the painting staff of the RCA, most of whom were later to become RAs. Bernard wasn't part of this group but, like so many RAs at that time, had supported his painting career through teaching. Bernard taught me much about the Academy's history and culture and I enjoyed his company a great deal.

We didn't get off to a good start, however. My introduction to Bernard was a letter in which he outlined for me the basic tenets of editing, number one being to spell people's names correctly, particularly those people that readers might have heard of. I had misspelt a well-known art historian's name in a headline – at least it wasn't on the cover! From there things fortunately got better. Bernard became a regular contributor to the magazine. He had written books on Impressionism and brought this knowledge to bear in his writing on late nineteenth-century art, particularly the work of Bonnard, Vuillard and Degas. His writing was jargon-free and illuminating to the many Friends of the RA who read the magazine and for whom the Academicians were distant beings. His support of the magazine also helped establish the publication in the eyes of his fellow RAs.

Bernard's essay on Walter Sickert's technique was a wonderfully lucid account of an artist with whom Bernard had a great affinity. He wrote of Sickert's handling of paint, applied full brush, laid down and left undisturbed. The description could equally well apply to much of Bernard's practice. Bernard's subject-matter could be seen as commonplace: intimate interiors with delicately draped figures seen through a doorway or across a bed, musicians in rehearsal, street scenes in Venice. His subjects were always authentically conveyed and the product of genuine perception. Through 'Impressionist' light he could

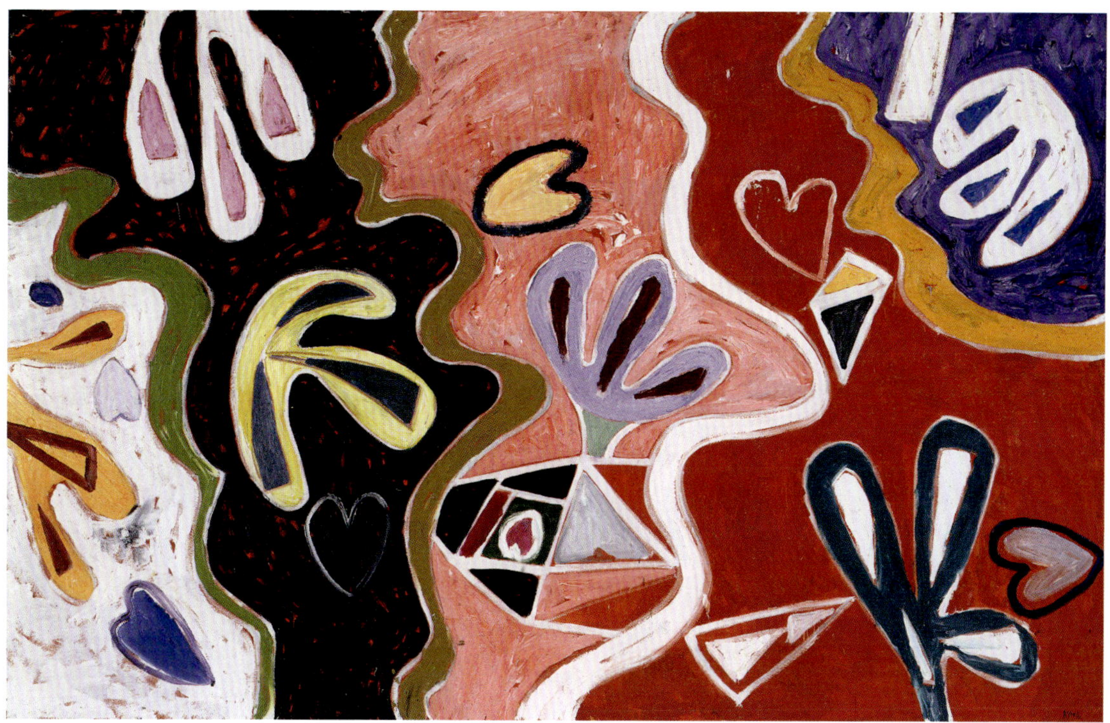

transform the mundane into the magical. His was an art that didn't so much redefine pictorial language as provide a genuine response to the traditions he held dear. The results brought him many admirers, and his pictures were always greatly sought after in the Summer Show and treasured by those quick-witted enough to find them on Buyers' Day.
Nick Tite

Gillian Ayres CBE RA (1930–2018)
Gillian Ayres began to paint as a schoolgirl and carried on painting her whole life long. She always said it was the best thing in the world, but it can't have been easy in the early days, the way the world was then. She hit her stride as a young painter in the 1950s, making large-scale abstract work, very radical in the context of post-war Britain and the art of the time. The first poured and puddled paintings made on boards laid out on the floor began as delighted improvisations, when an unexpected commission came her way, but she had already absorbed and understood important lessons in visual art – there was much from Europe and beyond that she was looking at, taking in, being excited by. They herald what came later – expansive, spacious pictorial exploration, increasing richness of colour, sensuous handling, physicality, immersion, a life of painting, a *raison d'être*.

Her work evolved over the decades, how it looked, the way it was made, but there is consistency, a full-blown head-over-heels kind of facture that insists on arriving at celebration or gorgeousness, however hard to achieve, however long the pauses must have been in the decision-making process of painting. Her prints are a beautiful counterpoint to the weight and density of the paintings, the woodblocks especially, their sharp colour dancing across the delicate surfaces of wafer-thin Japanese paper.

In early April, the day after I heard that Gillian had died, I listened to some archive recordings, *Artists' Lives*, excellent interviews with Mel Gooding, who knew her well. I must have wanted the illusion of being in her company again, hearing that inimitable voice, the pitch and pace and drawl of it, her chuckle. In one of the tapes she is hilarious about housekeeping, or rather the lack of it, and furious about what bureaucracy did to art schools; then she says something wonderful about *the secret inside painting, not to be spoken of too much, to be kept at the back of the mind so that it stays as questioning, as searching, as hope within us.* She was an inspiration, as an artist and as a person, and she will be greatly missed.
Mali Morris RA

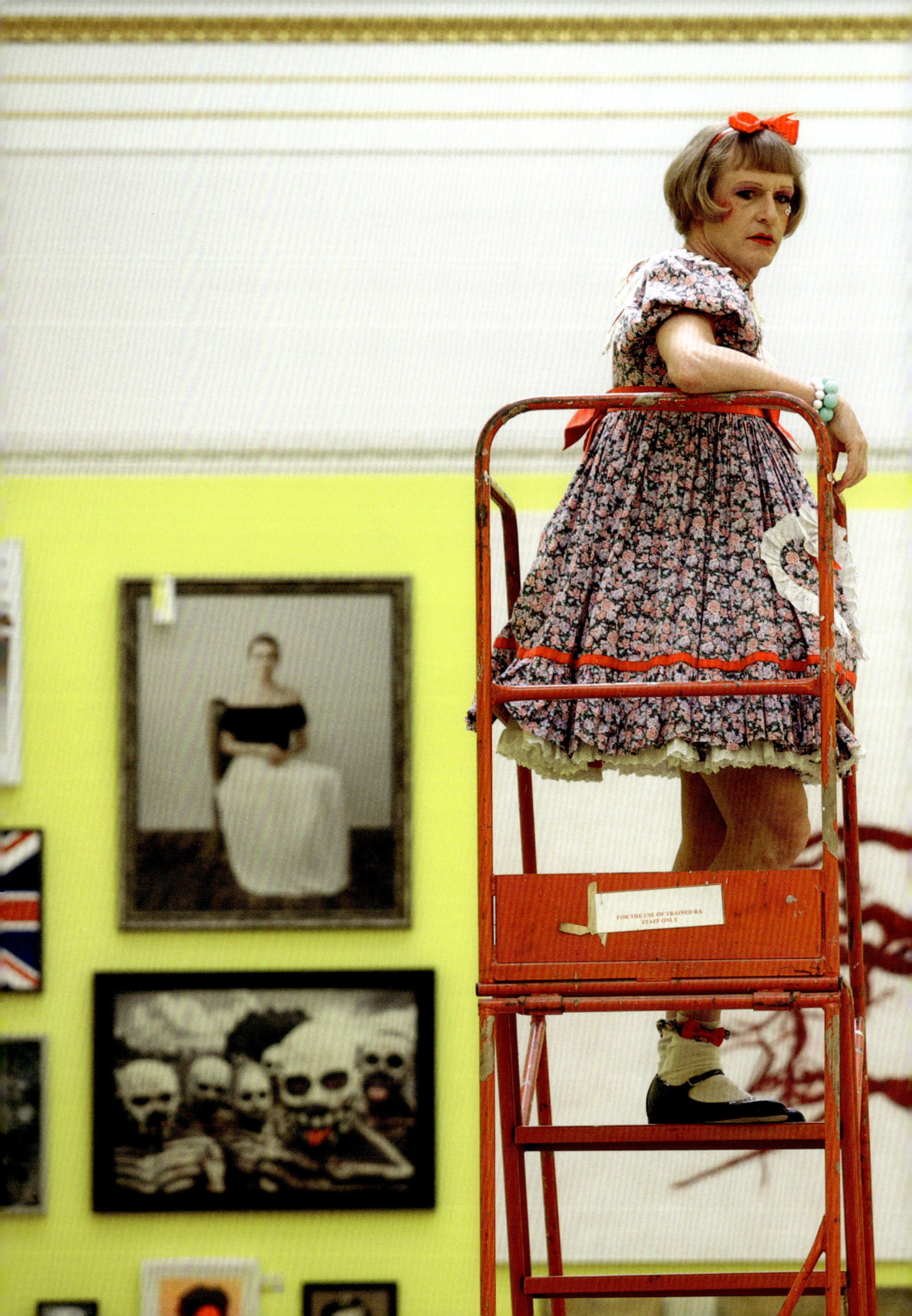
FOR THE USE OF TRAINED RA
STAFF ONLY

Mike Nelson RA
Untitled (Public Sculpture for a Redundant Space)
Sleeping bag, concrete and rubble
H 50 cm

Tim Shaw RA
Green Vine
Burnt newspaper, masking tape and cardboard
H 150 cm

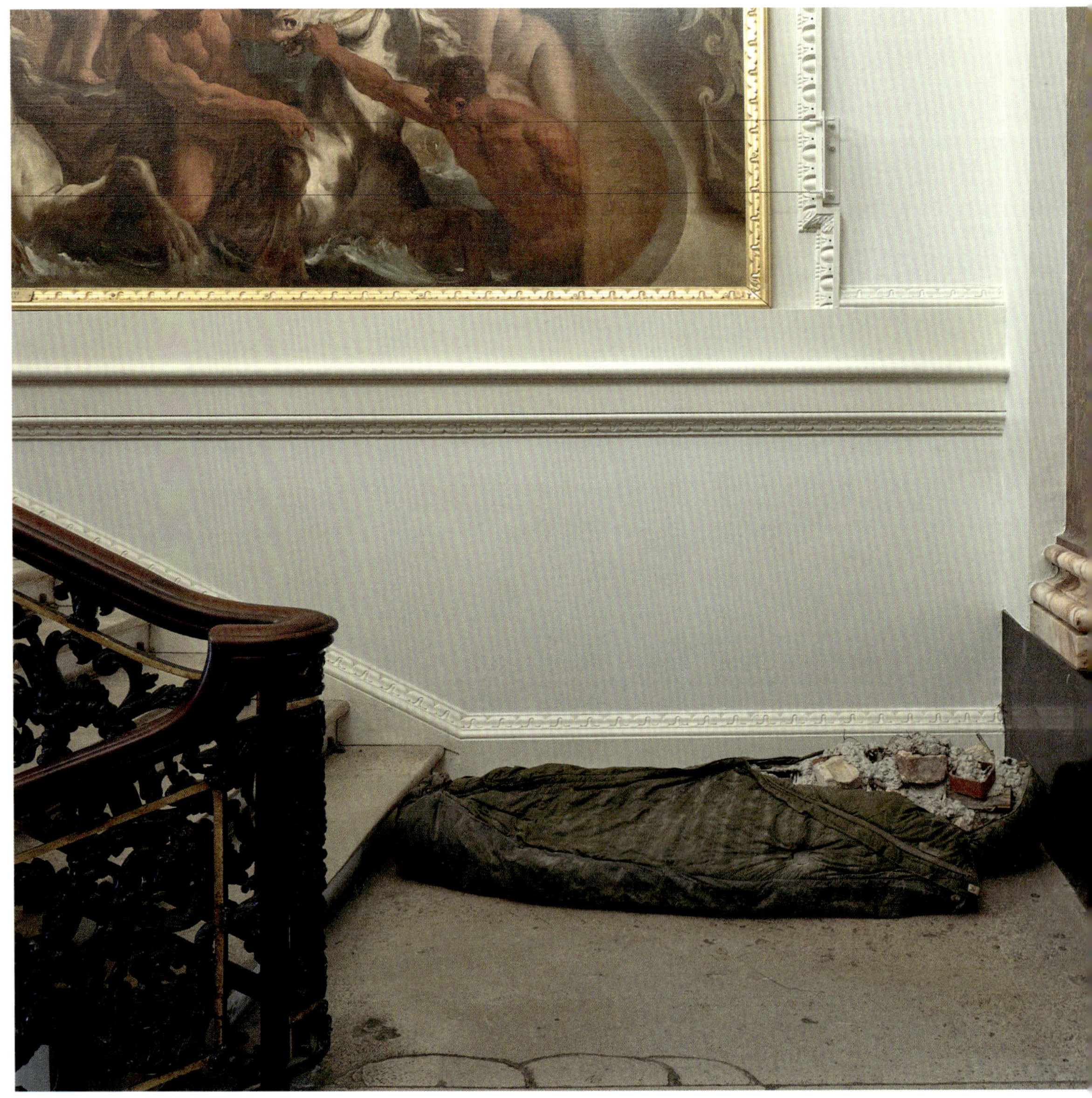

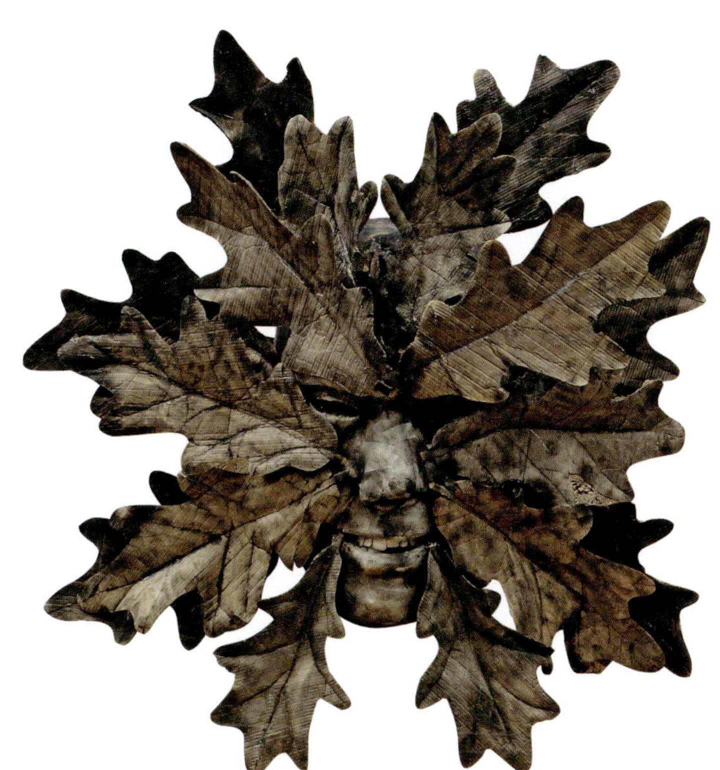

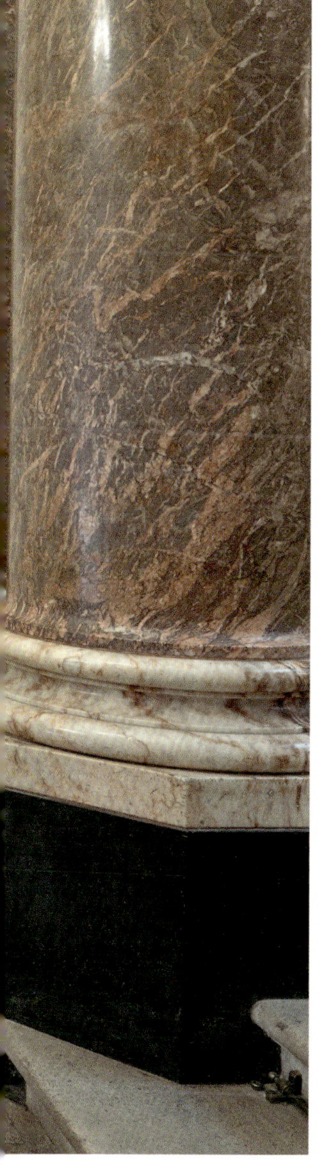

Dame Paula Rego DBE RA
Human Cargo
Conté pencil, conté and ink wash
135 × 100, 160 × 163, 135 × 100 cm

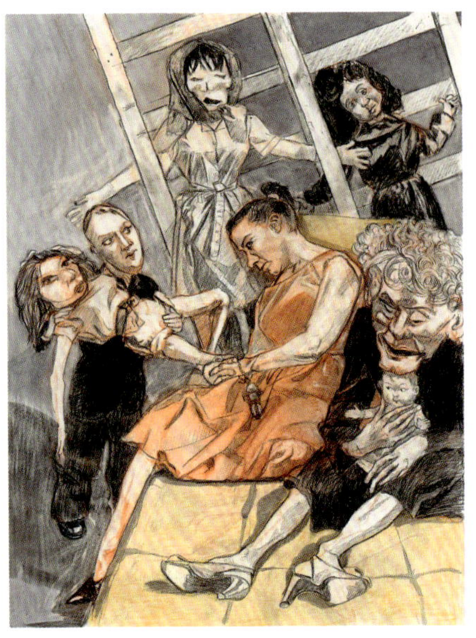

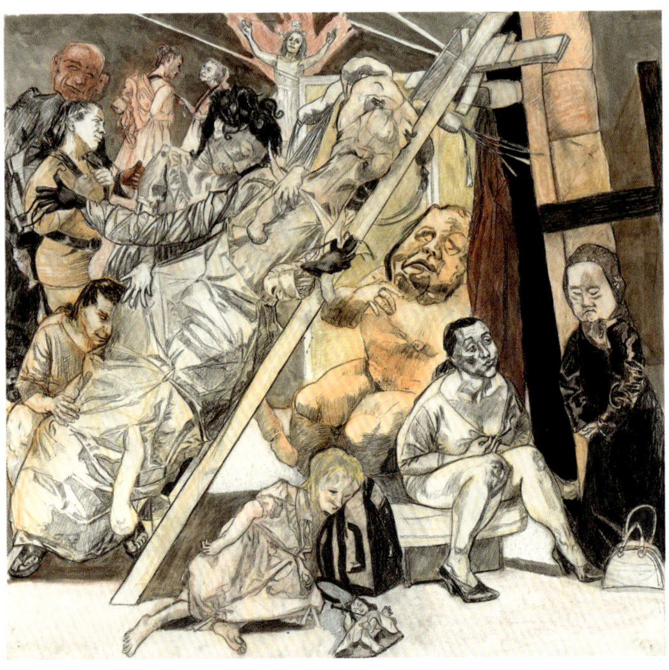

Prof Cathie Pilkington RA
Lovely Eyes
Mixed media
H 25 cm

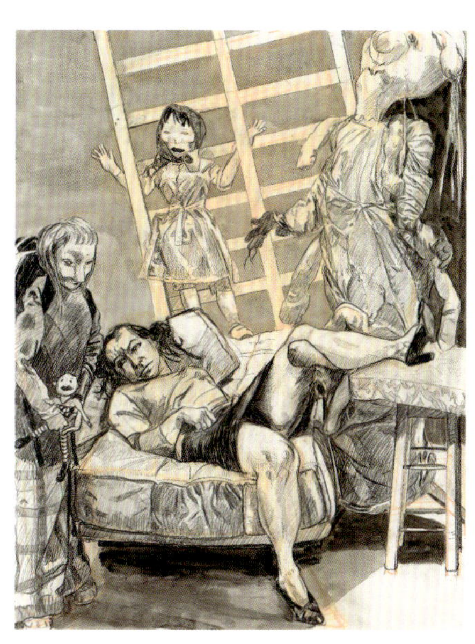

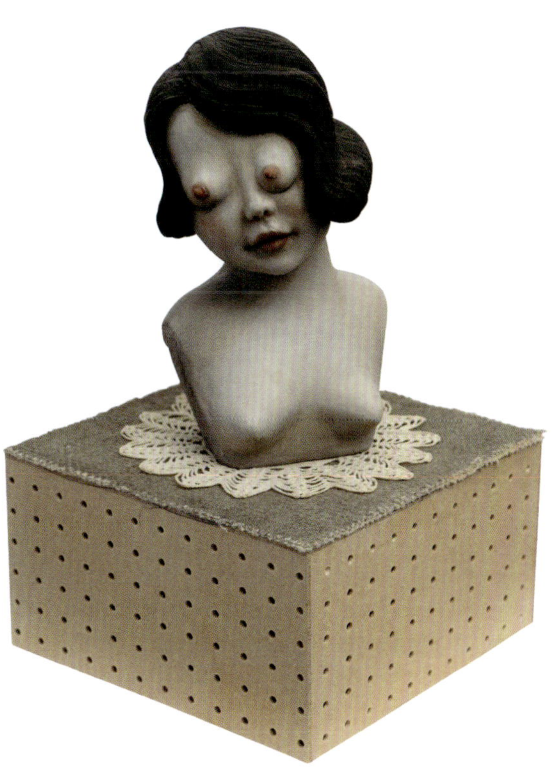

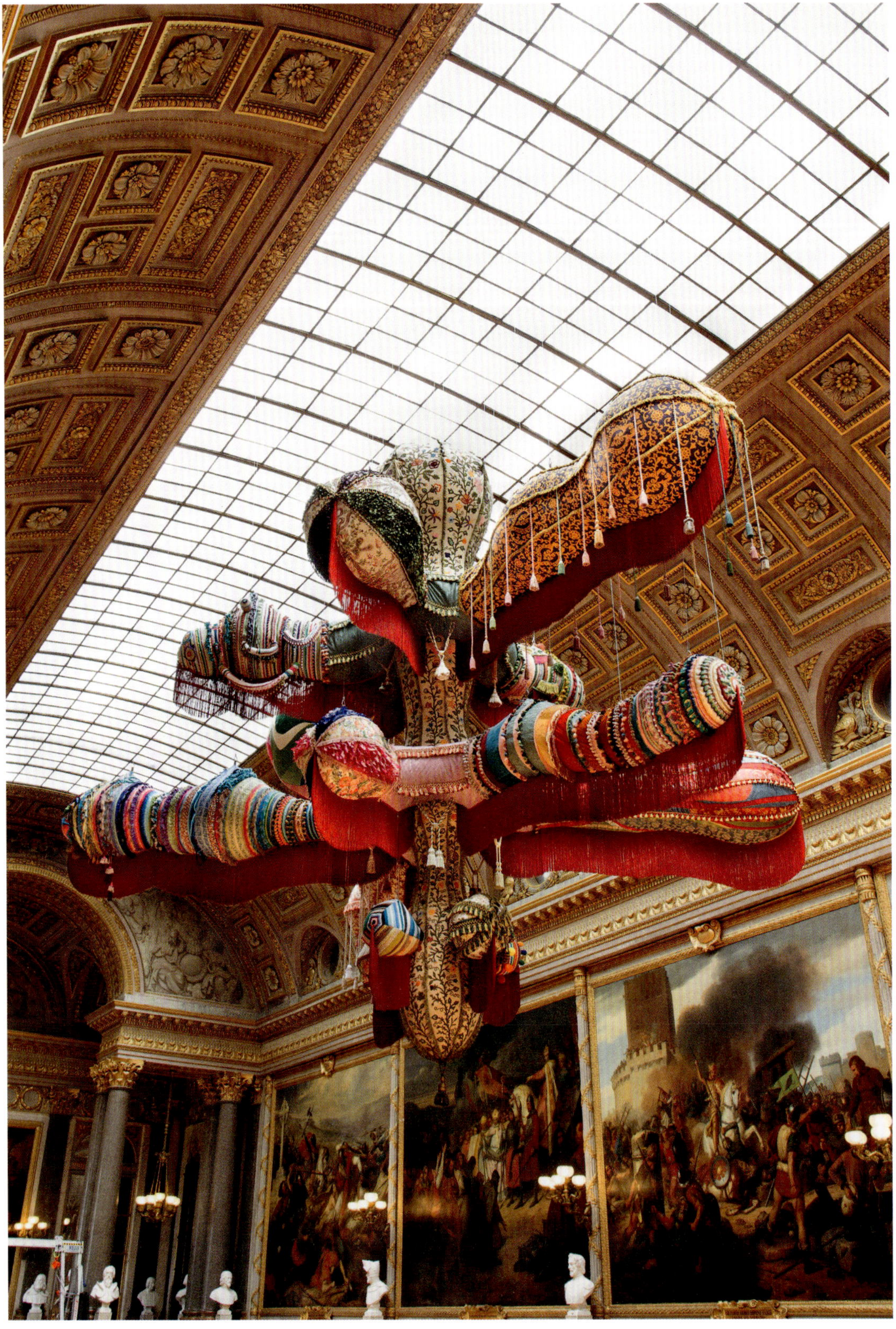

Joana Vasconcelos
Royal Valkyrie
Mixed media
H 625 cm

Prof Paul Huxley RA
Axis
Silkscreen
72 × 69 cm

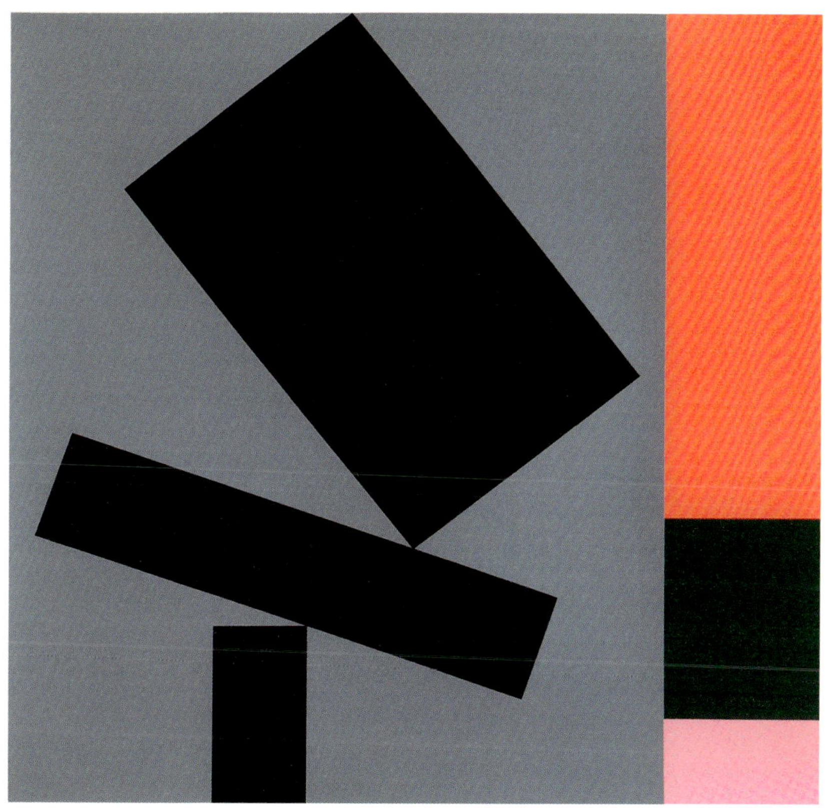

Renata Adela
Map Mundi I
Embroidery
71 × 69 cm

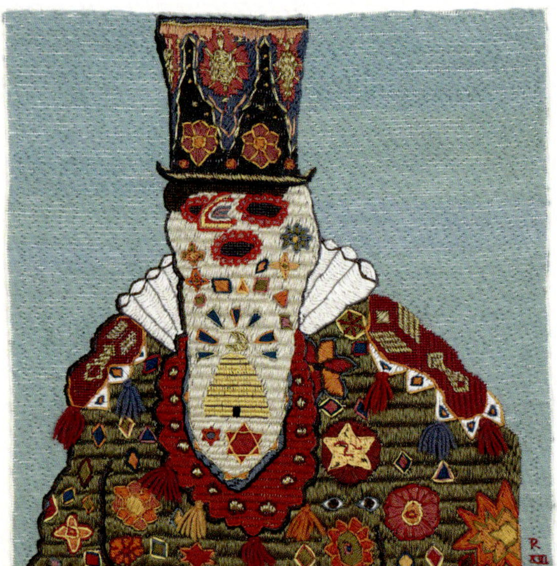

Emmely Elgersma
Ron
Papier-mâché
H 52 cm

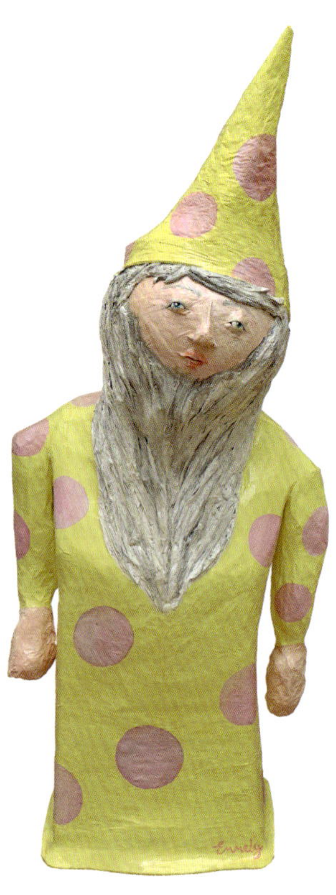

Bob and Roberta Smith OBE RA
The Art Issue!
Signwriters' paint on fridge door
80 × 60 cm

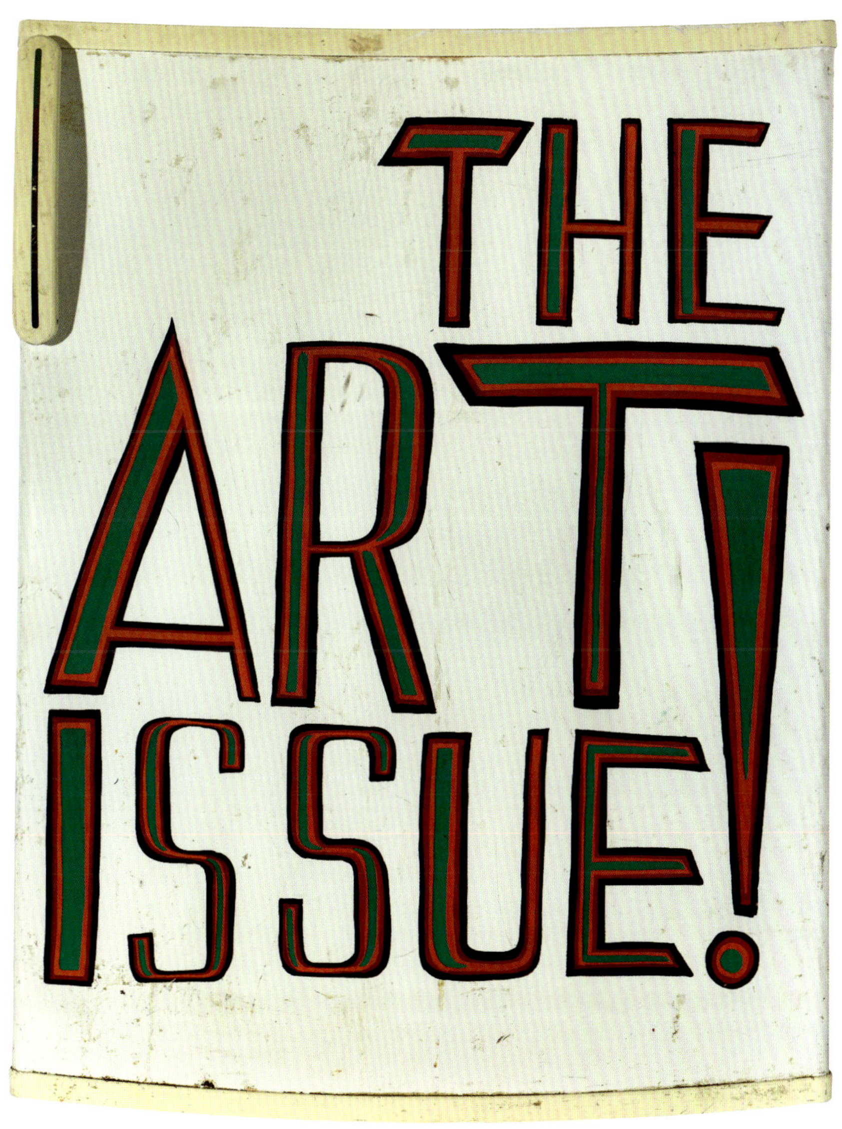

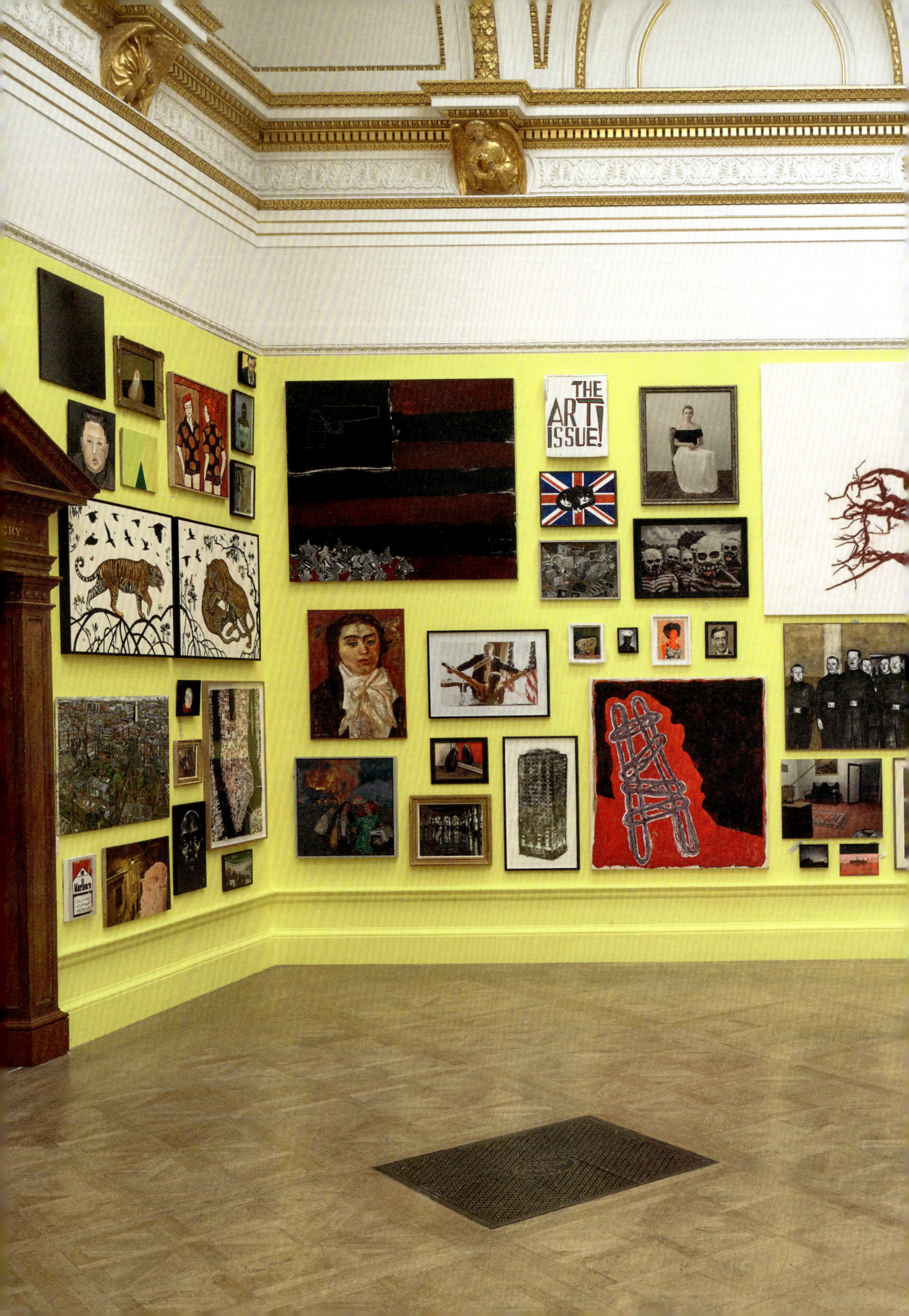
THE
ART
ISSUE!

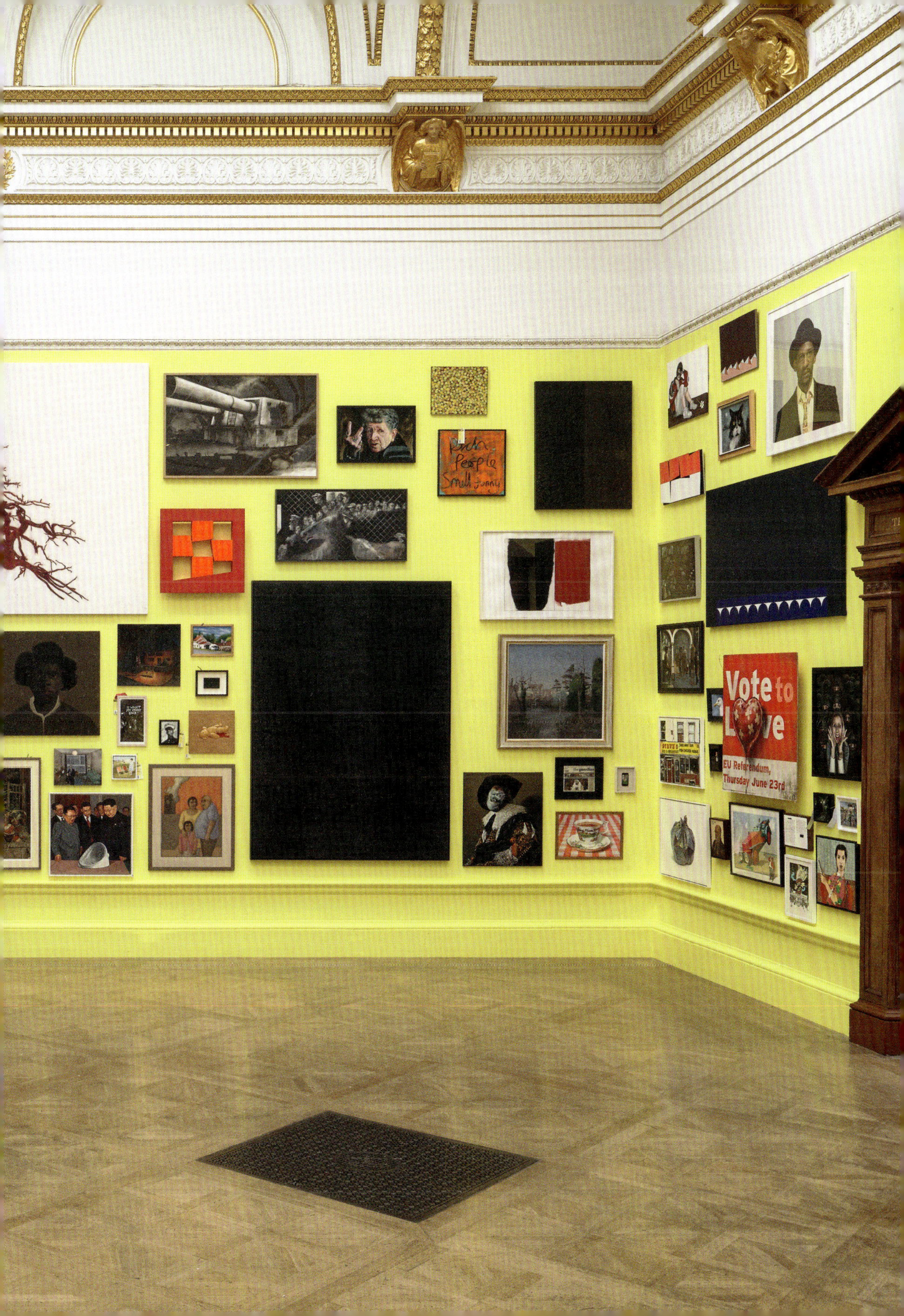
Vote to
EU Referendum,
Thursday June 23rd

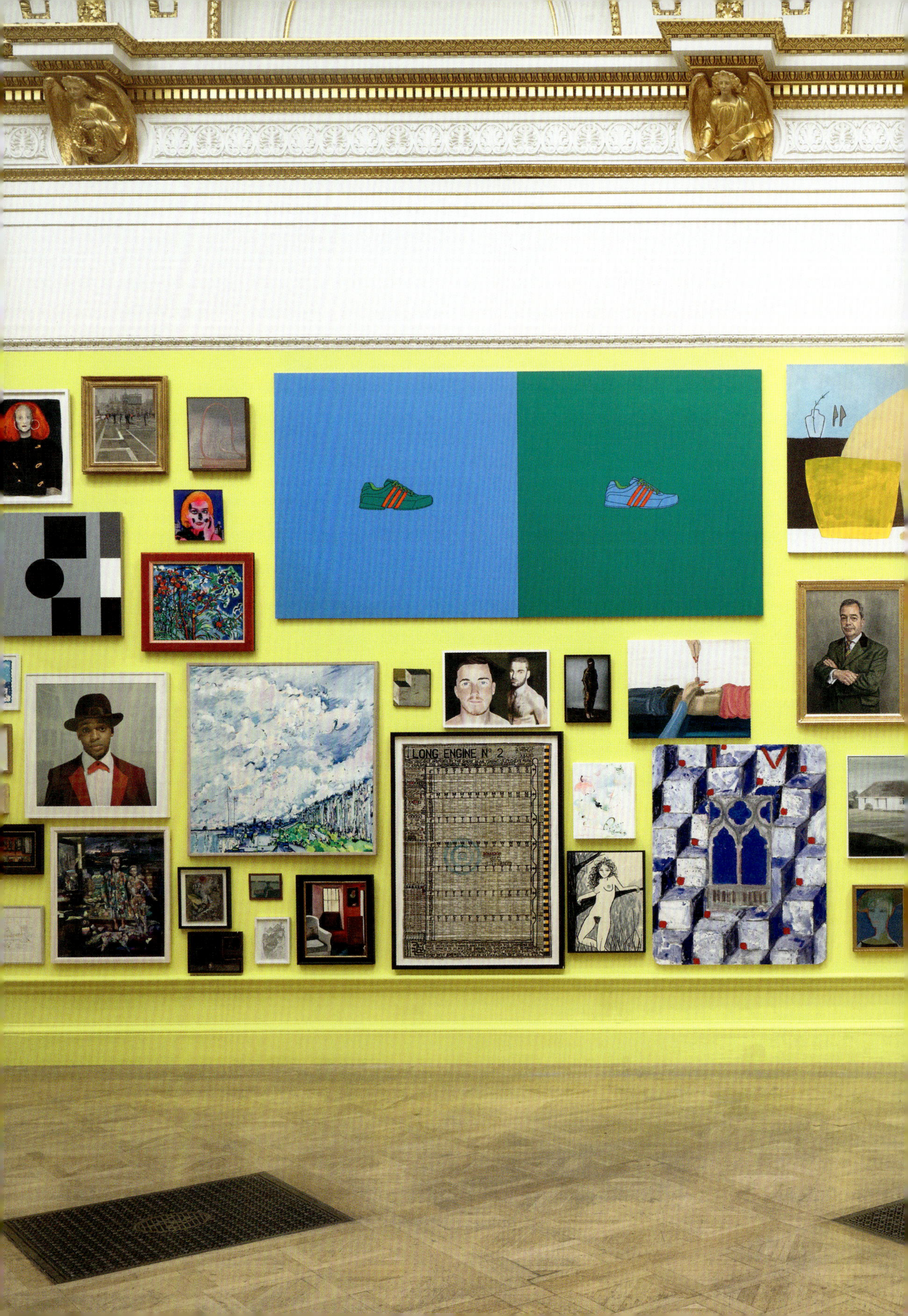
LONG ENGINE Nº 2

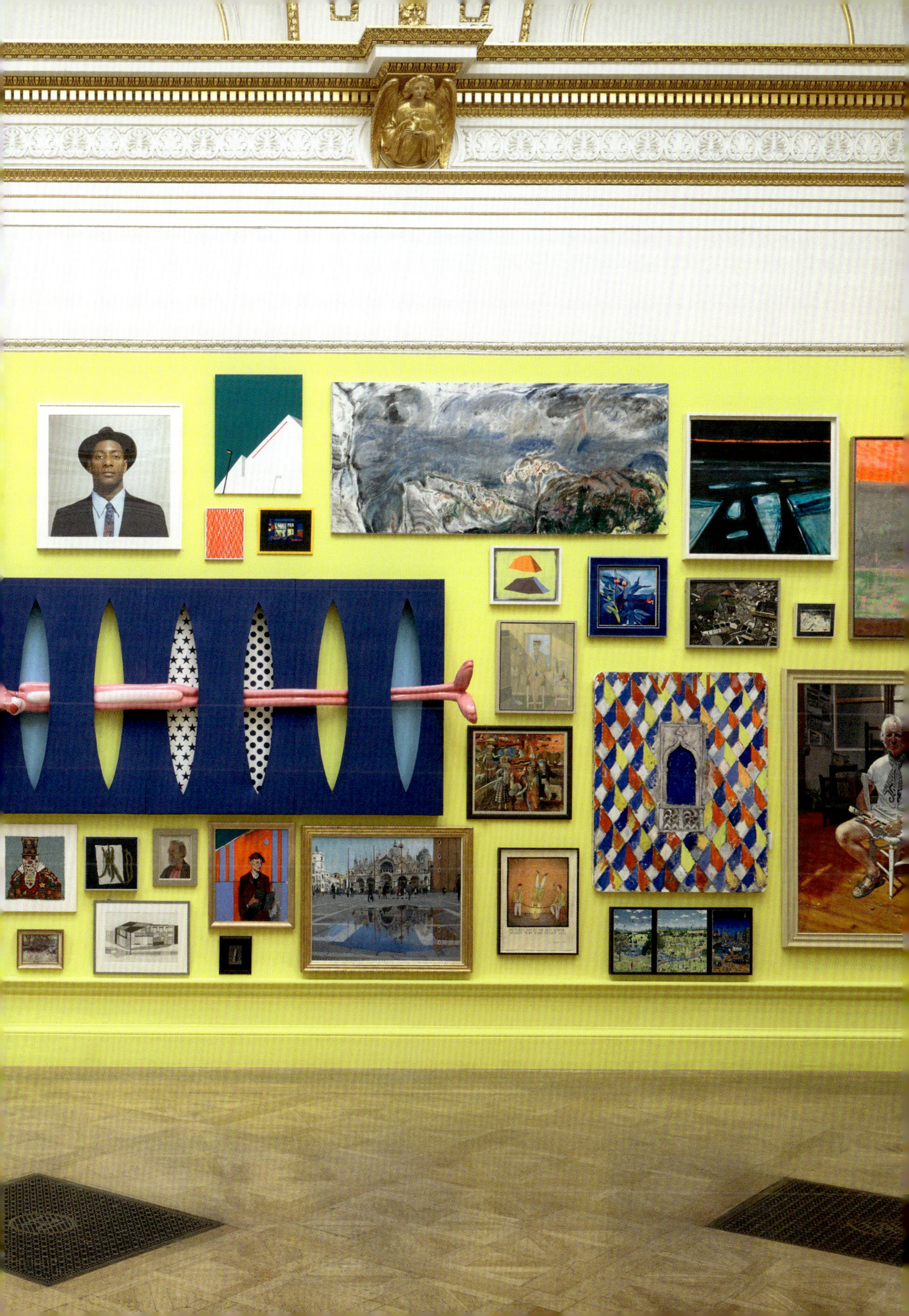

Anselm Kiefer Hon RA
Gehäutete Landschaft
Mixed media
190 × 280 × 37 cm

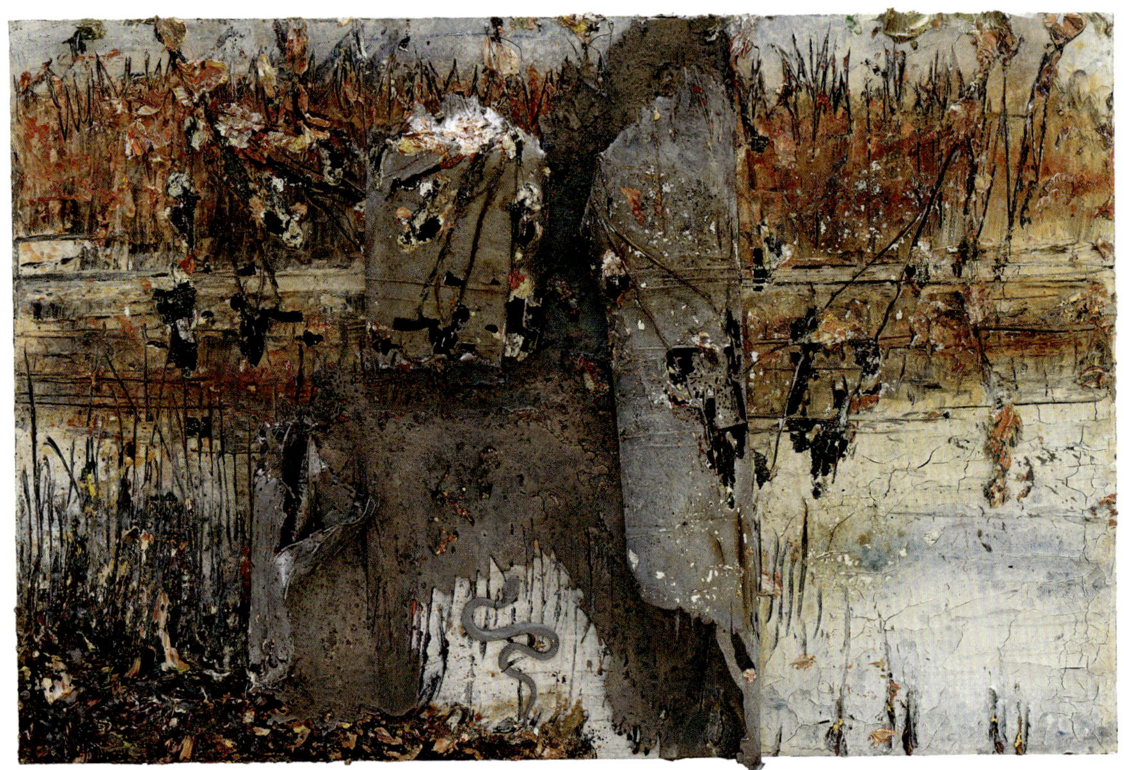

Tony Bevan RA
Tree No. 2
Acrylic and charcoal
239 × 331 cm

Kiki Smith Hon RA
Healers
Etching
24 × 30 cm

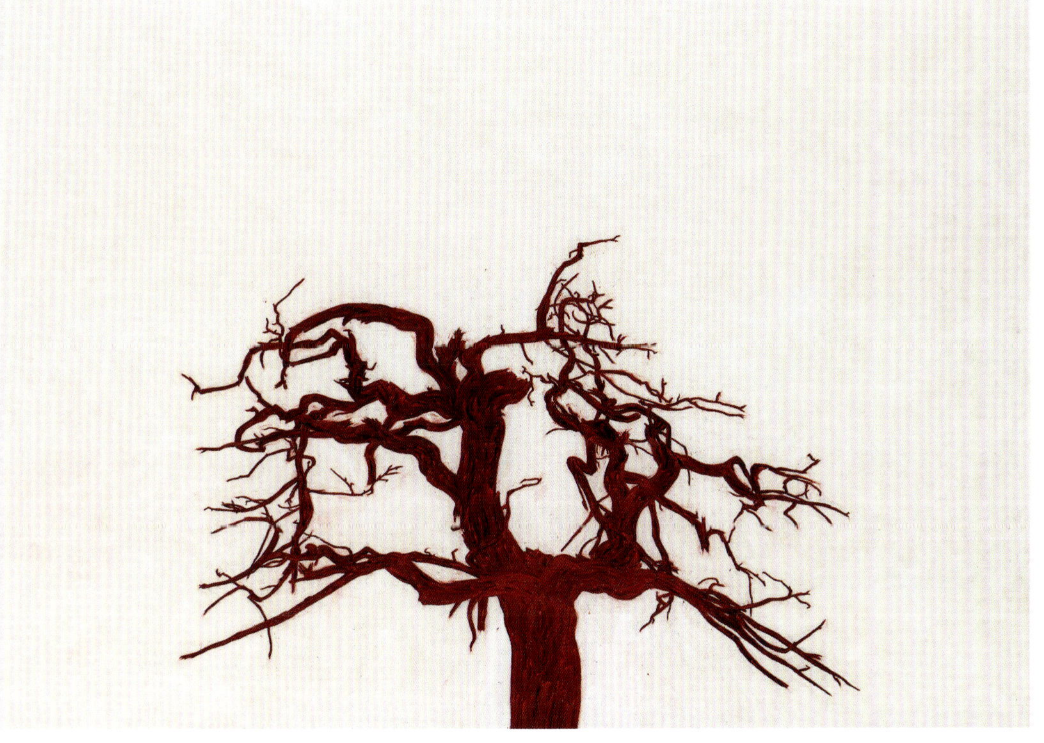

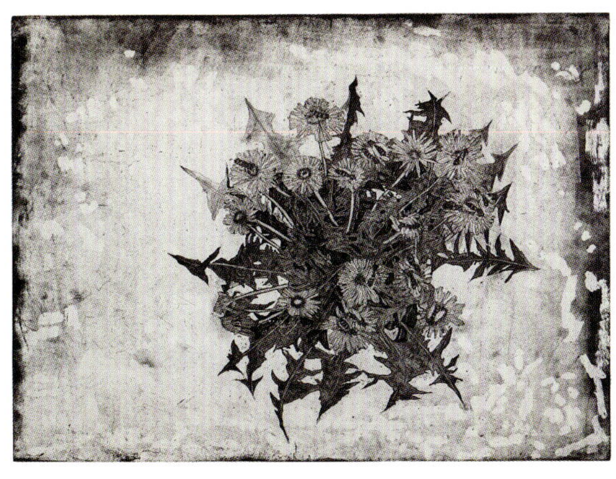

Bill Jacklin RA
Into the Waves
Monotype
70 × 55 cm

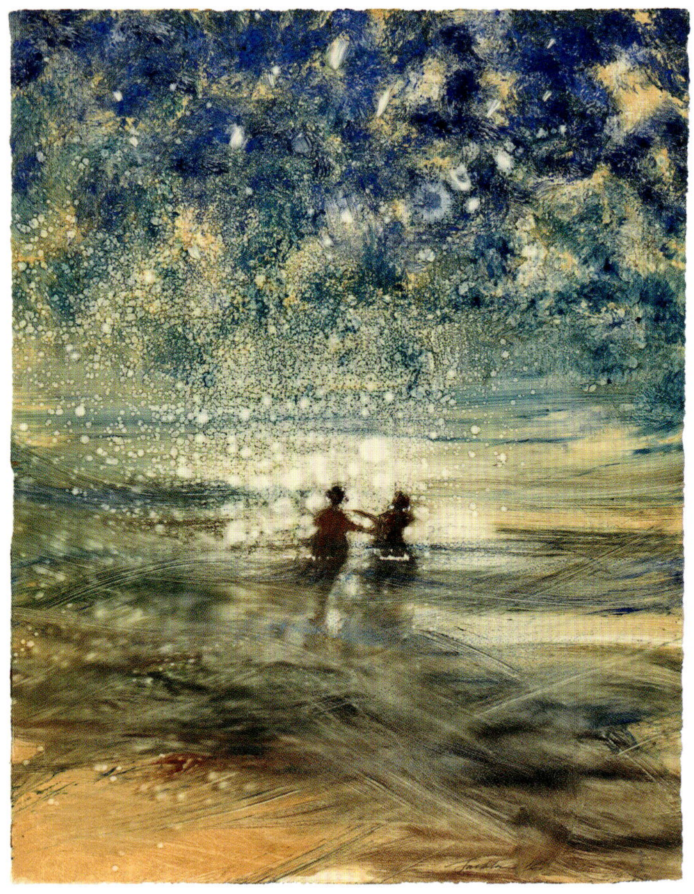

Dr Barbara Rae CBE RA
Ice Floes – Peel Sound
Mixed media
183 × 183 cm

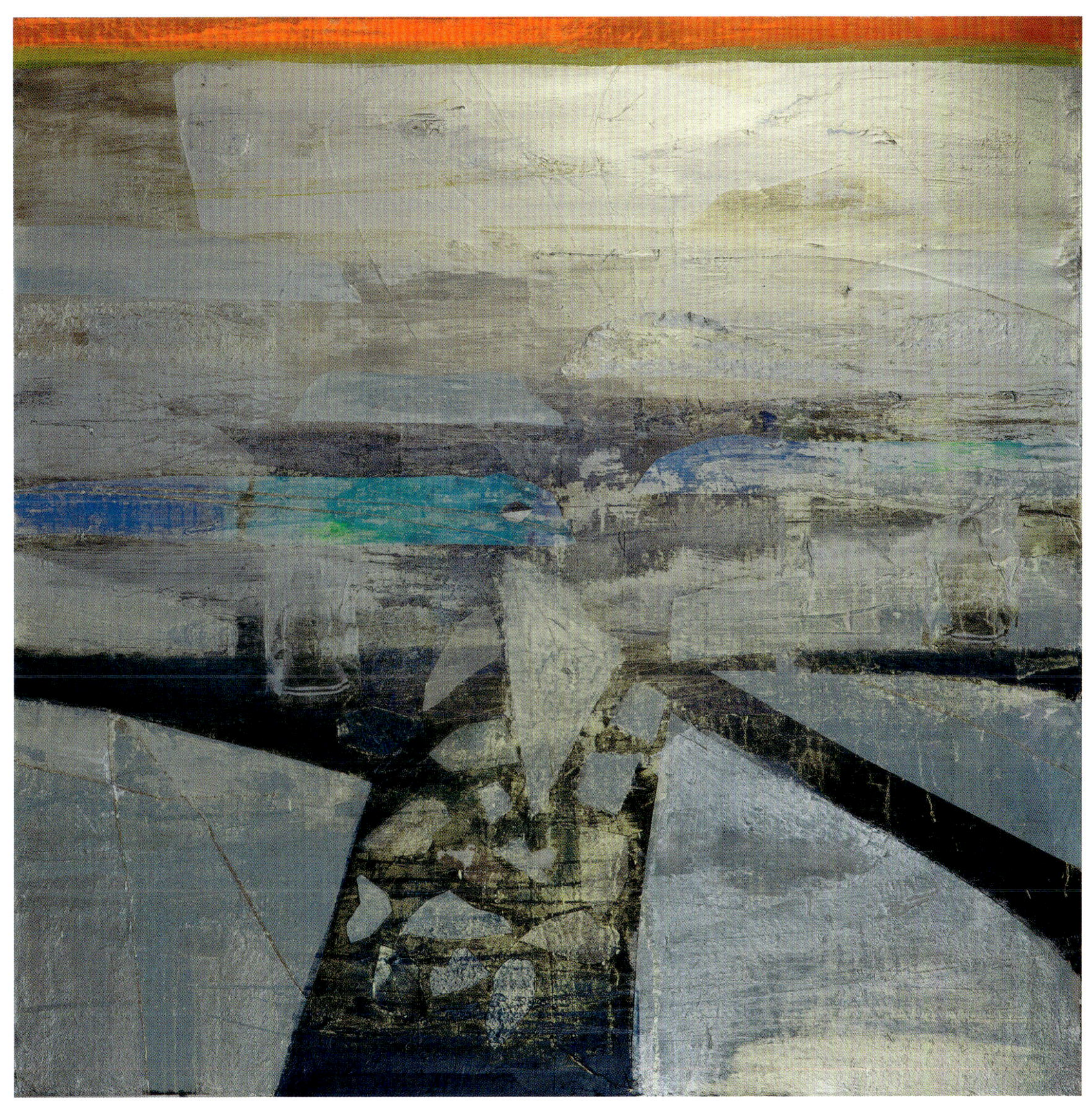

Rose Wylie RA
African Barber Shop Sign
Oil
183 × 341 cm

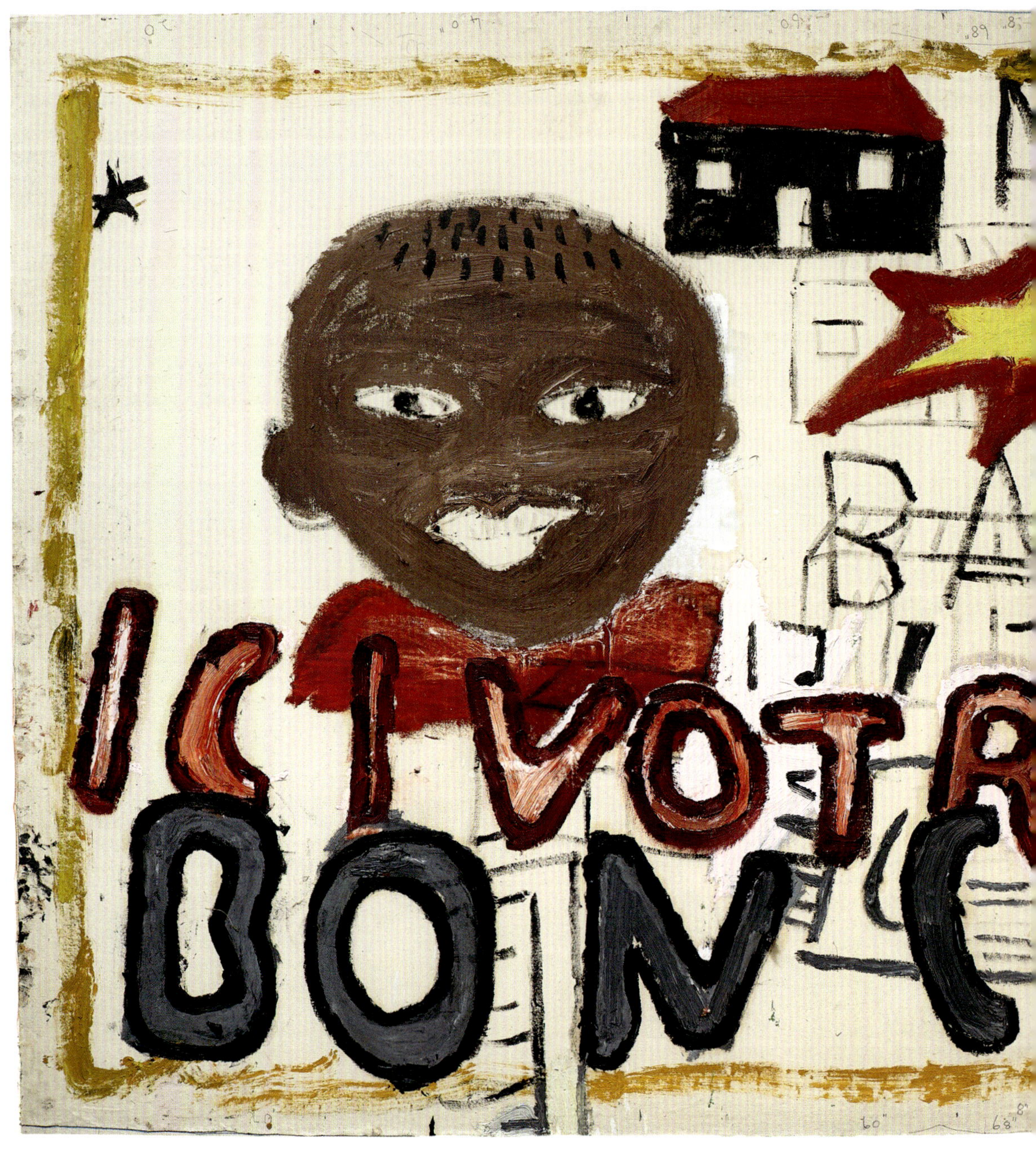

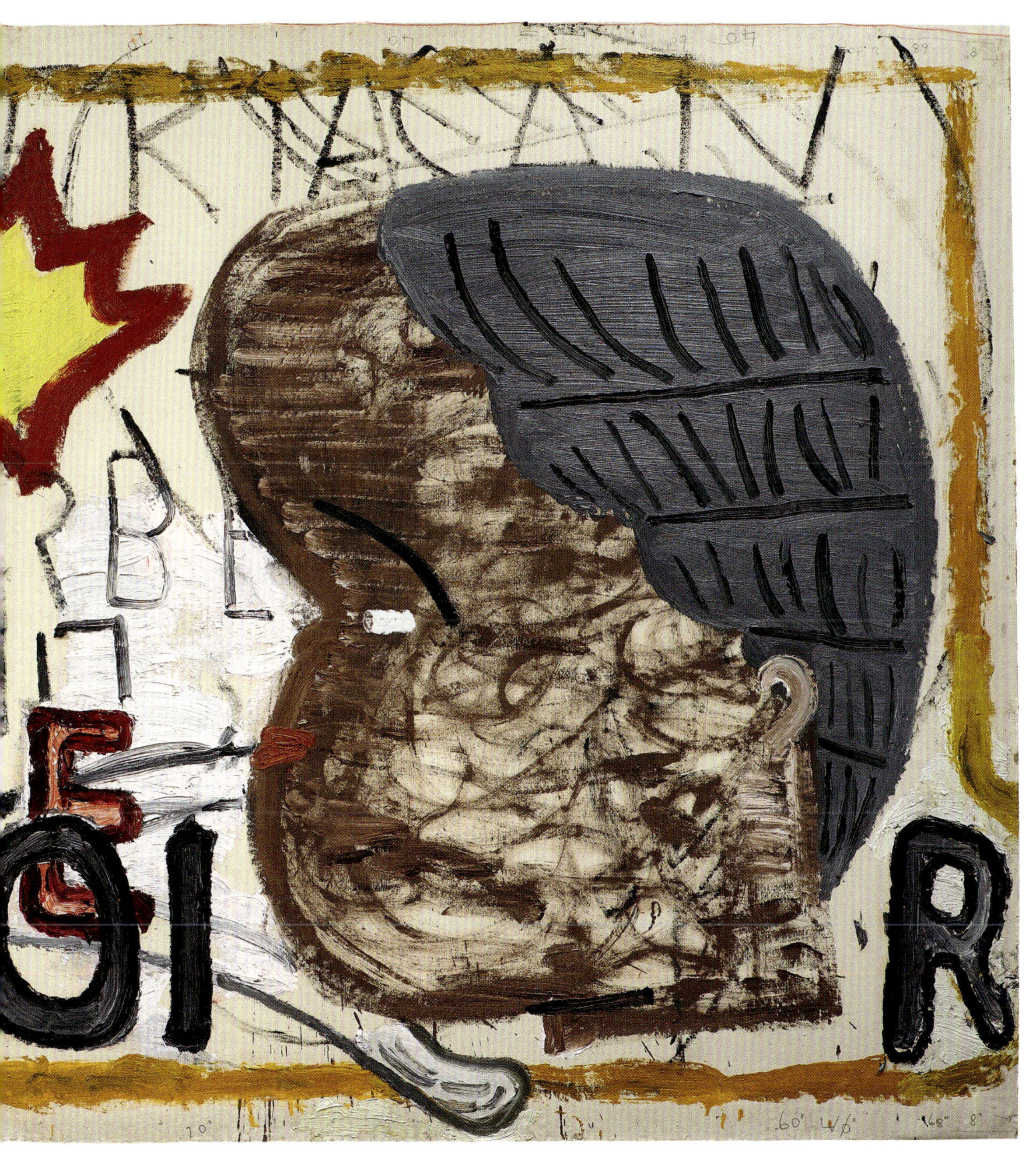

Prof Humphrey Ocean RA
Half Timber
Oil
73 × 92 cm

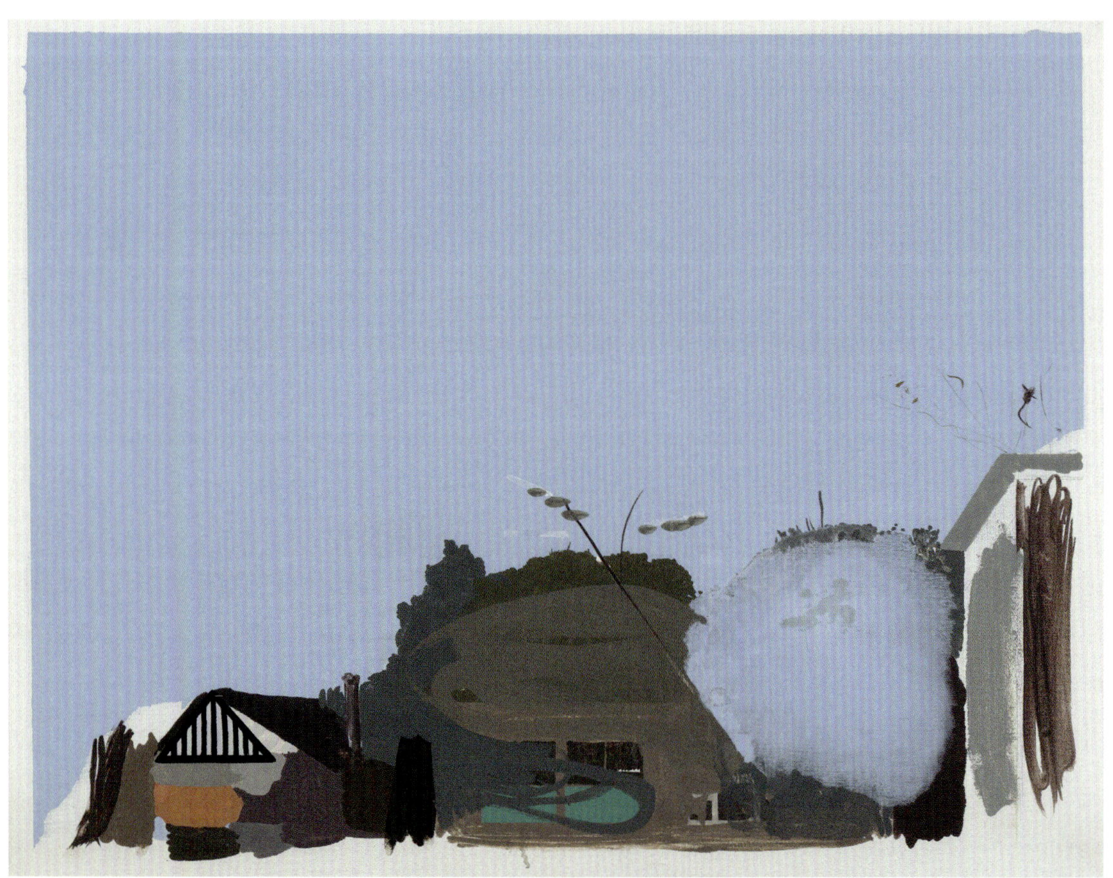

Lisa Milroy RA
Memory
Oil and acrylic
184 × 233 cm

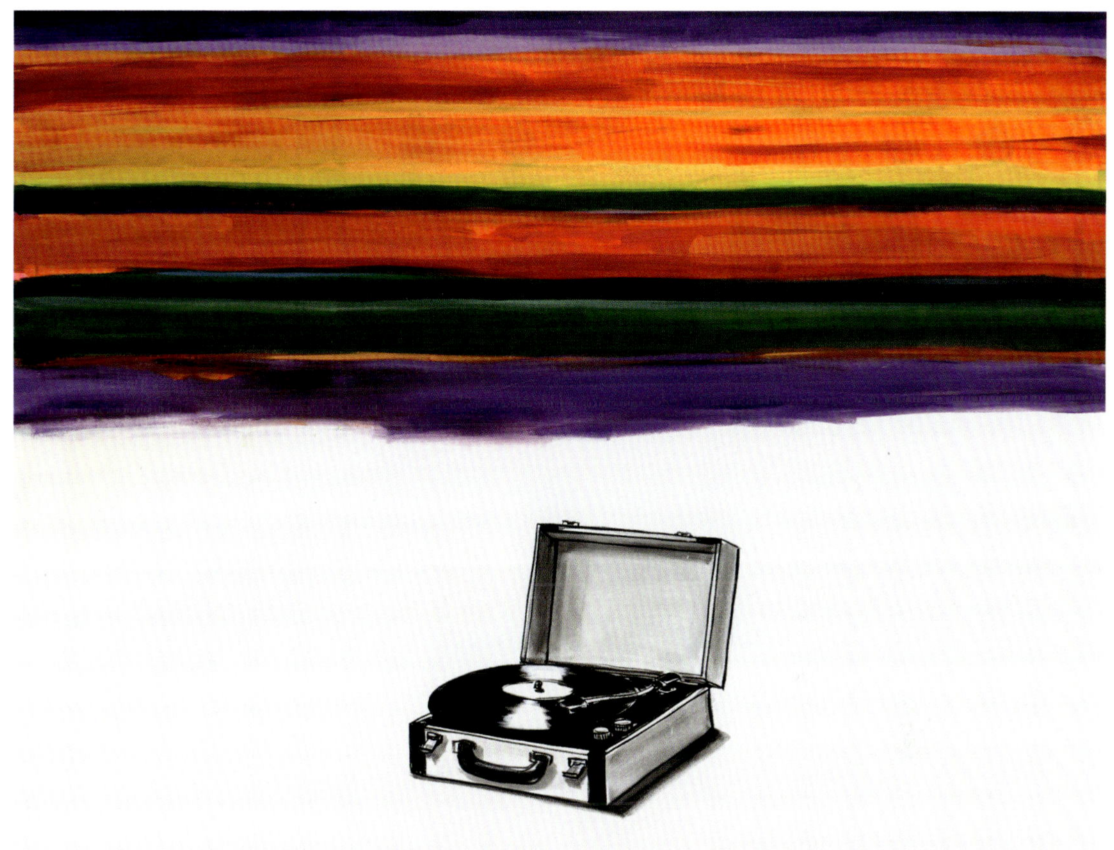

Ken Howard OBE RA
Aqua Alta, Venice
Oil
102 × 122 cm

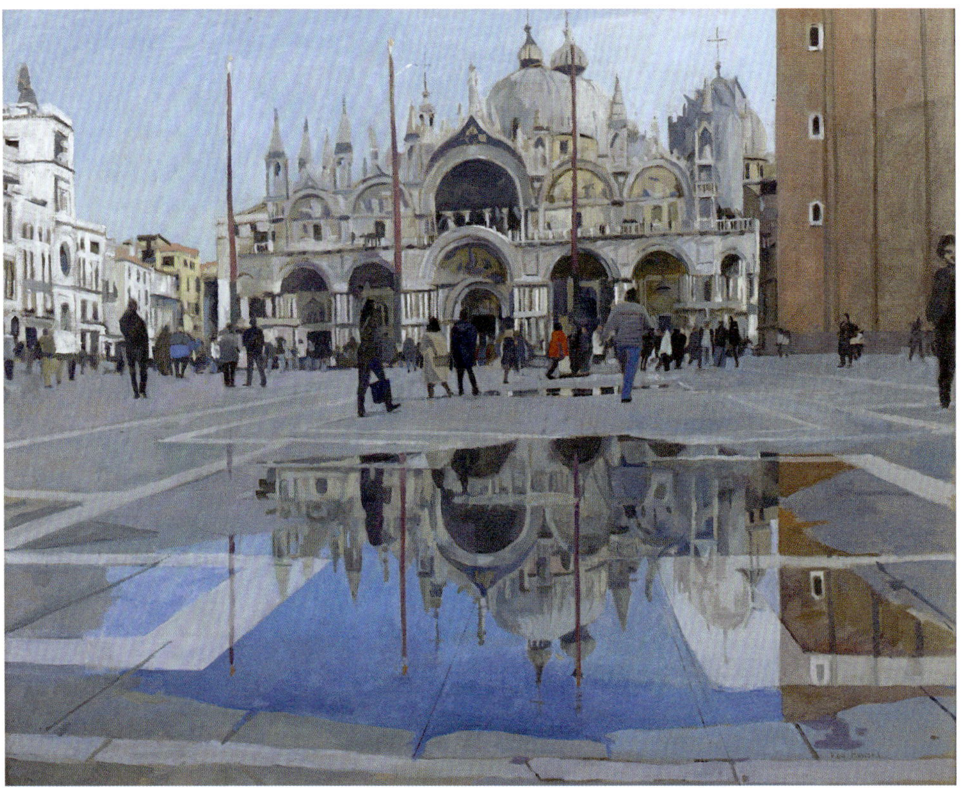

Joe Tilson RA
The Stones of Venice Ca' Foscari 2
Acrylic
178 × 142 cm

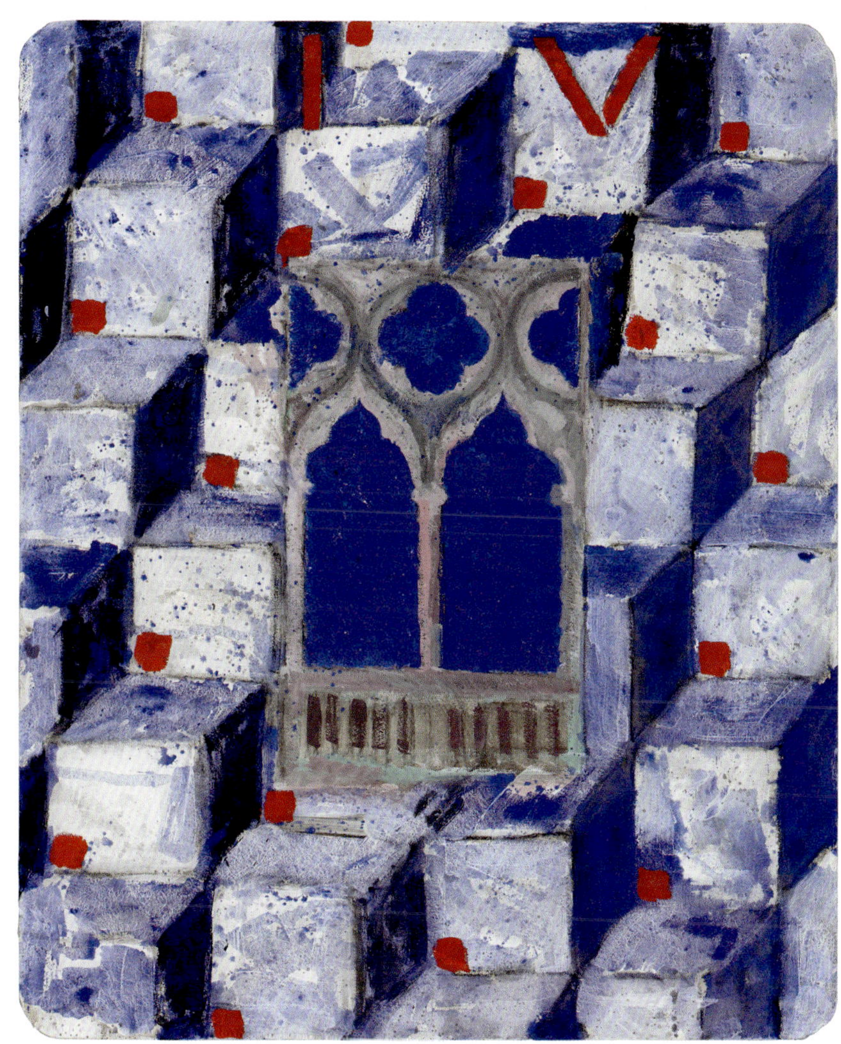

Michael Rooney RA
Curtain Call
Gouache and tempera
65 × 72 cm

Jeffery Camp RA
Rouge
Oil
30 × 41 cm

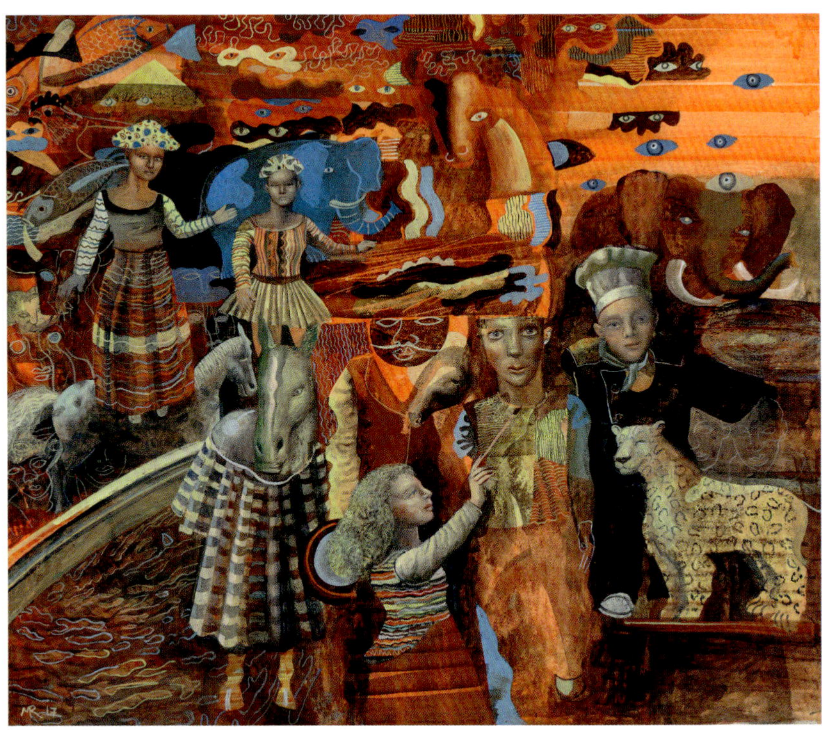

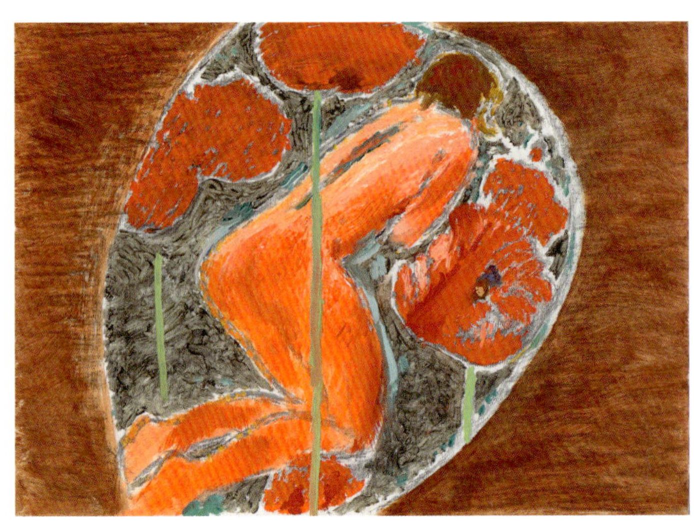

David Remfry MBE RA
Solong Salon
Oil
137 × 122 cm

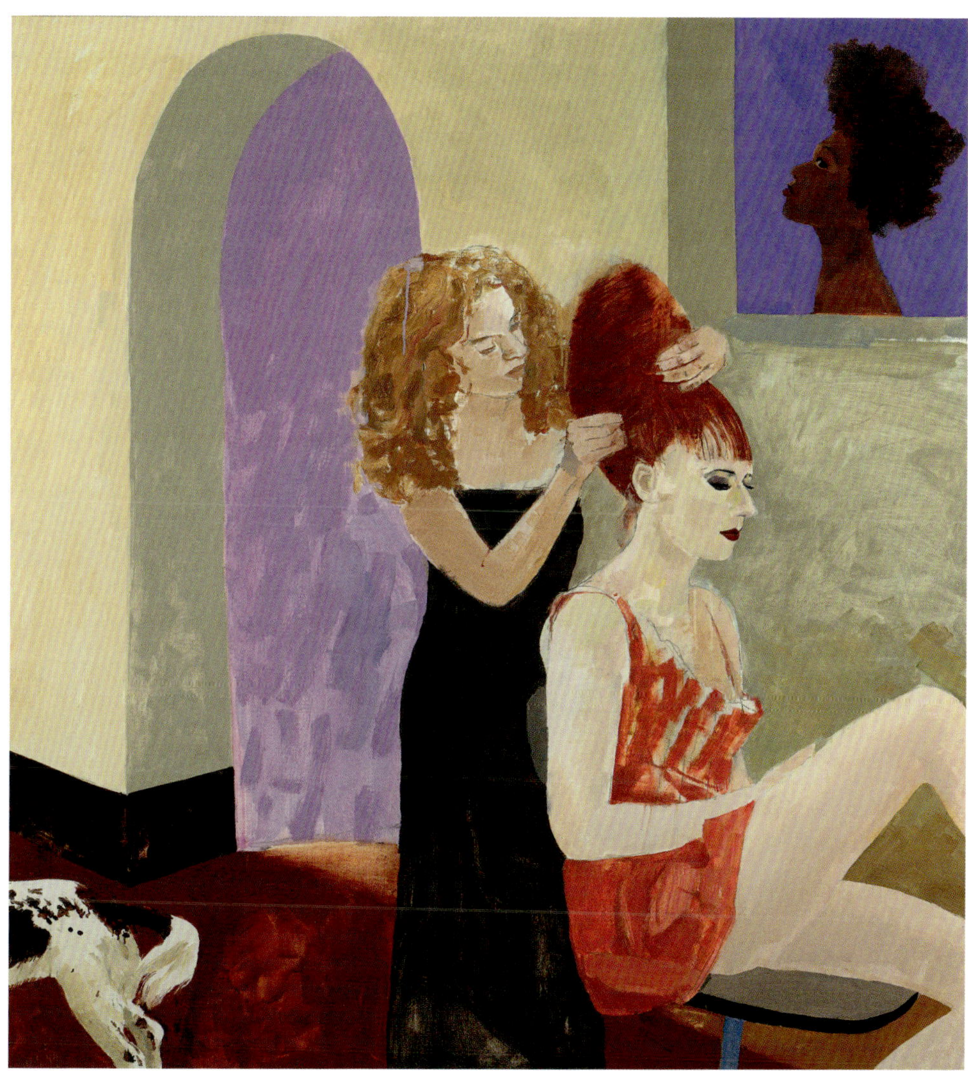

Olwyn Bowey RA
Gardener's World – Autumn
Oil
87 × 90 cm

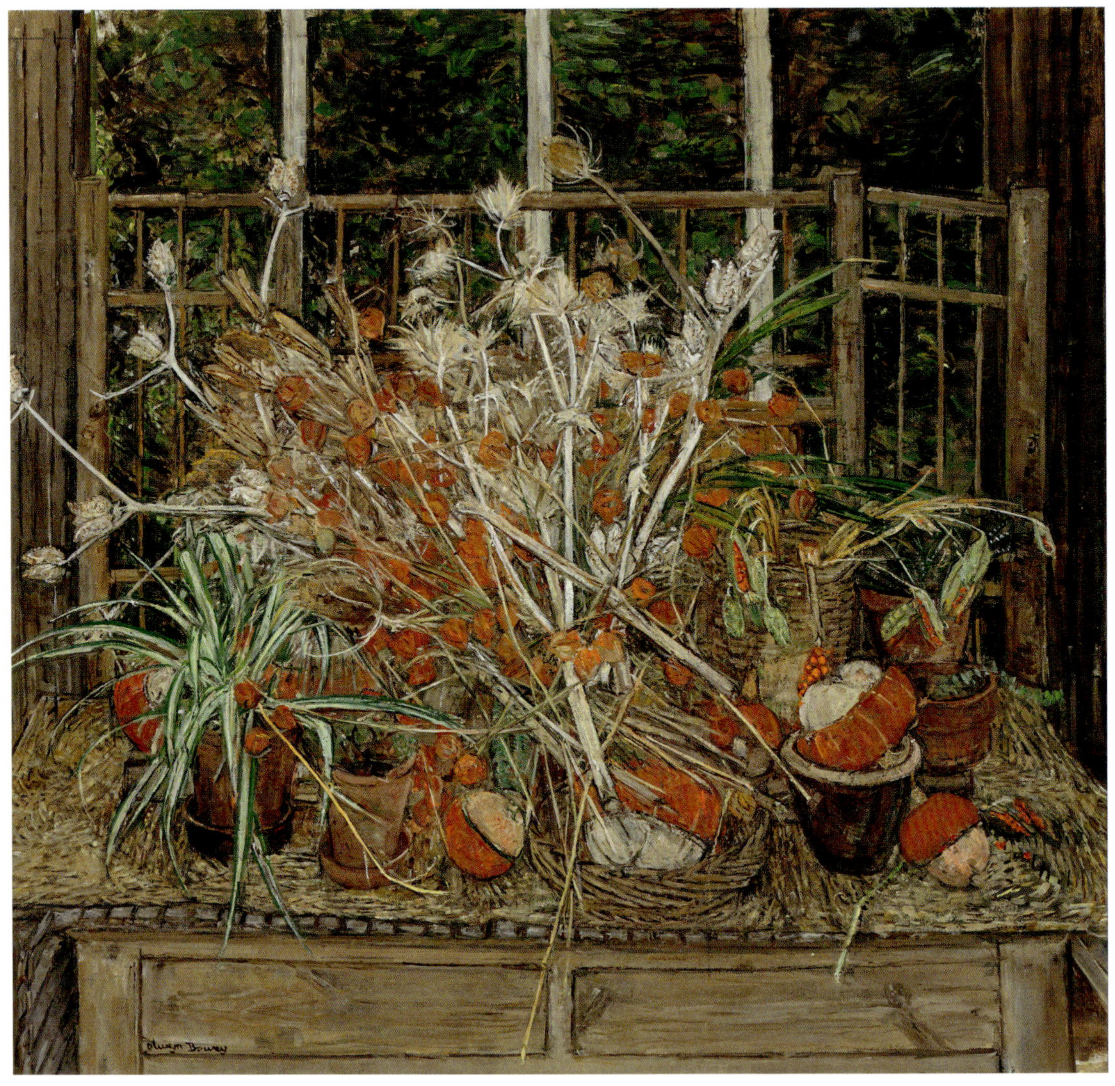

Frederick Cuming Hon D Litt RA
April Landscape
Oil
92 × 92 cm

Diana Armfield RA
Dawn over Snow, Llwynhir
Oil
22 × 27 cm

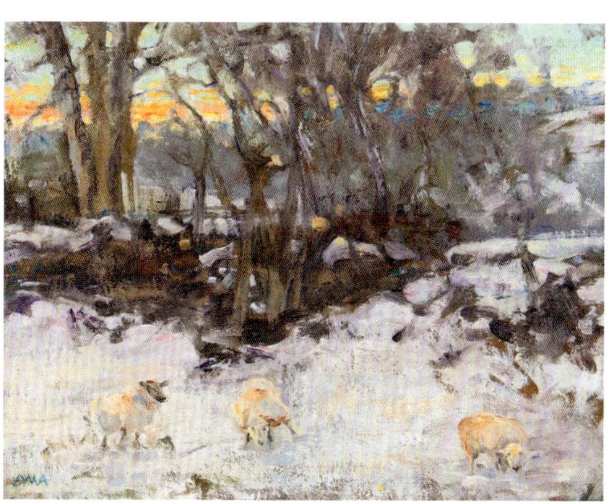

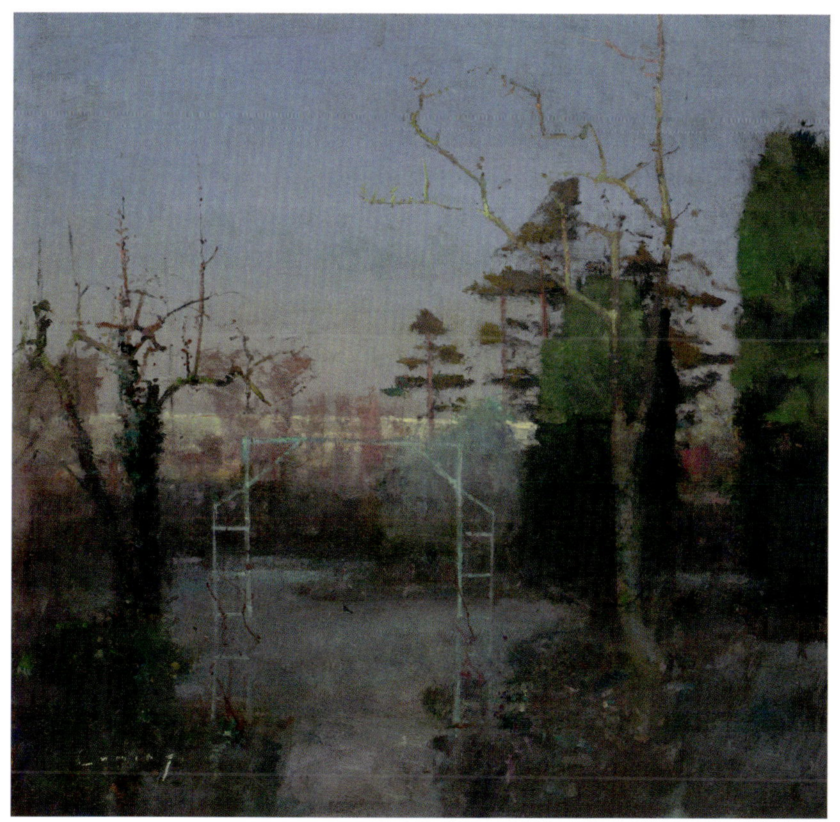

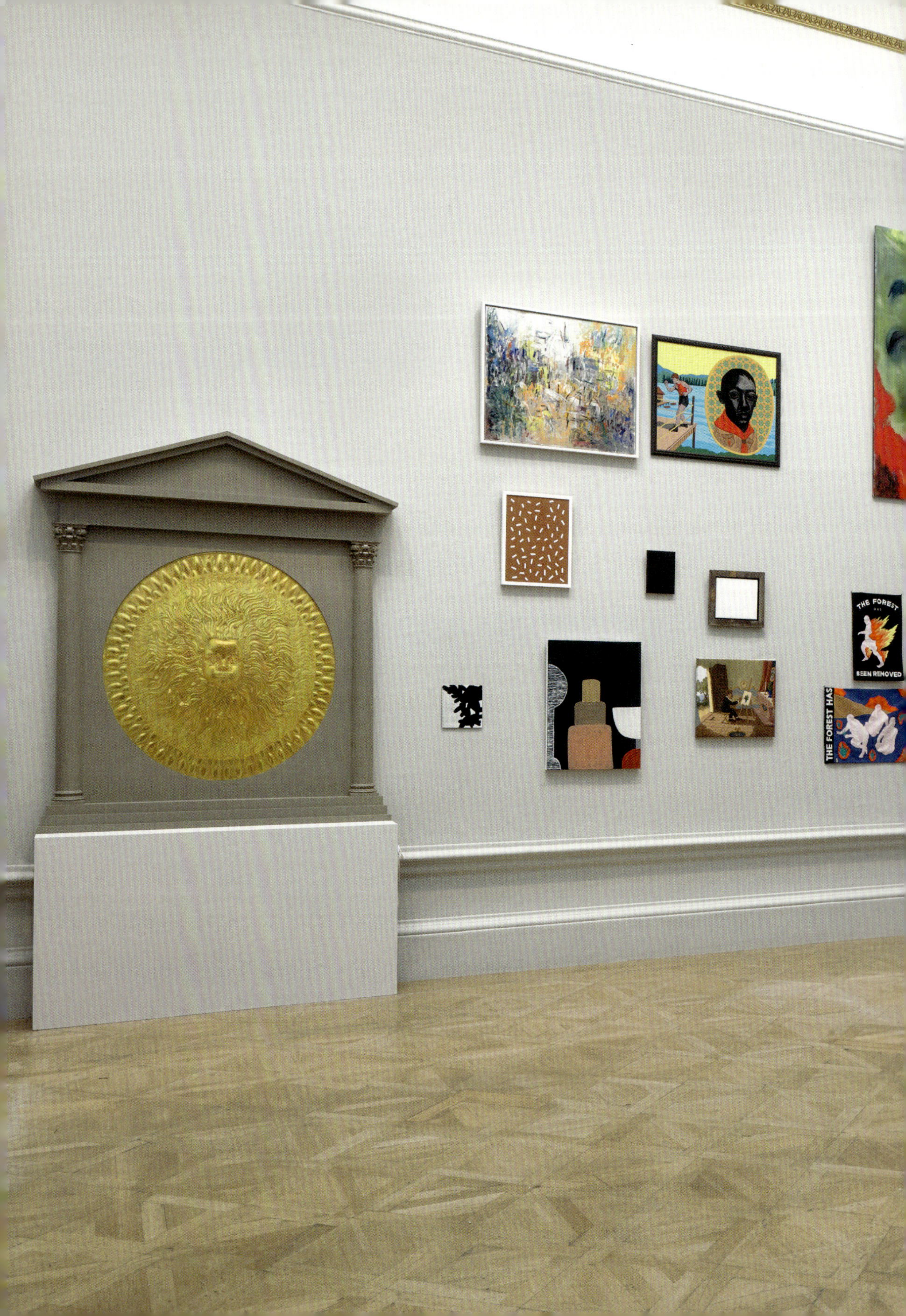
THE FOREST
HAS
BEEN REMOVED
THE FOREST HAS

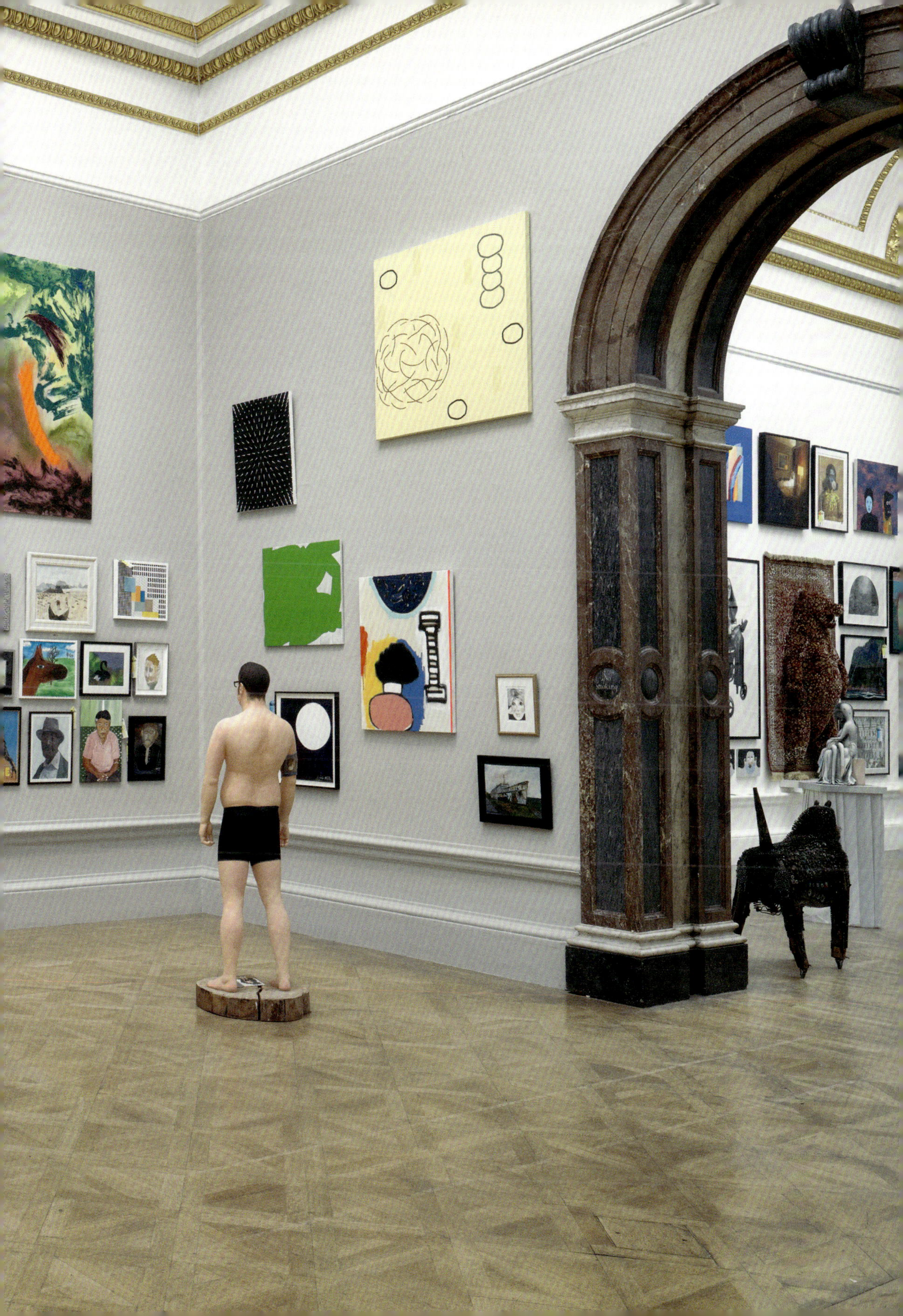

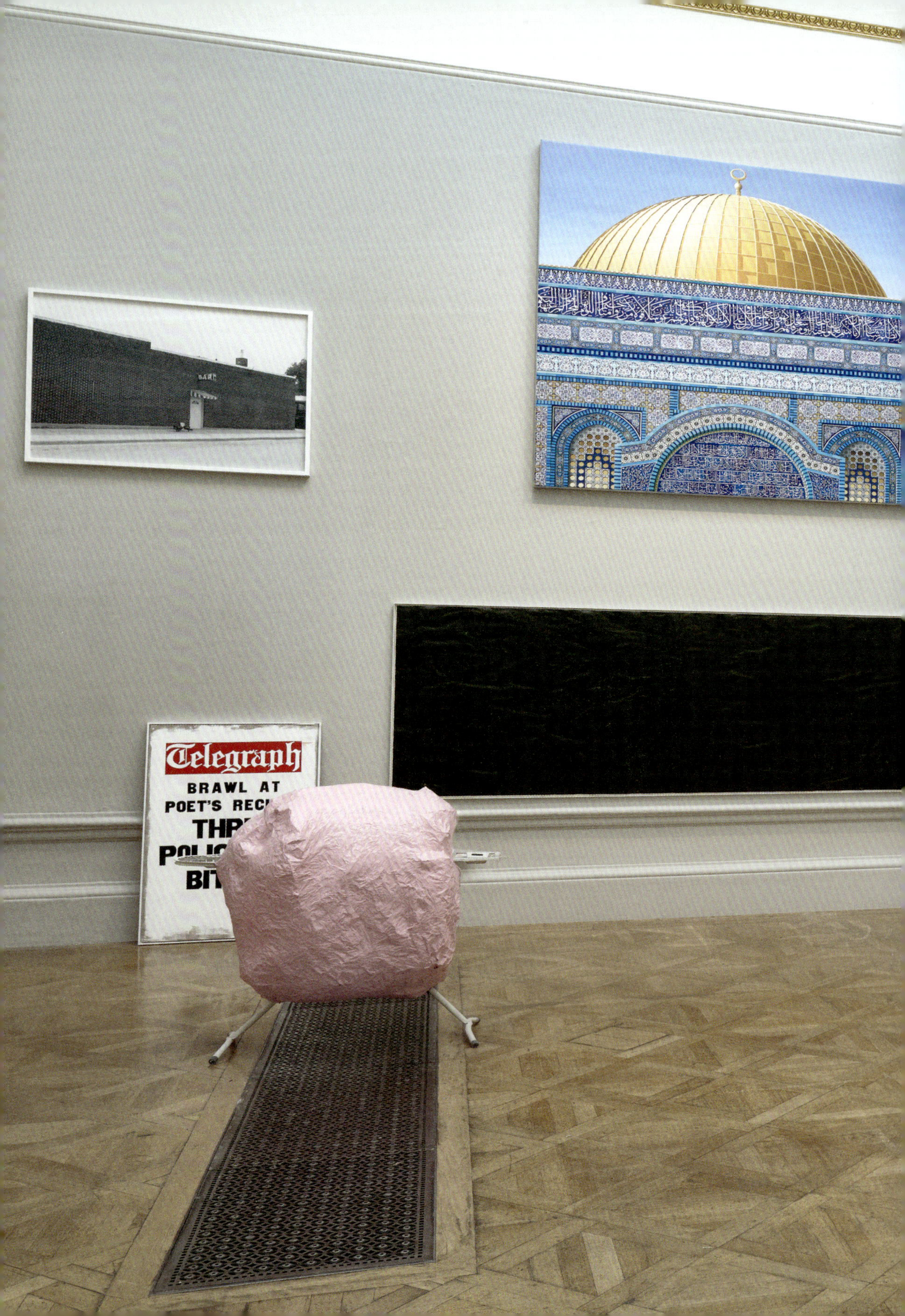
Telegraph
BRAWL AT

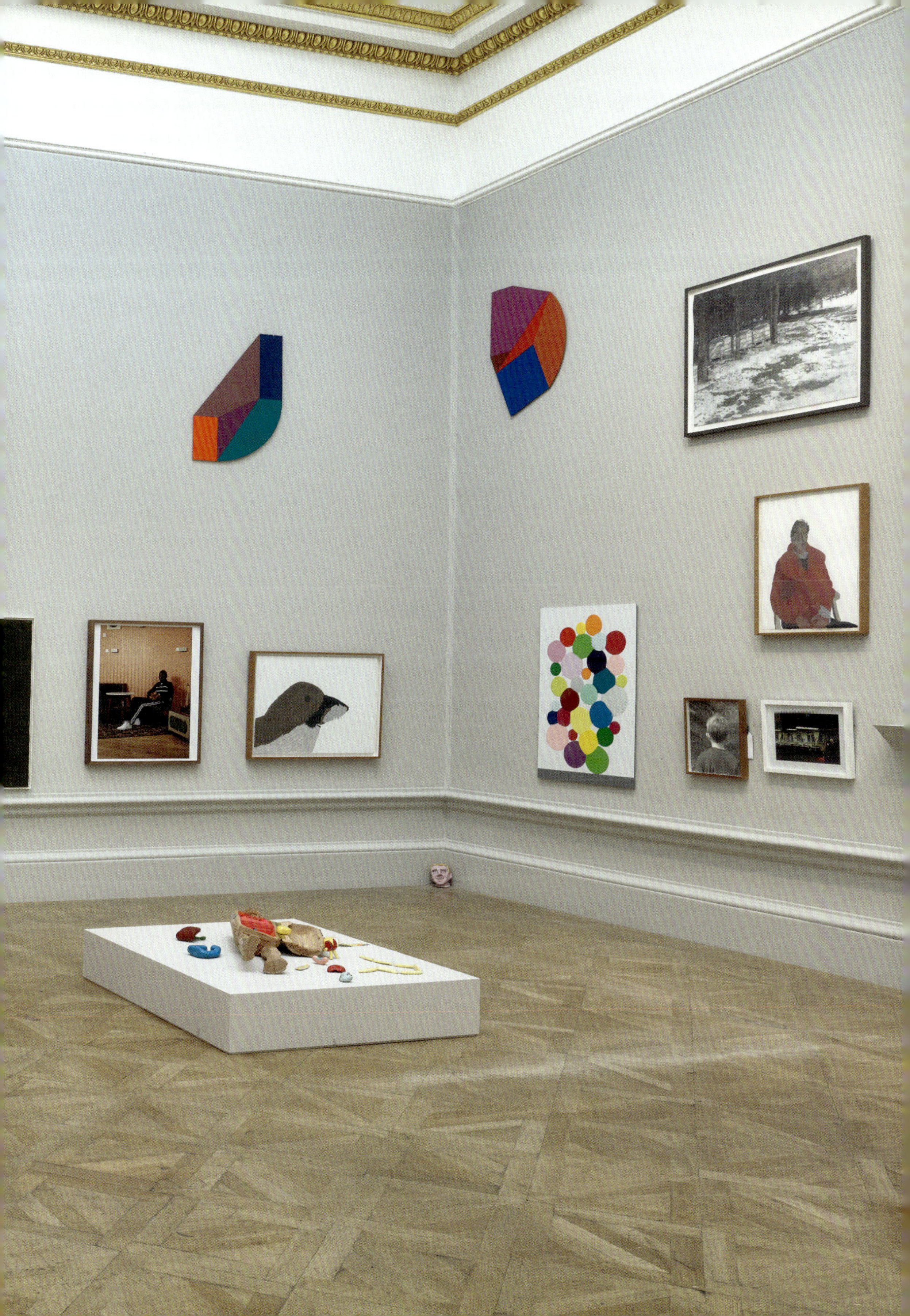

Christopher Le Brun PRA
Changing Light 4
Handmade woodcut
75 × 105 cm

Fiona Rae RA
Snow White with colours fairer painted
Oil
183 × 130 cm

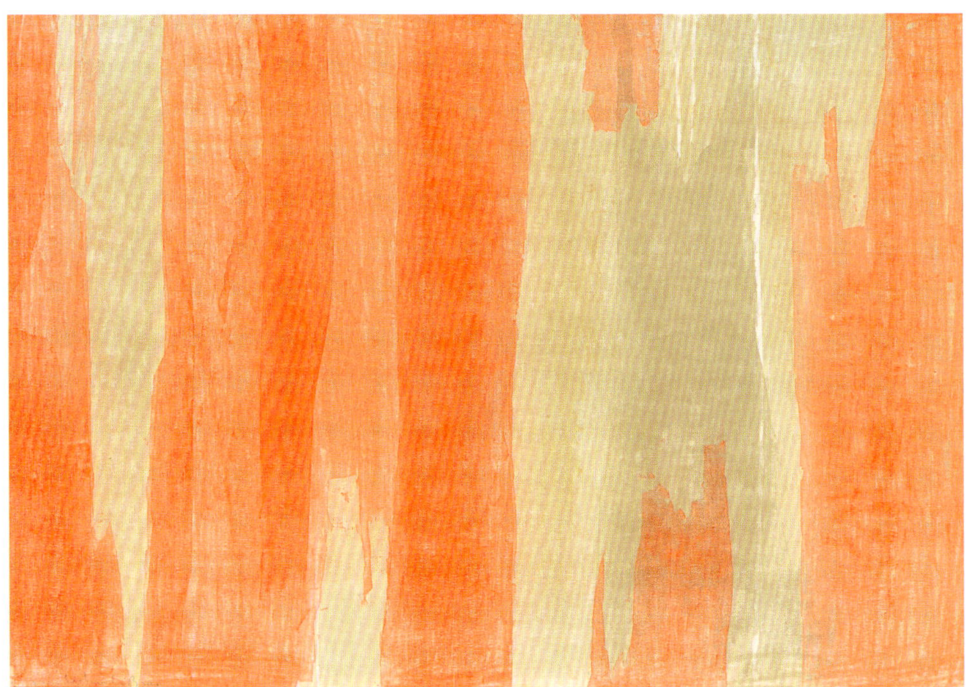

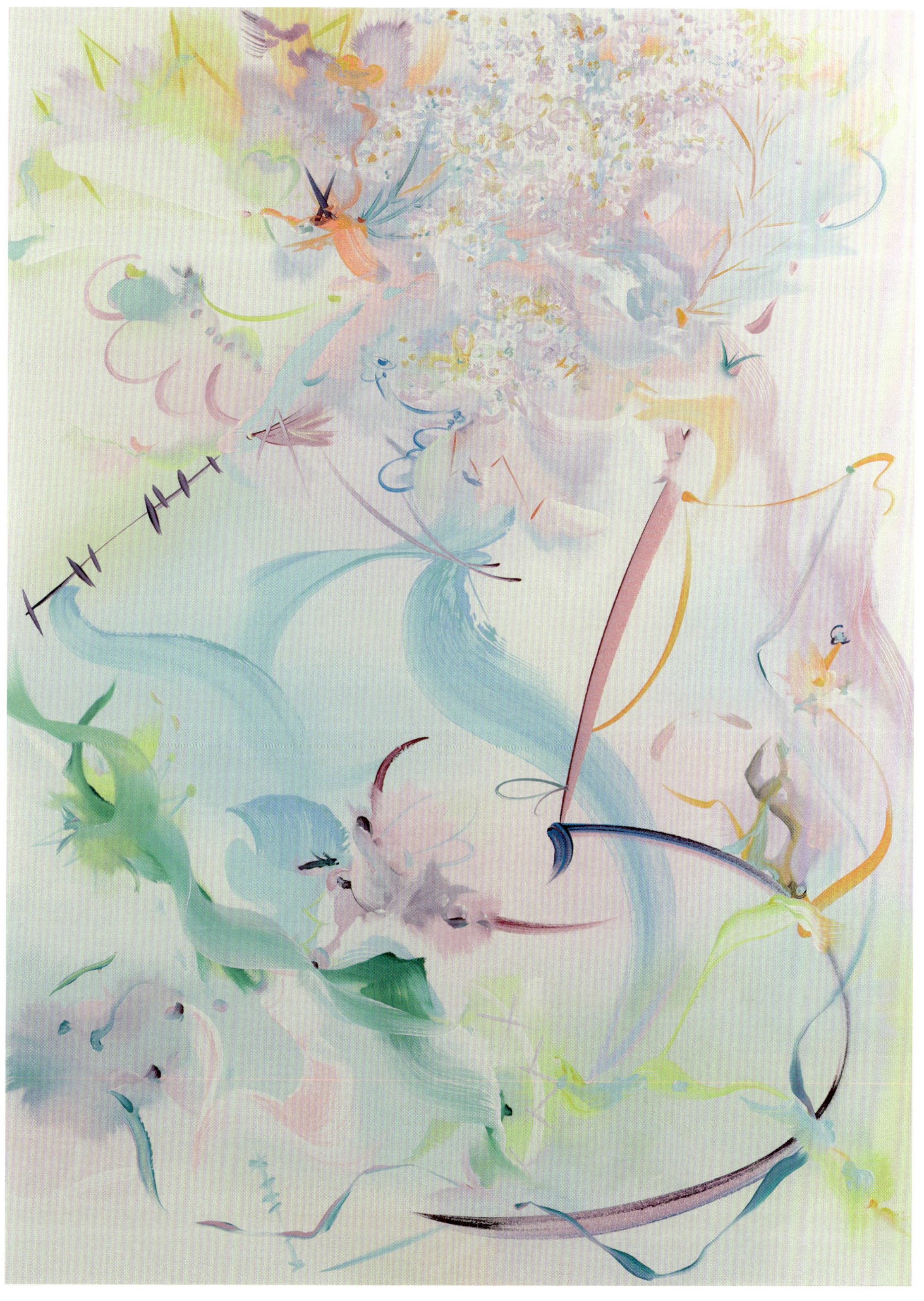

Stephen Chambers RA
Somewhere
Screenprint
112 × 76 cm

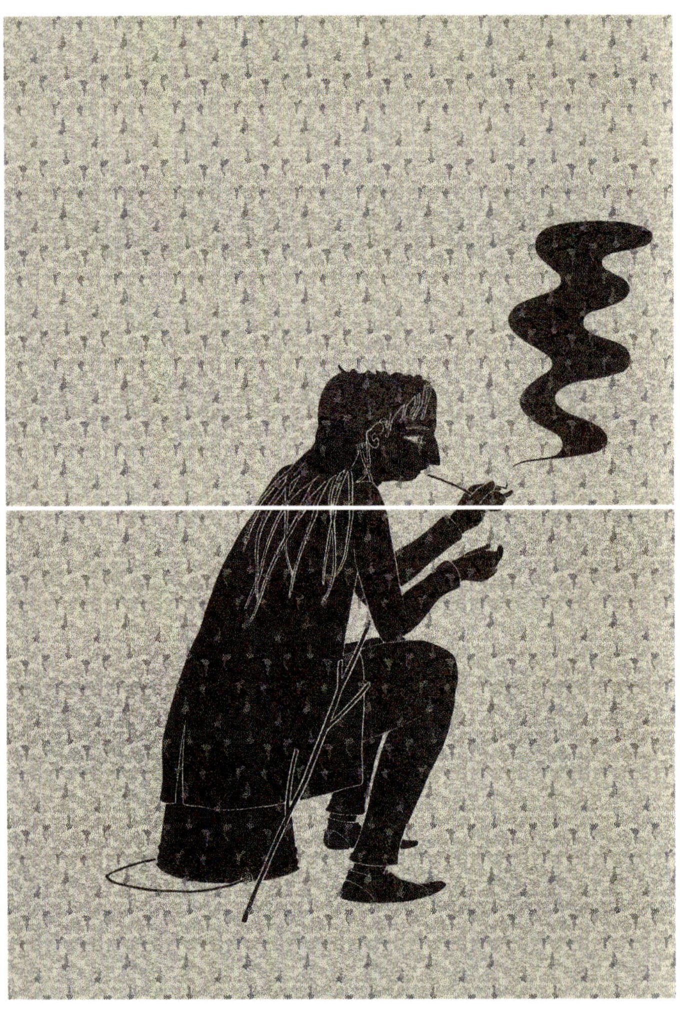

Tom Phillips CBE RA
After W. H. Davies
Oil
153 × 153 cm

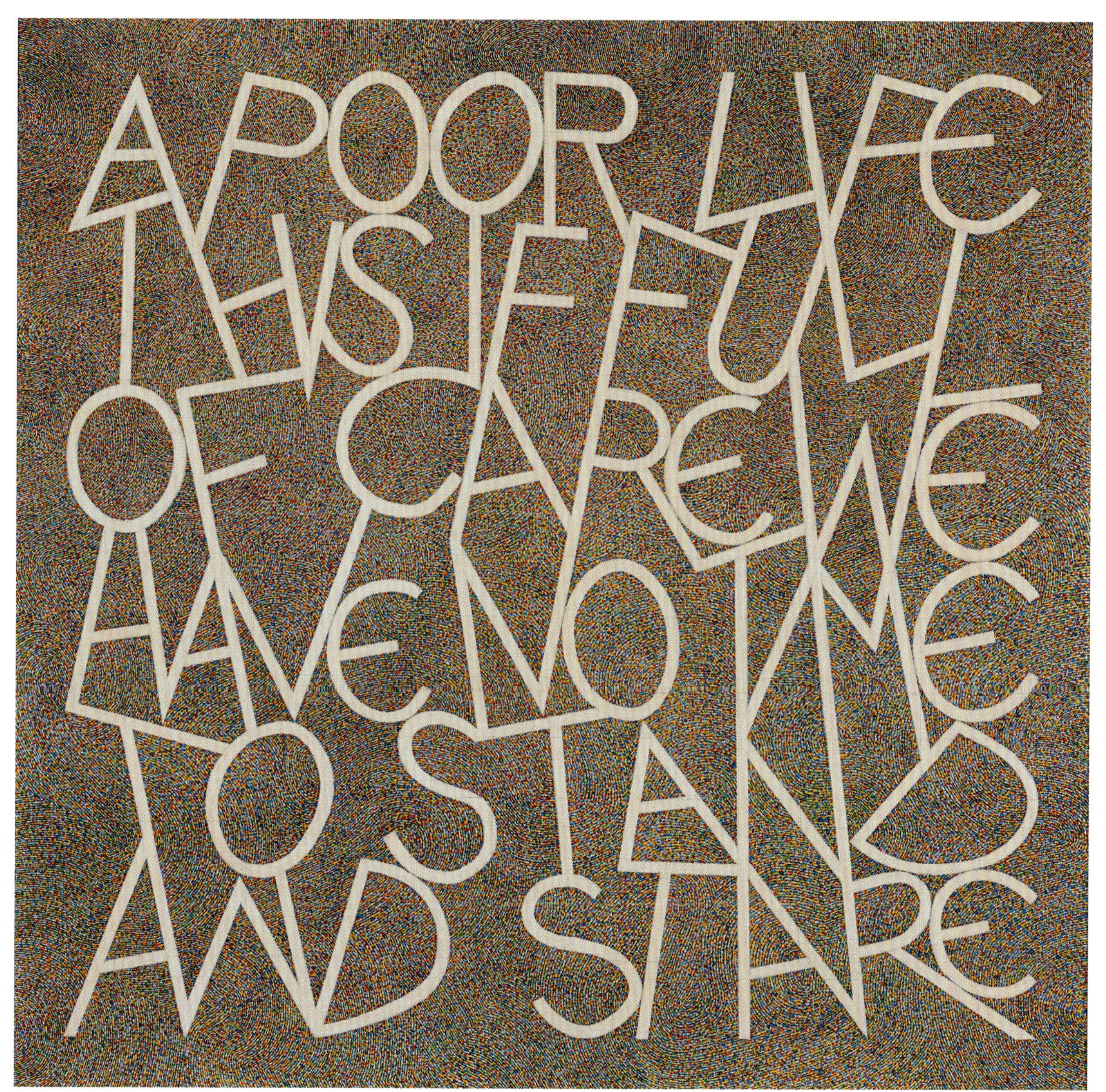

Michael Landy RA
Closing Down Sale
Mixed media and audio
H 165 cm

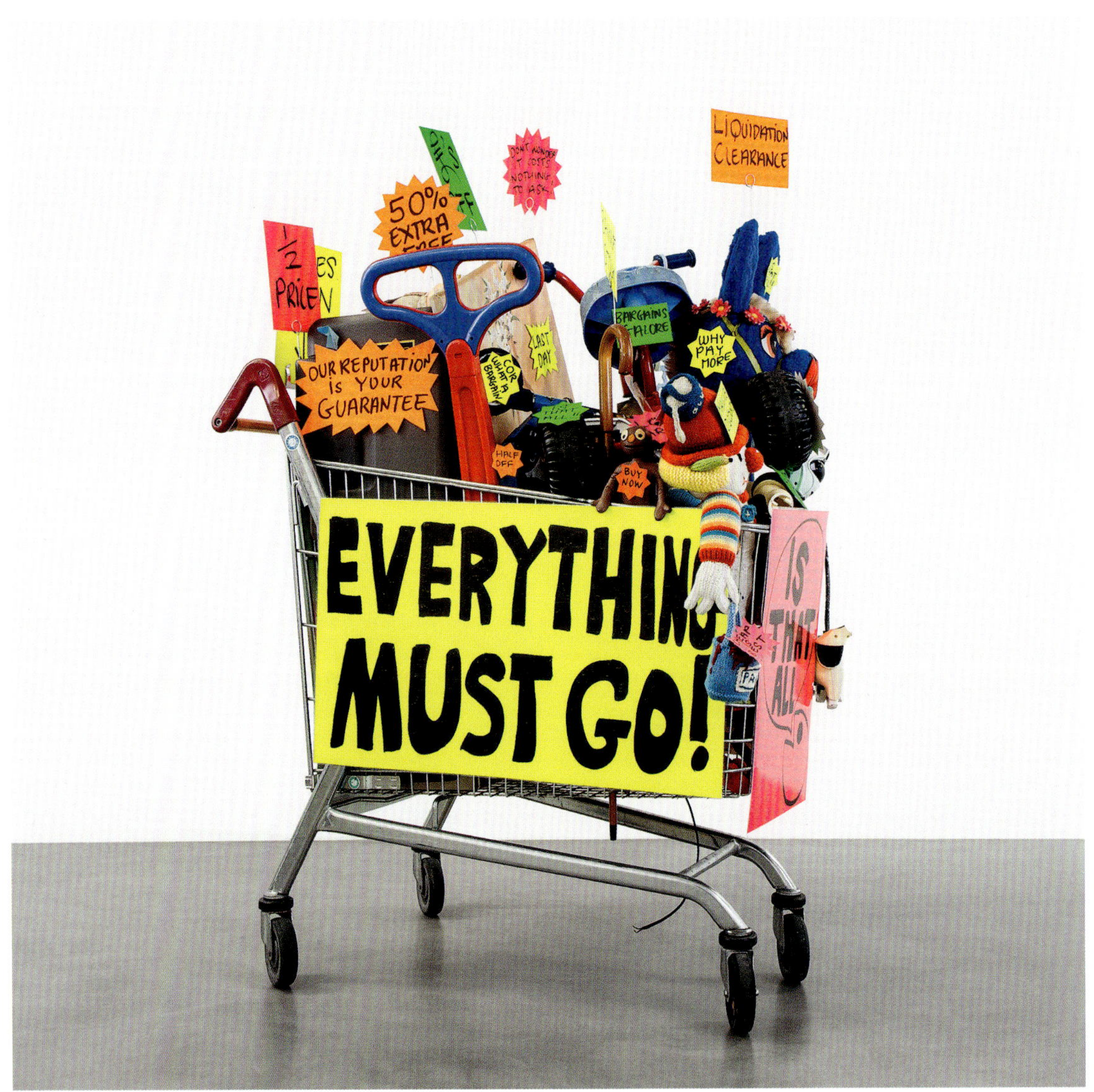

Tracey Emin CBE RA
Open Heart
Acrylic
182 × 182 cm

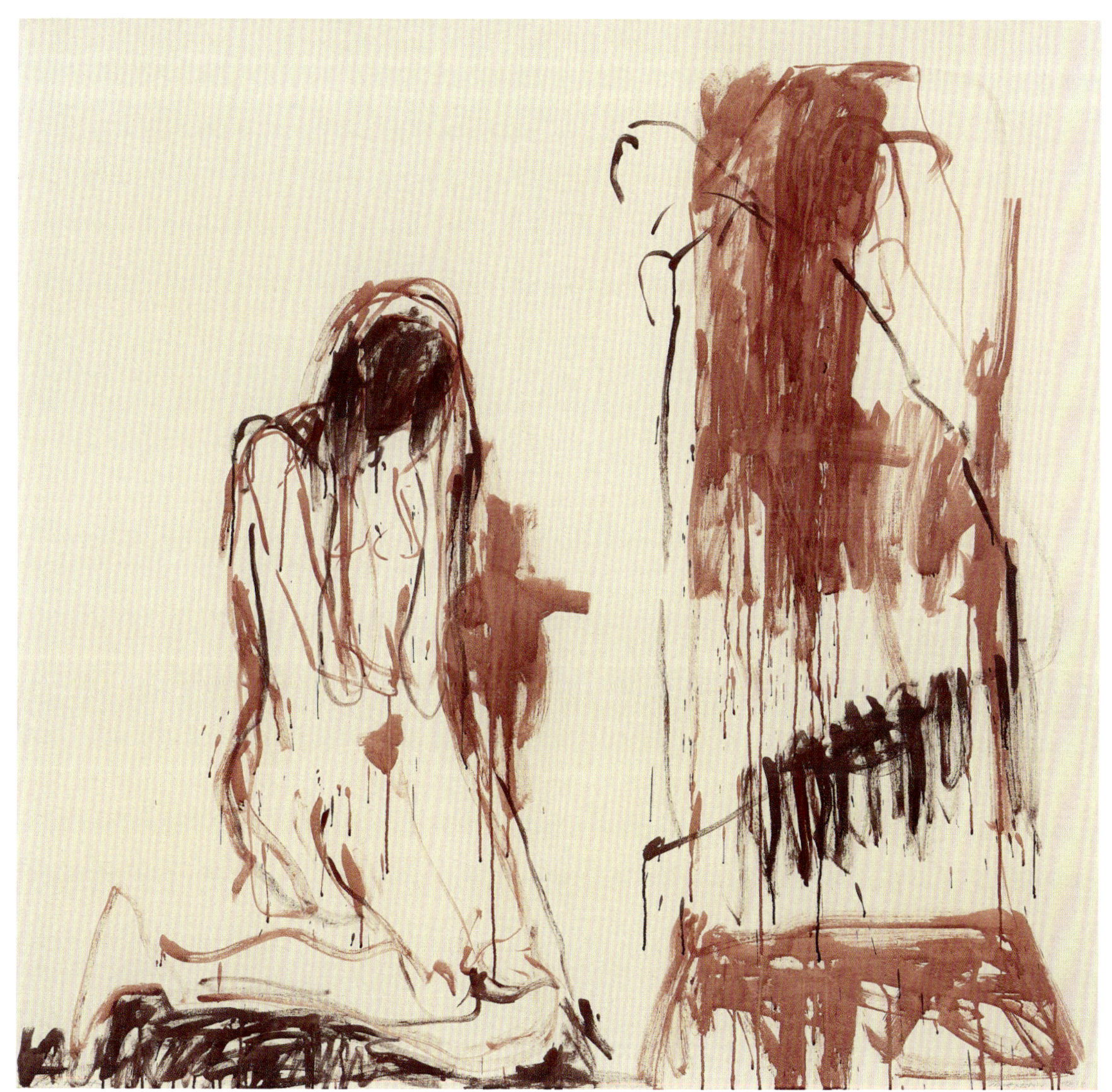

John Maine RA
Panel for Ascension
Gouache
92 × 75 cm

John Wragg RA
Poet
Acrylic
76 × 61 cm

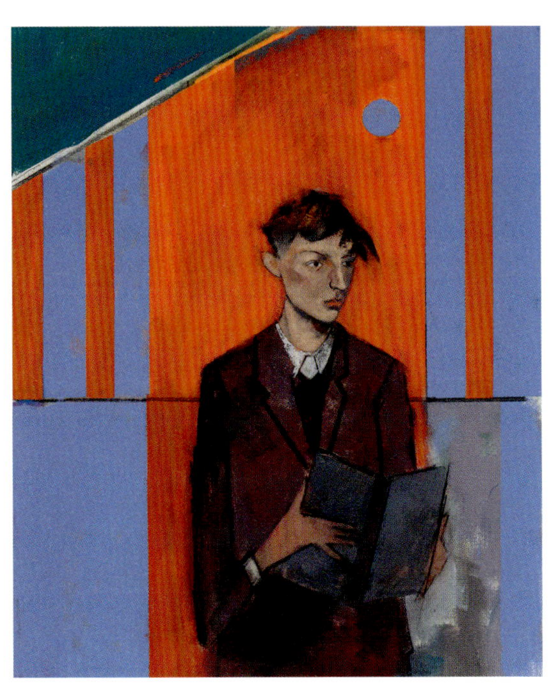

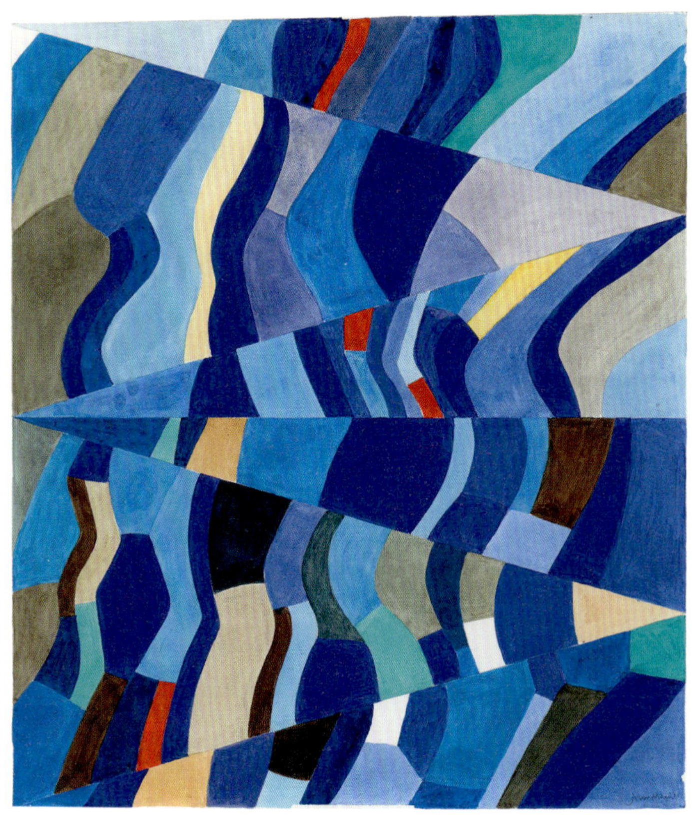

Philip Sutton RA
From Seeds of April Sowing
Oil
64 × 77 cm

Sonia Lawson RA
Coleridge
Oil
122 × 90 cm

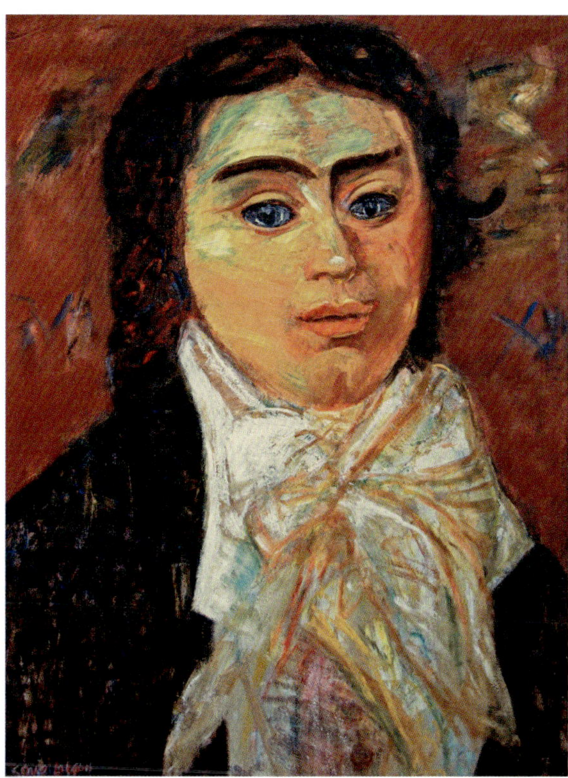

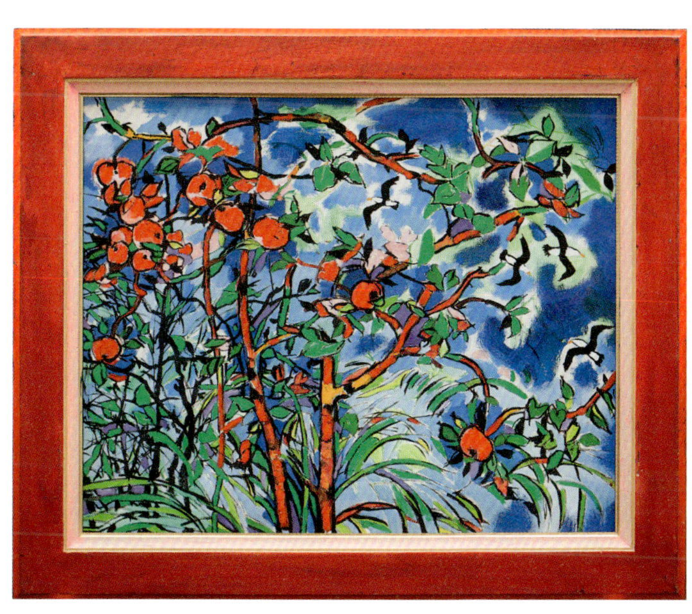

Anthony Eyton RA
Horse on Piano
Oil
40 × 38 cm

Dr David Tindle RA
Eve, her Father and a Passing Shadow of her Mother
Acrylic
46 × 61 cm

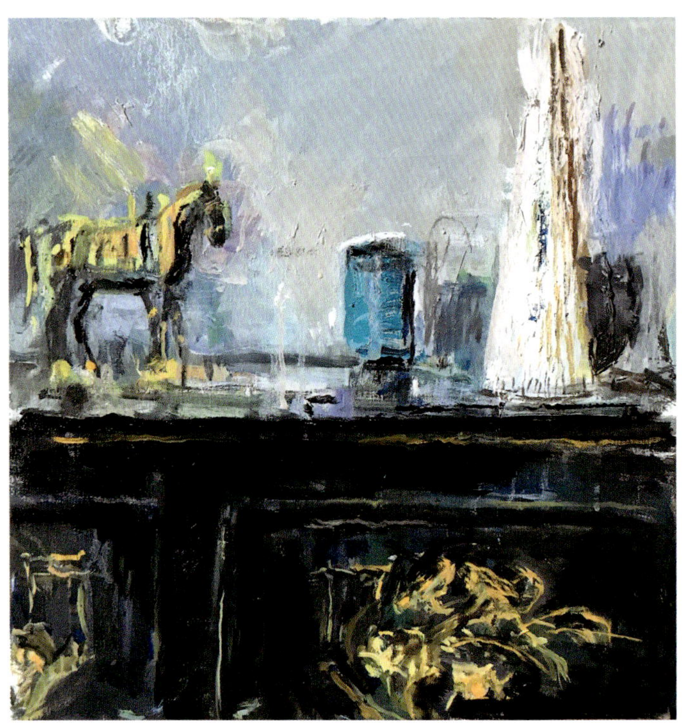

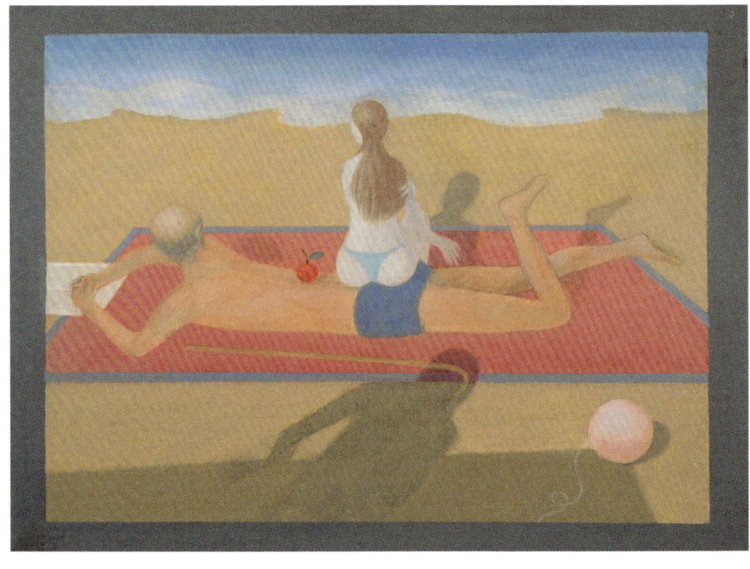

Gus Cummins RA
Pavilion Erehwon
Gouache
56 × 76 cm

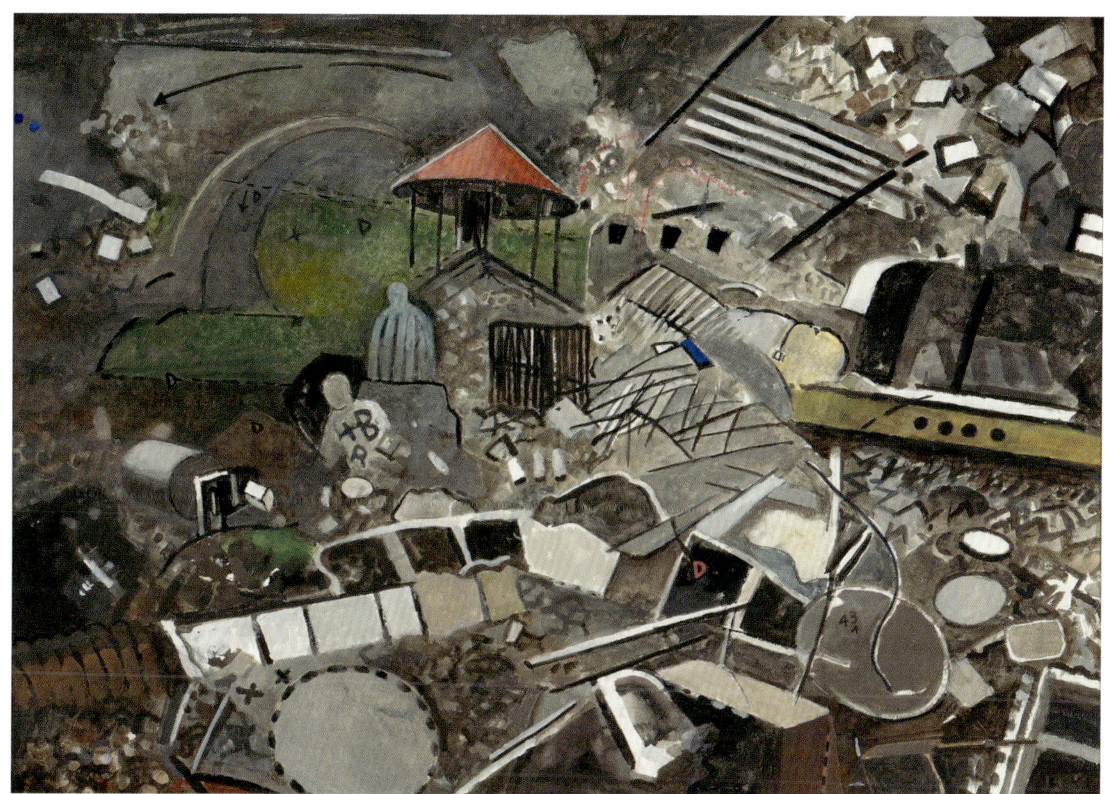

Mali Morris RA
Second Ghost
Acrylic
169 × 193 cm

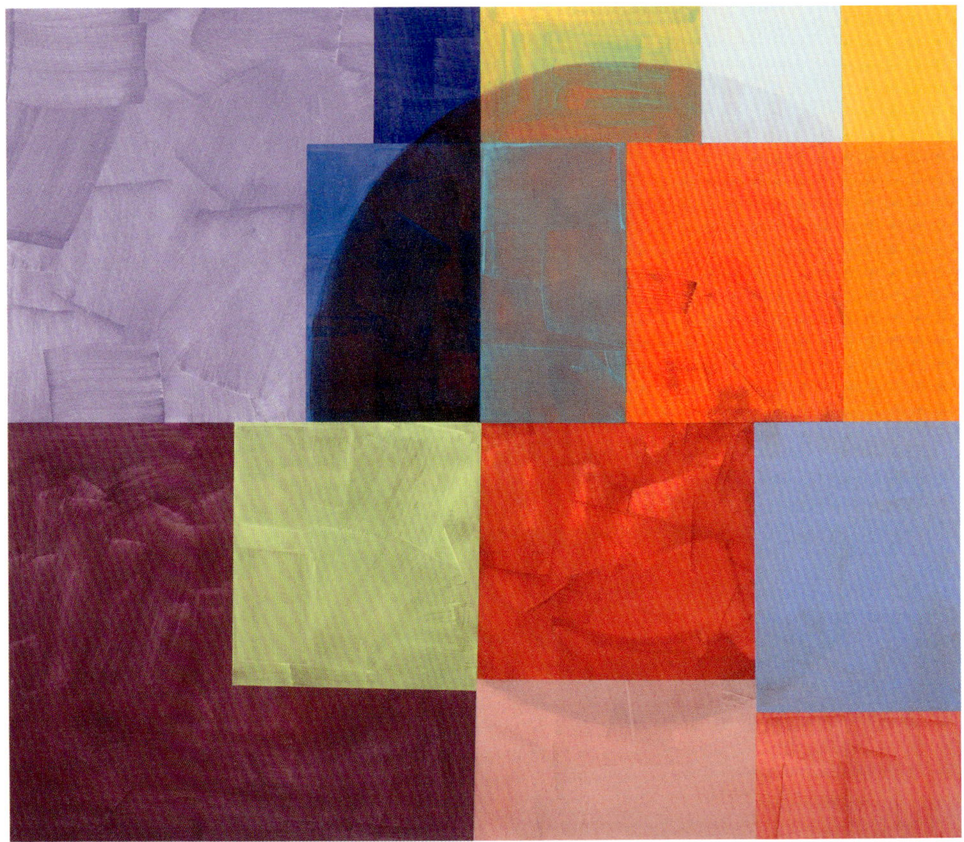

Frank Bowling OBE RA
All Fall Down (for Karl Ltony, Old Pals)
Mixed media
194 × 155 cm

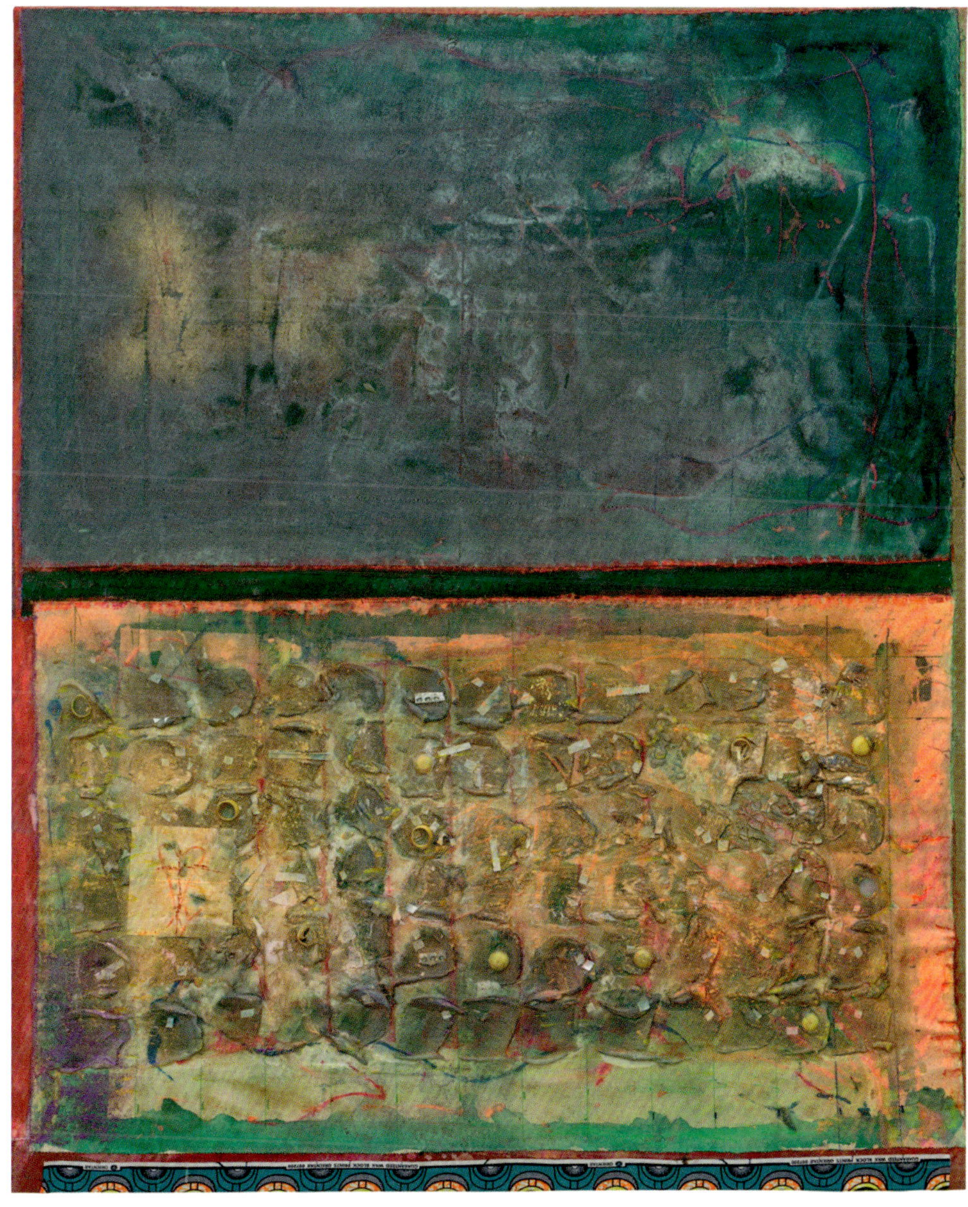

David Axtell

The Inspection: Kim Jong Un and Kim Jong Il Inspecting Lady Gaga's Homage to Duchamp Urinal

Oil

76 × 76 cm

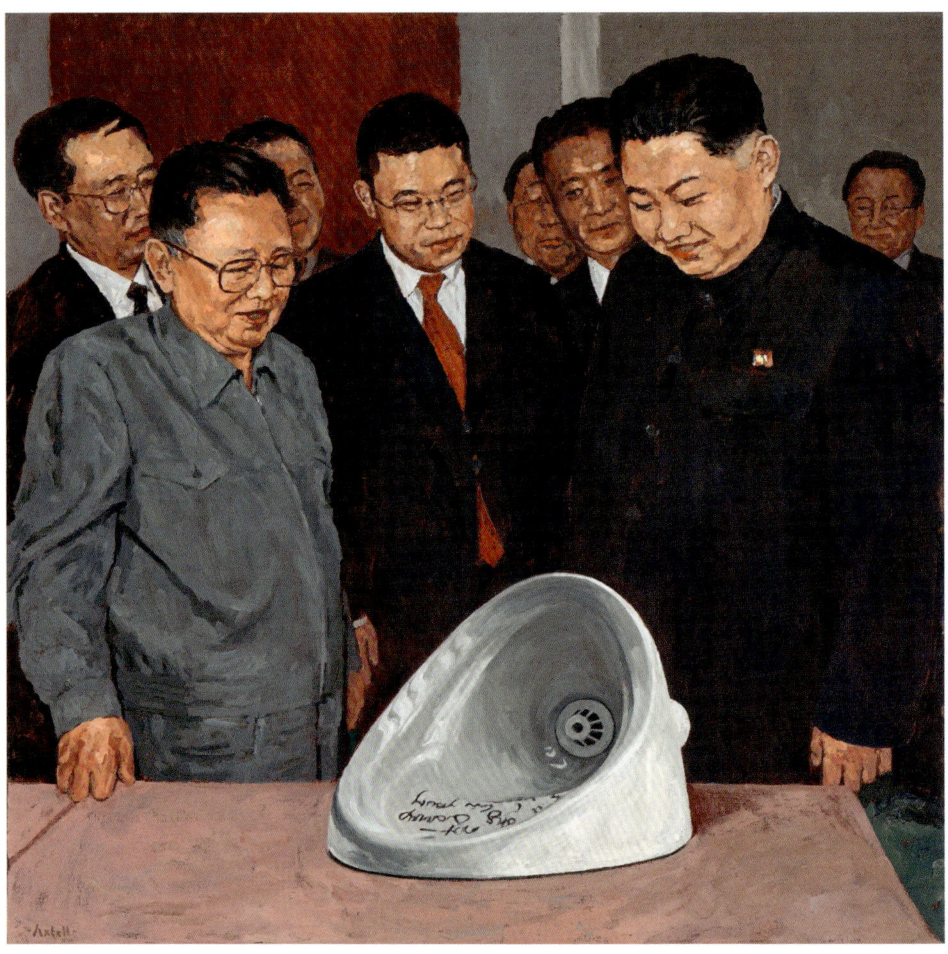

Angela O'Connell
Spaghetti Girls
Acrylic
100 × 100 cm

Mu Tian
Beardman
Marble, granite and chain
H 29 cm

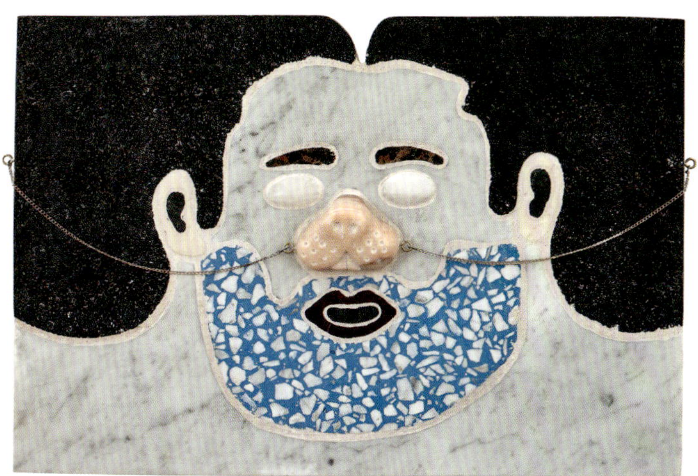

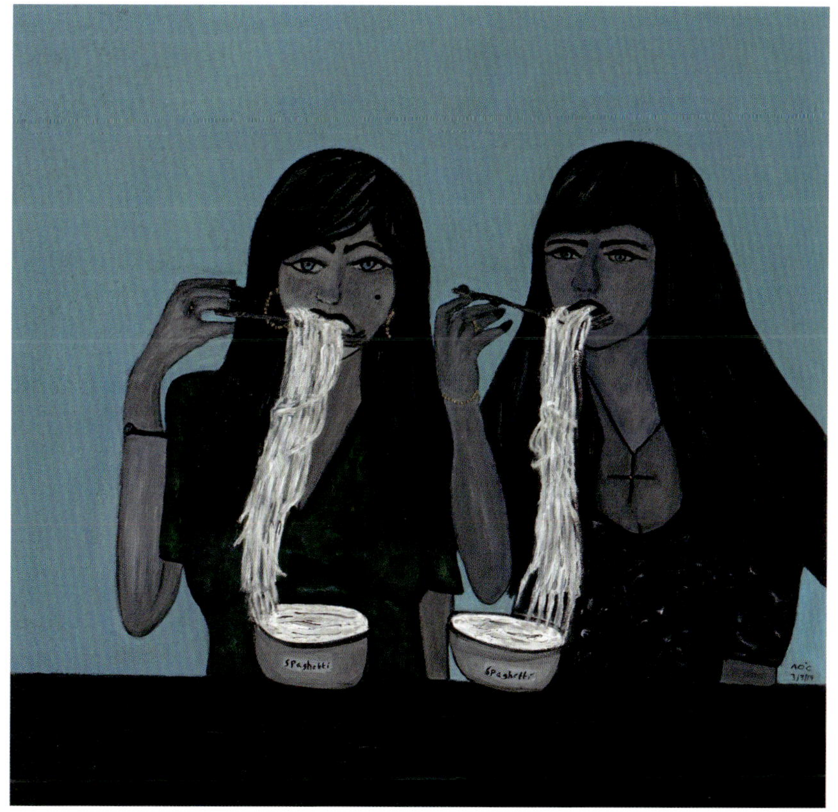

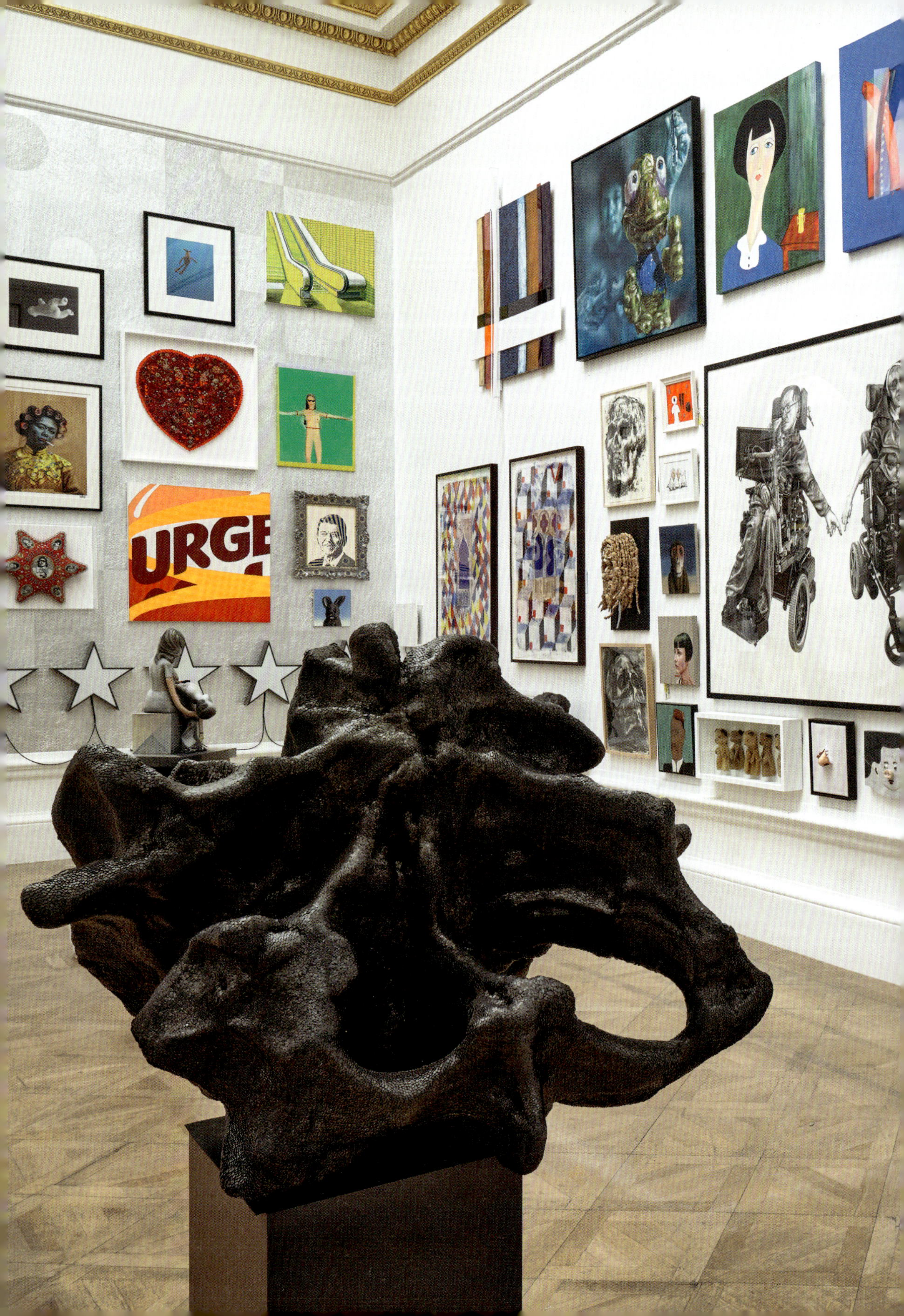
URGE

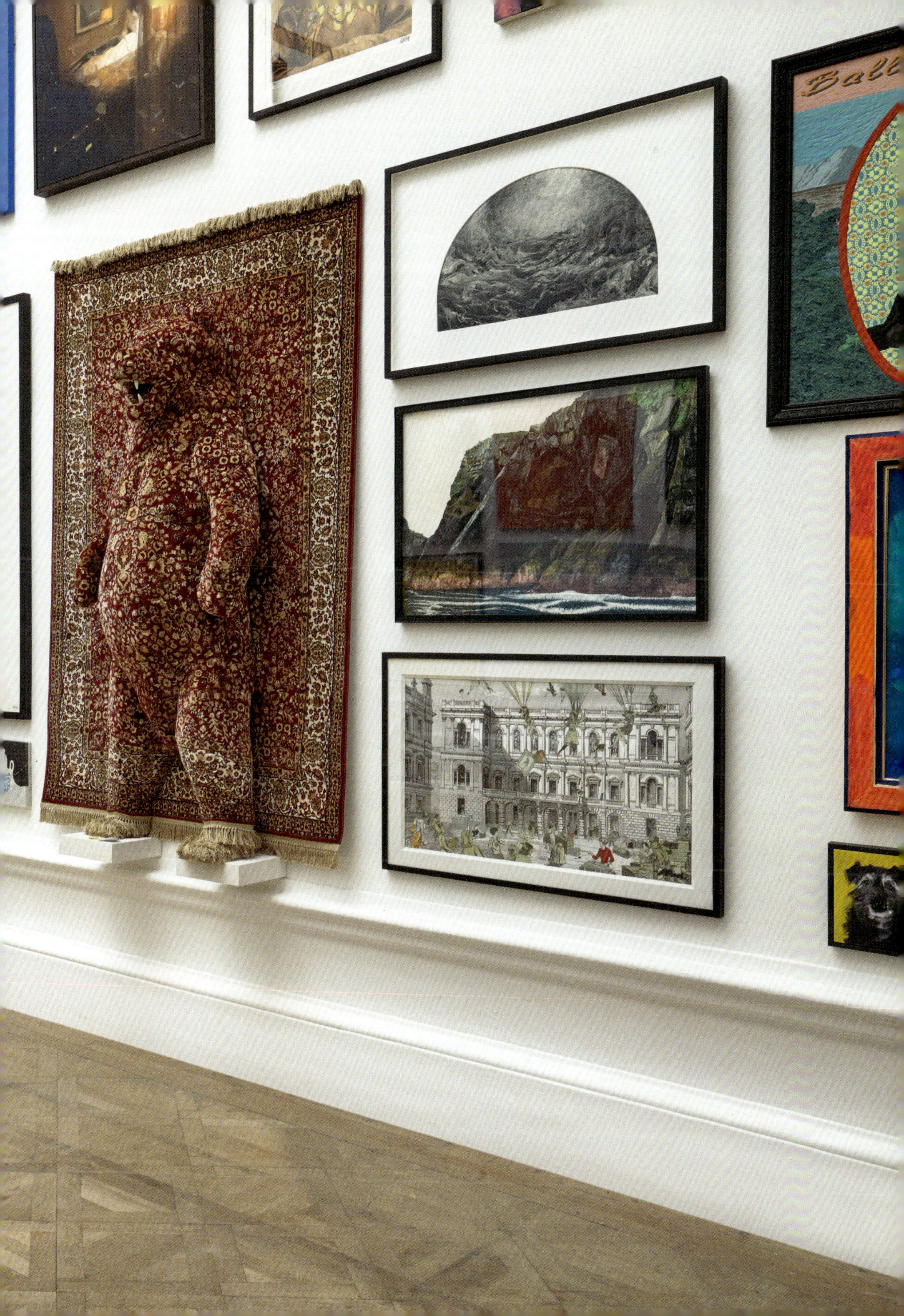

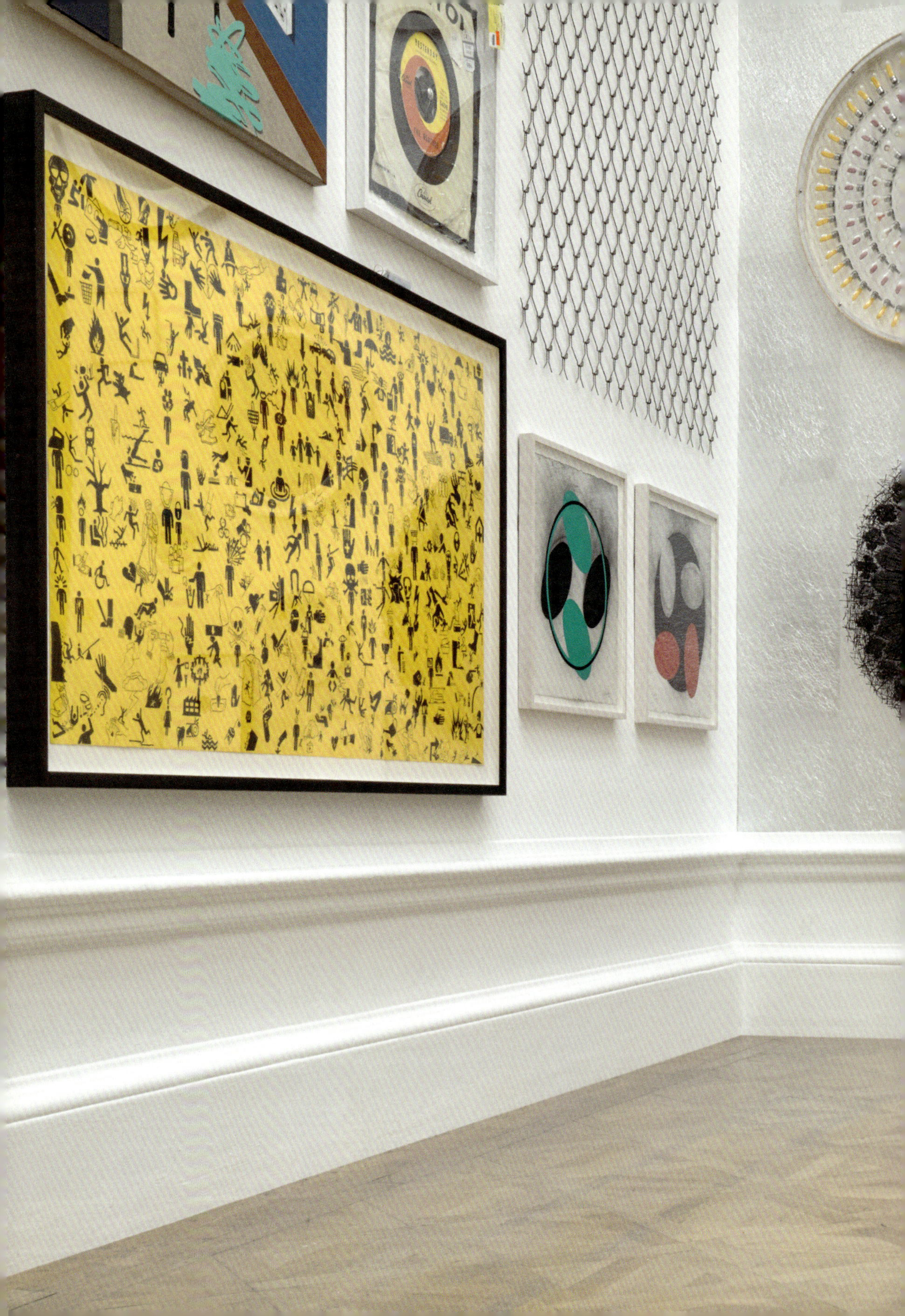

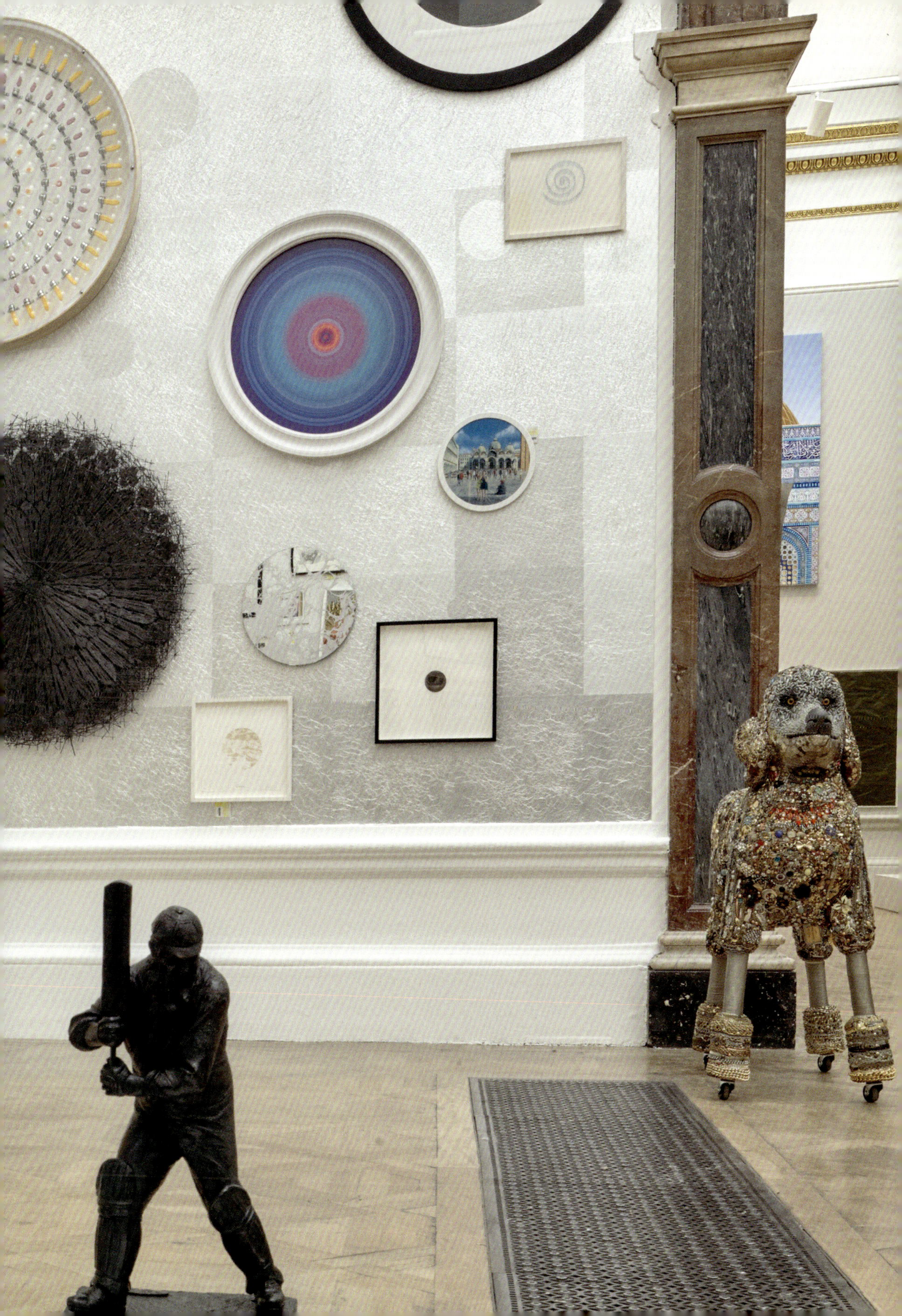

John Carter RA
Identical Shapes, Two Rows, Red and White
Acrylic with marble powder
40 × 80 cm

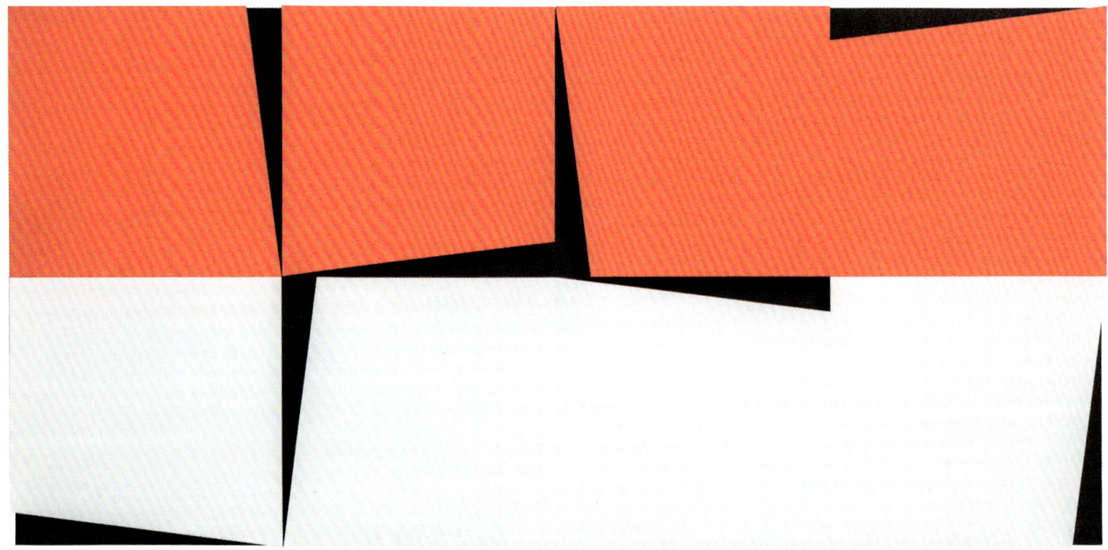

Vanessa Jackson RA
Ignite
Oil
183 × 153 cm

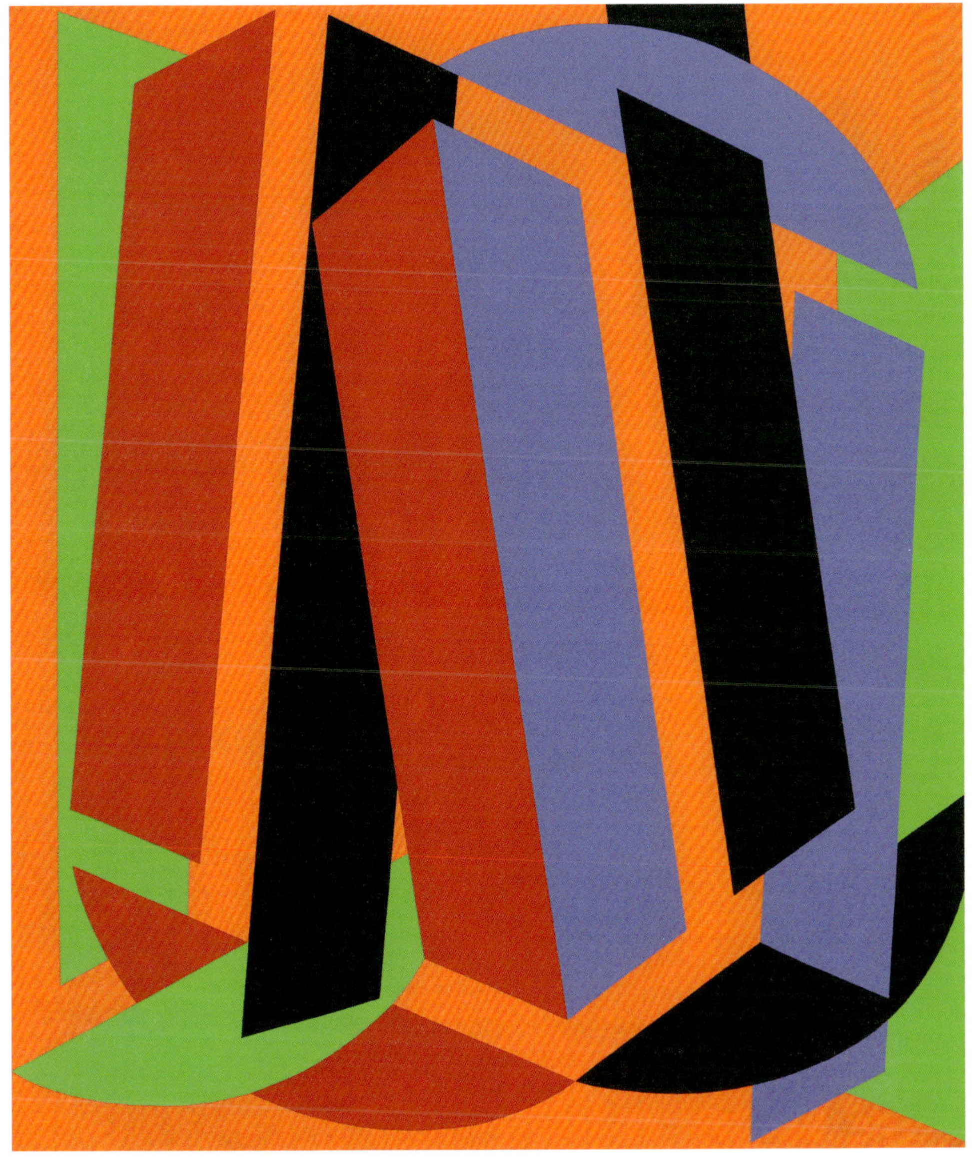

Anthony Green RA
L'Equipe II
Inkjet and screenprint
60 × 60 cm

Ron Arad RA
Where are my Glasses – Under (Green)
Hand-blown glass and metal
H 25 cm

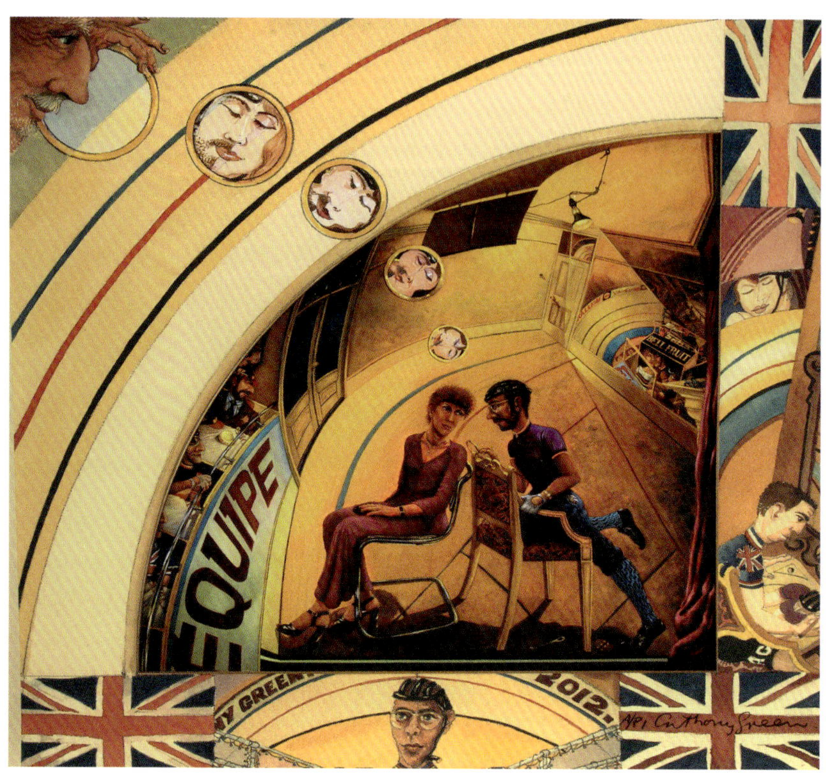

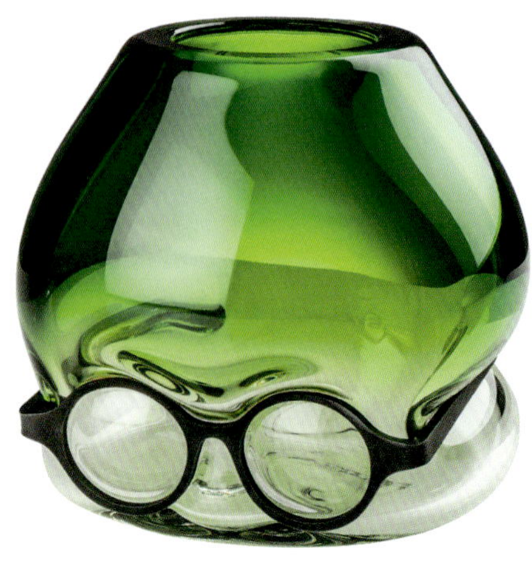

Kenneth Draper RA
Dawn Chorus
Mixed media
70 × 70 cm

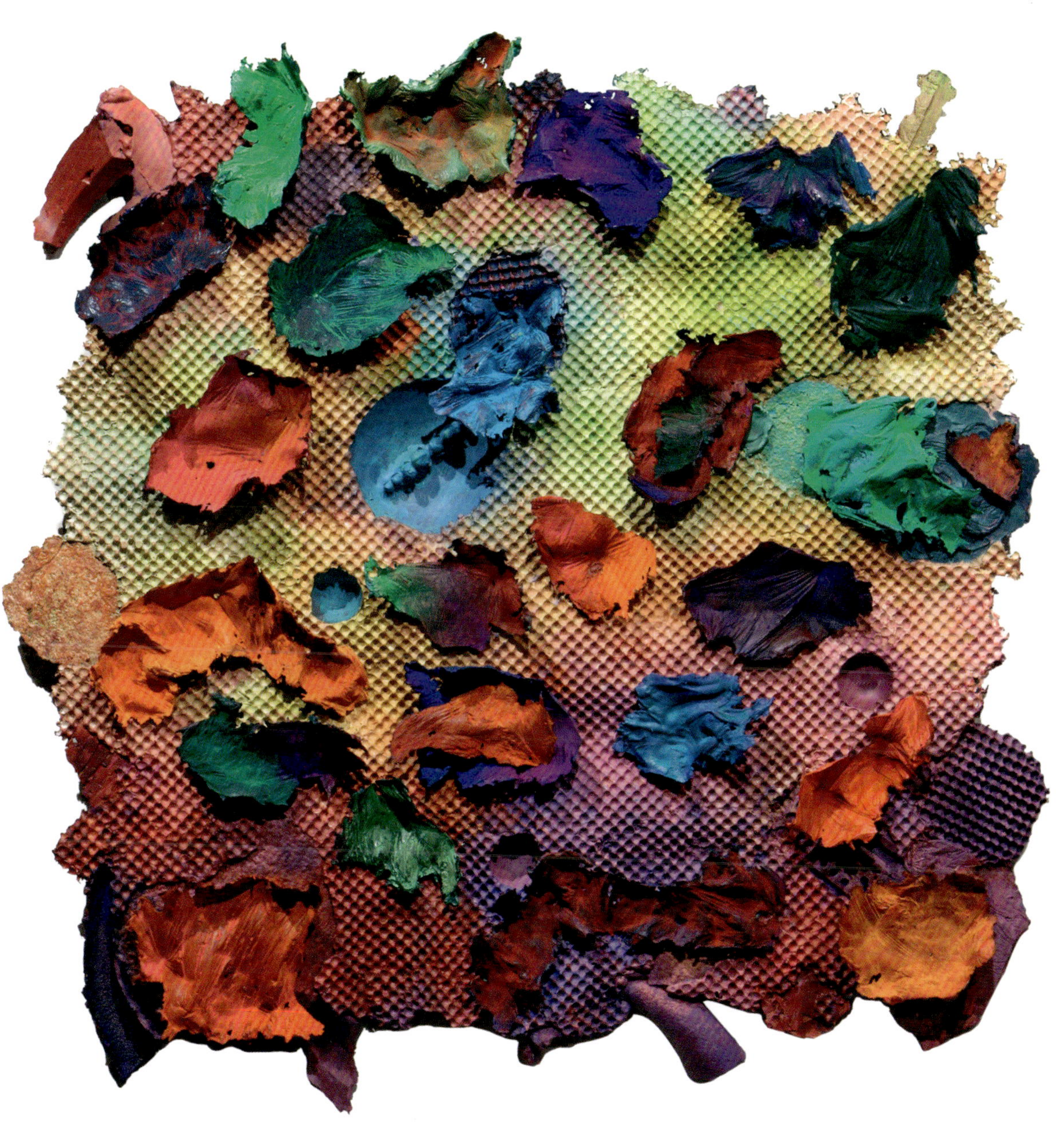

Tess Jaray RA
Predella (Wide)
Acrylic
122 × 209 cm

Sir Richard Long CBE RA
Time and Tide
Screenprint
59 × 148 cm

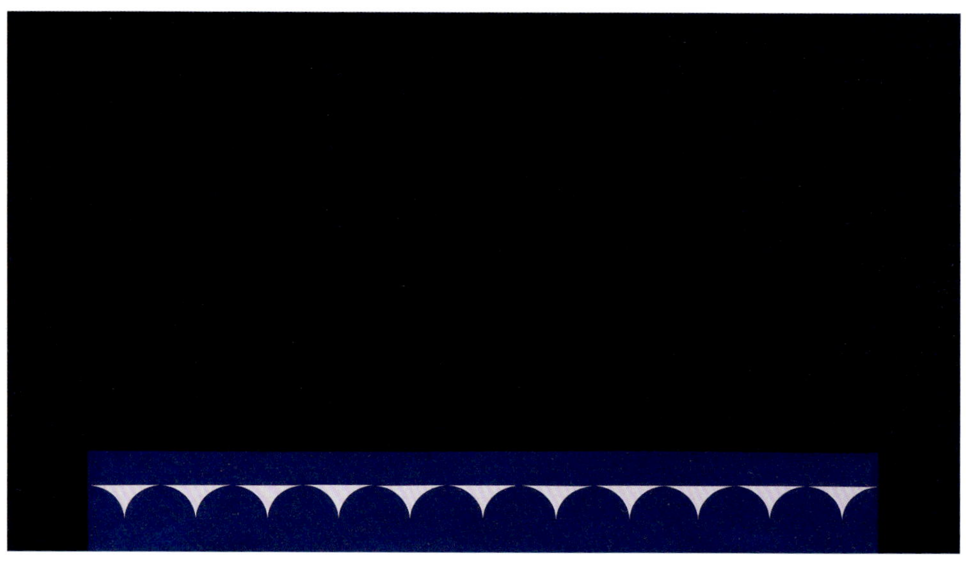

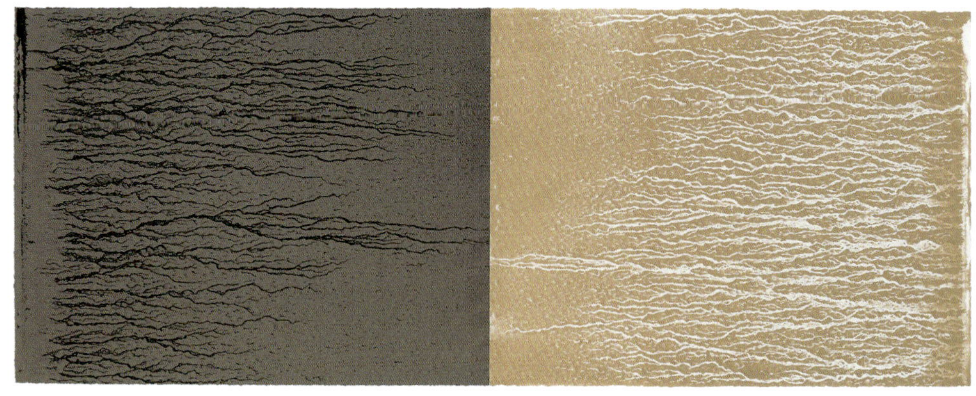

Prof Ian McKeever RA
Henge VIII (Diptych)
Acrylic and oil
240 × 285 cm

Basil Beattie RA
A Mazed (Ladder Series)
Oil and wax
153 × 122 cm

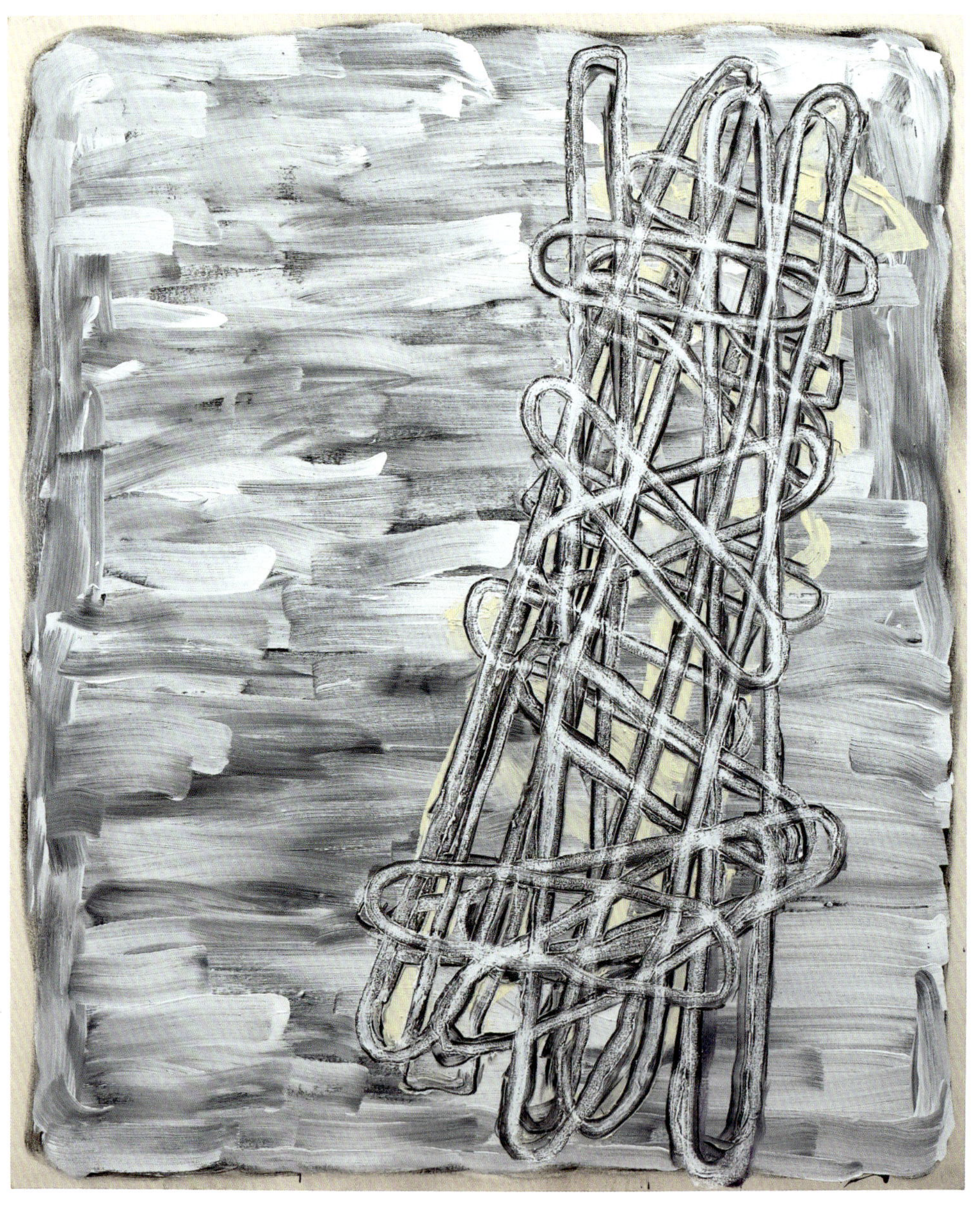

Prof Bryan Kneale RA
Flute
Patinated bronze
H 28 cm

Jock McFadyen RA
Calton Hill
Digital print and acrylic
57 × 51 cm

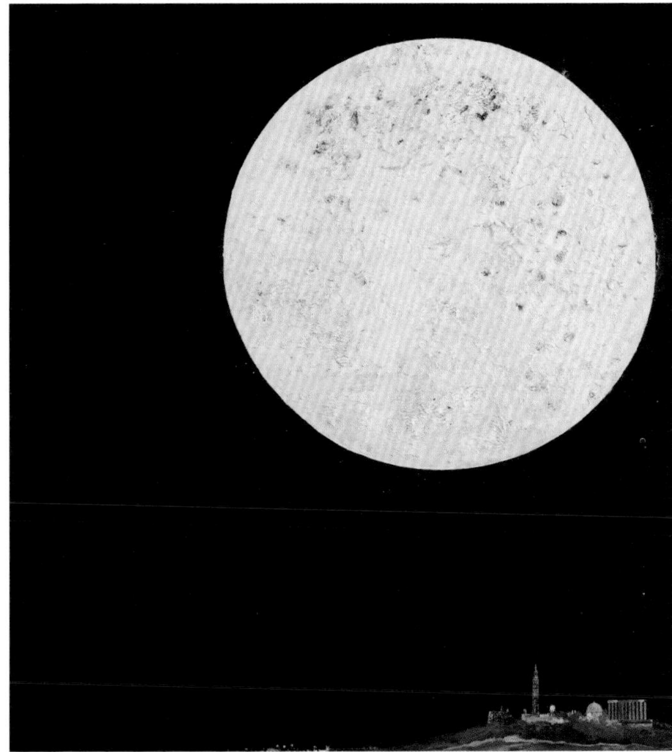

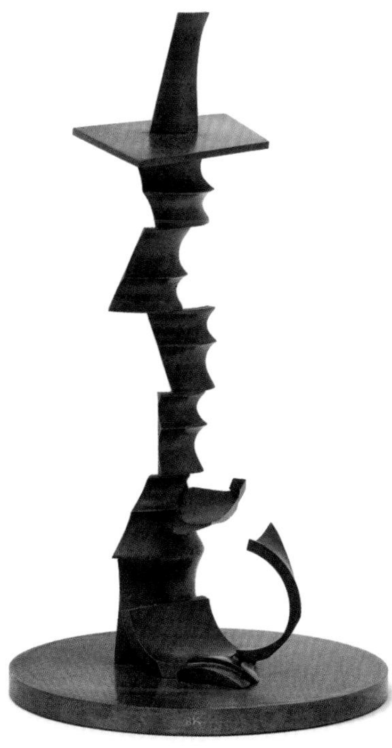

Prof Chantal Joffe RA
Ishbel
Oil
60 × 50 cm

Prof Dhruva Mistry CBE RA
Recline, 1PX (Study), Vermillion
Stainless steel with oil
H 28 cm

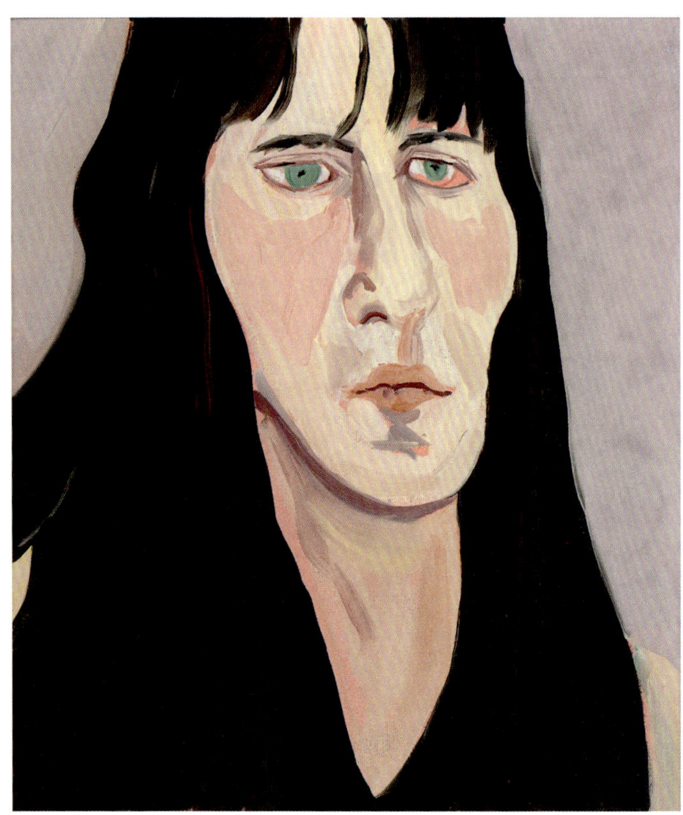

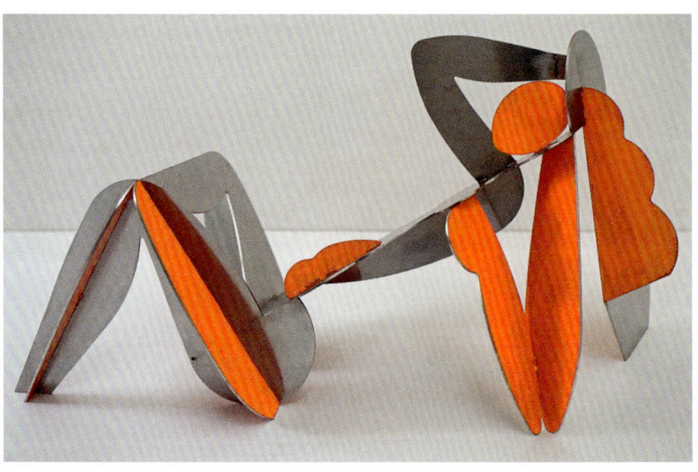

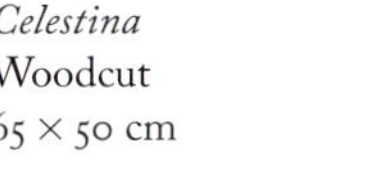

Eileen Cooper OBE RA
Celestina
Woodcut
65 × 50 cm

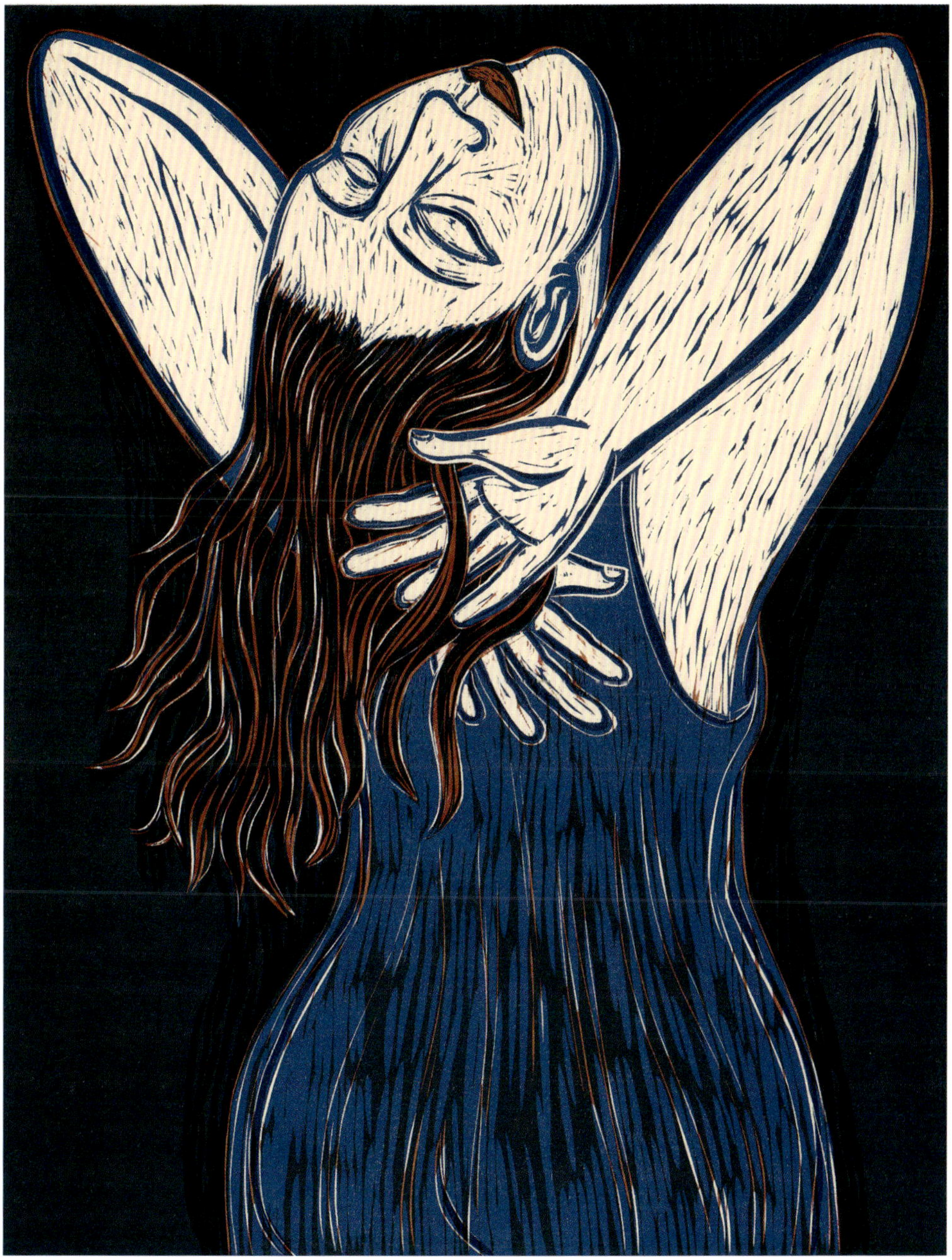

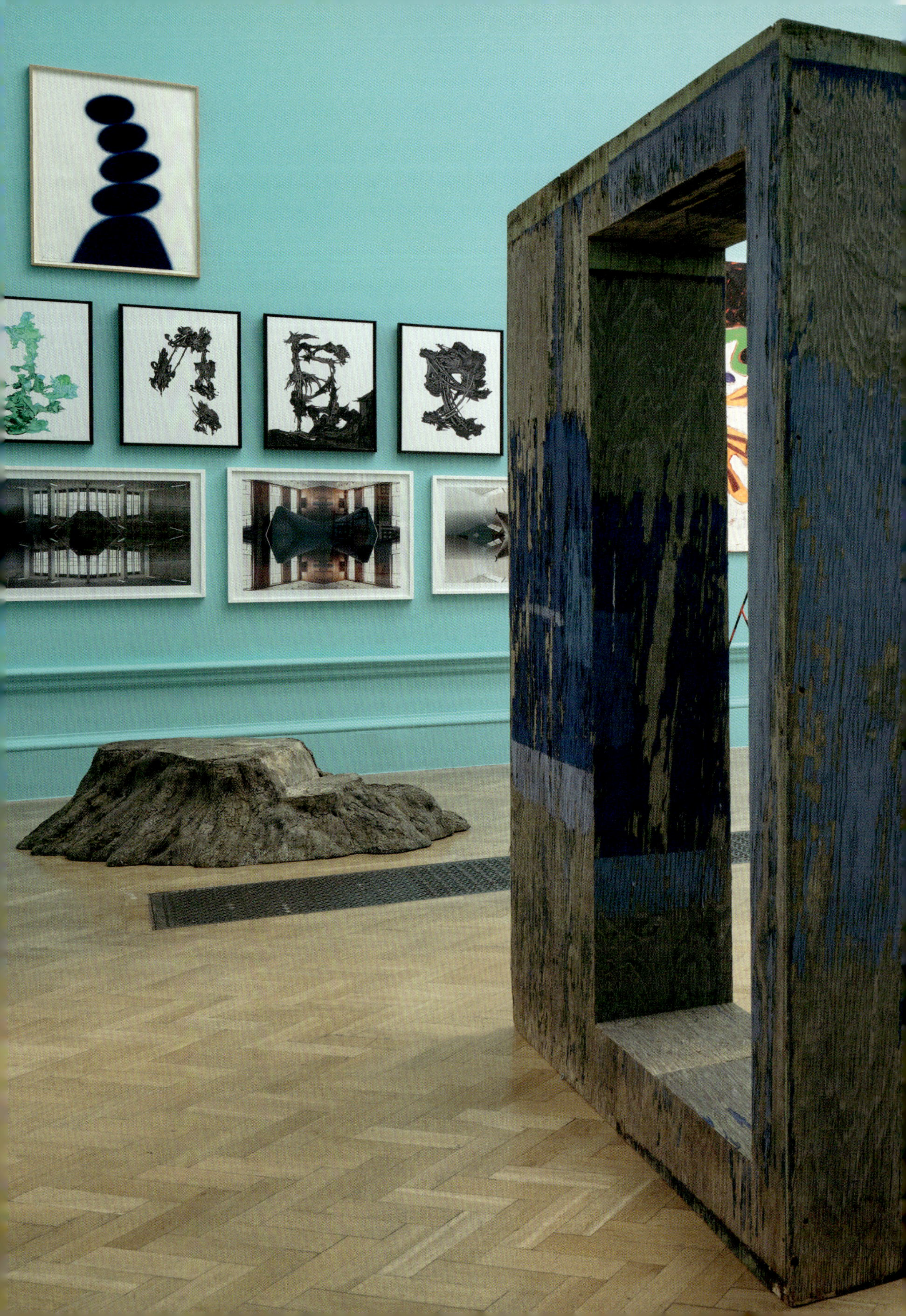

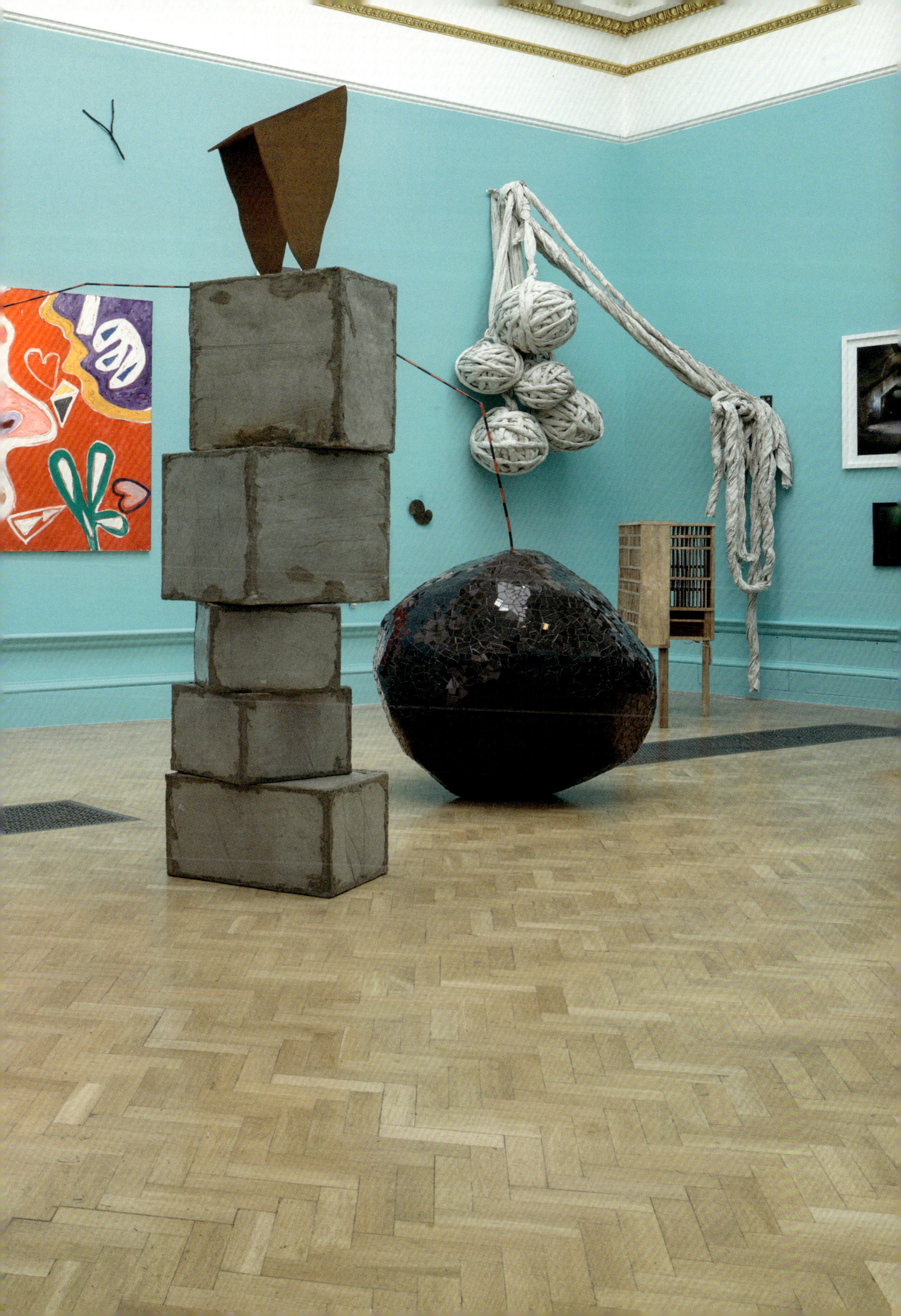

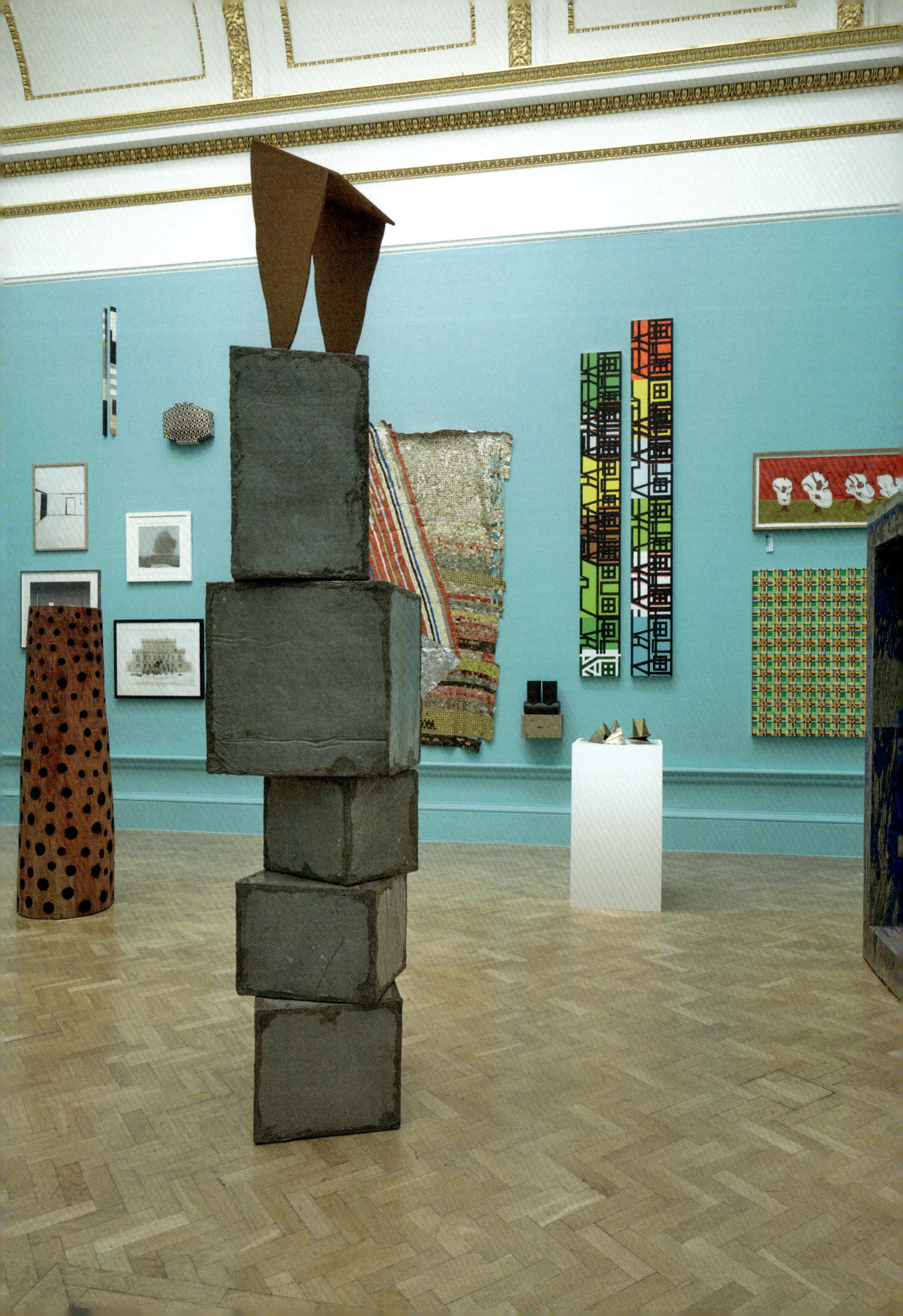

Bill Woodrow RA
Untitled
Mixed media
60 × 84 cm

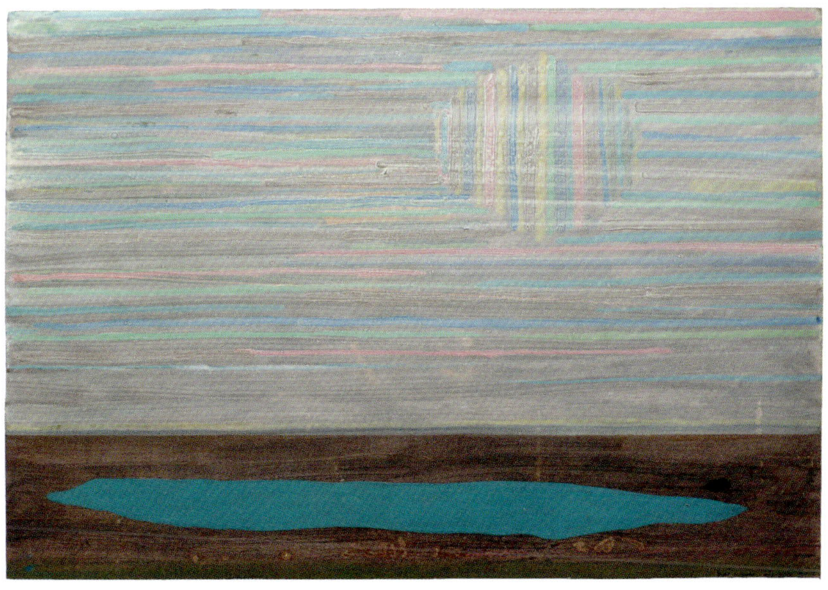

Sir Michael Craig-Martin CBE RA
Double Take (trainer)
Acrylic on aluminium in two panels
Each 200 × 200 cm

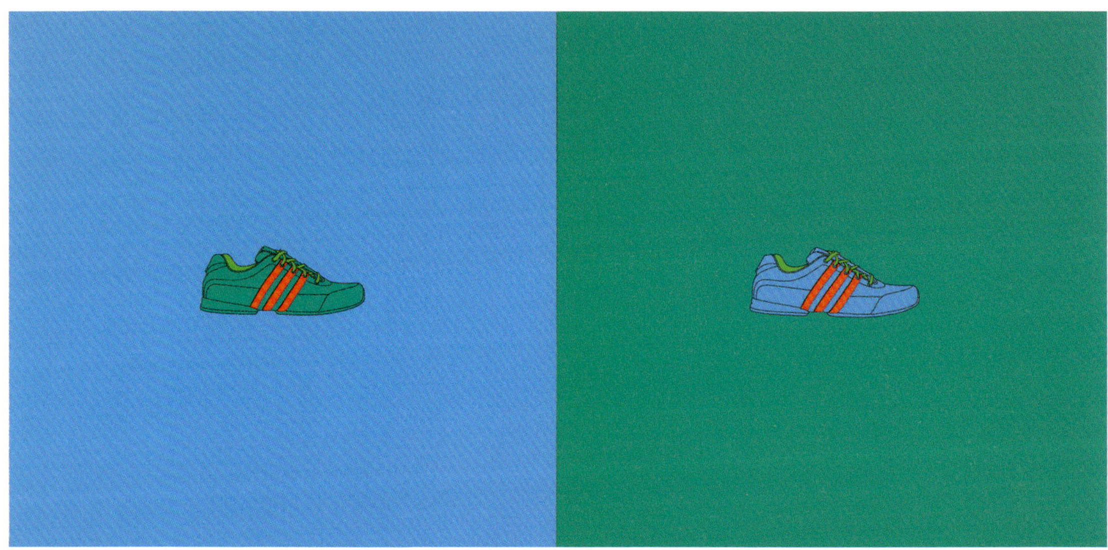

Nigel Hall RA
Square Dance
Corten steel
H 240 cm

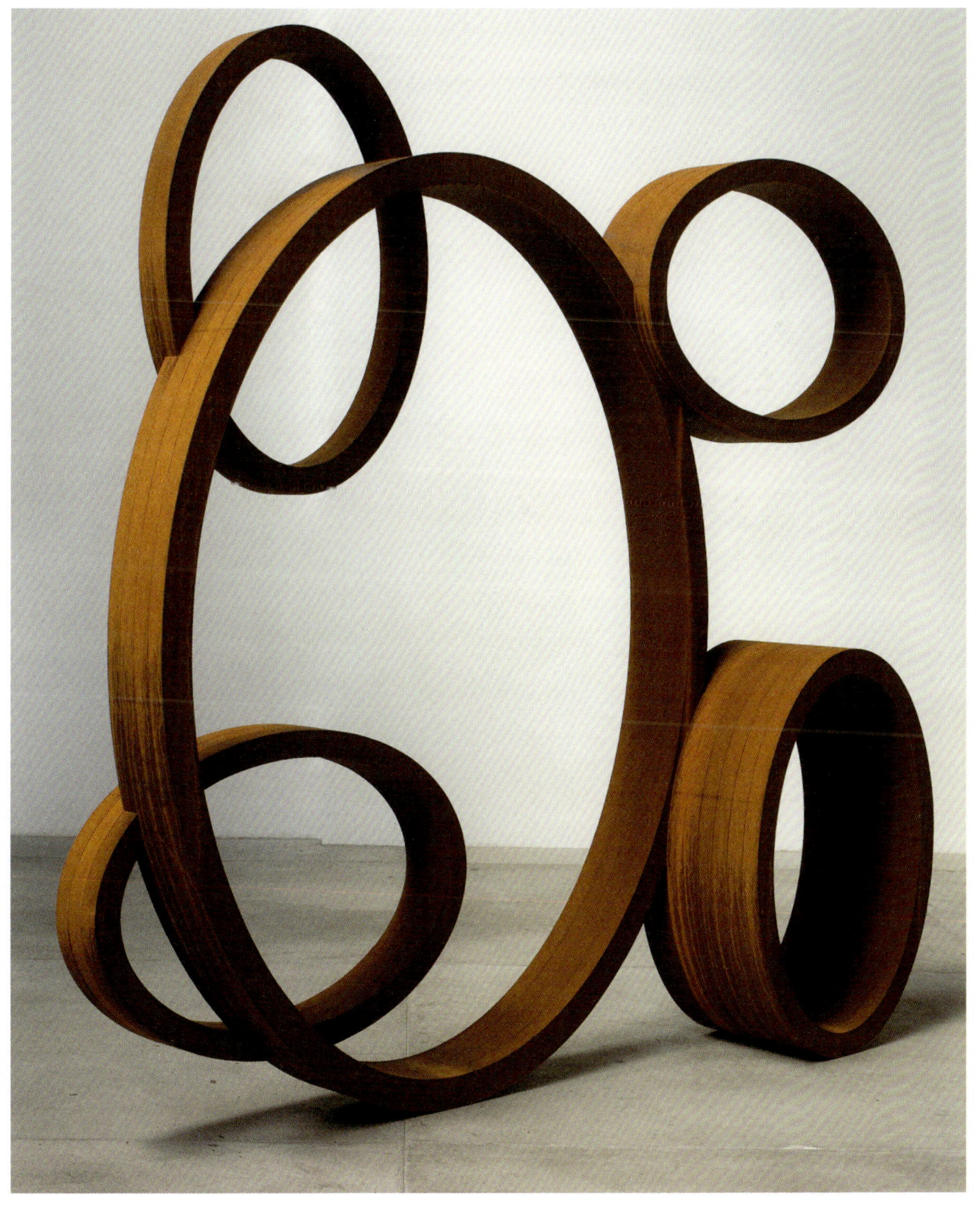

Timothy Hyman RA
The Academician
Oil
70 × 50 cm

Anne Desmet RA
RA Revolution
Stone lithograph
31 × 42 cm

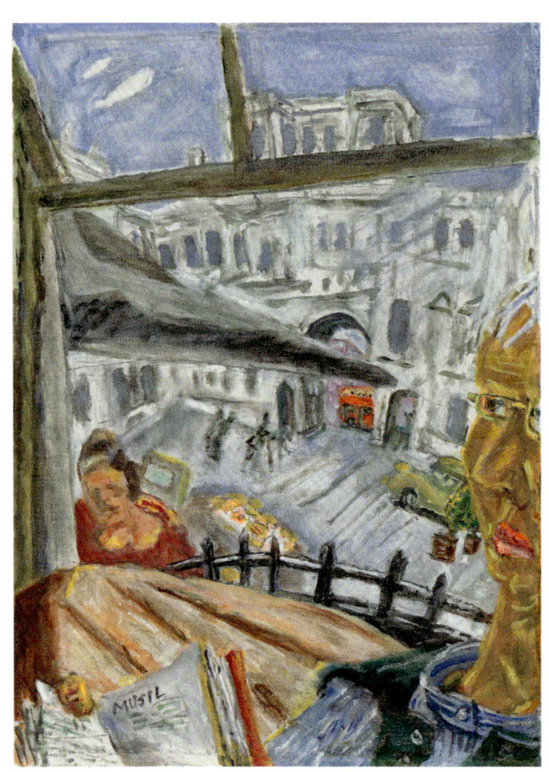

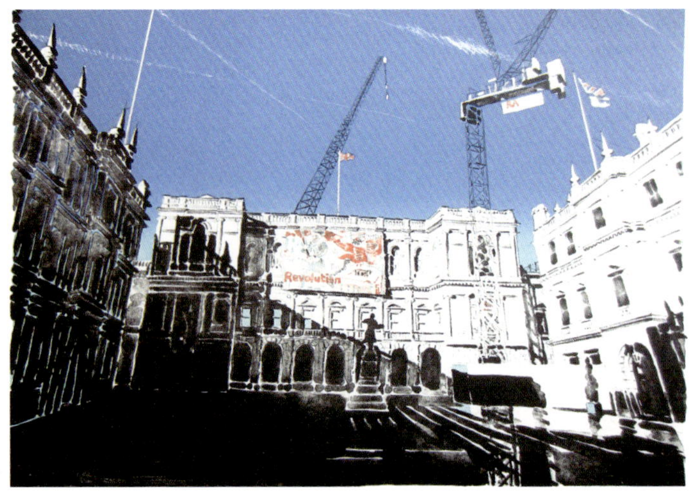

Prof Chris Orr MBE RA
The Fauves Picnic
Silkscreen
52 × 73 cm

Glen Baxter
My First Day at the New School Seemed to be Going Rather Well
Ink and crayon
79 × 57 cm

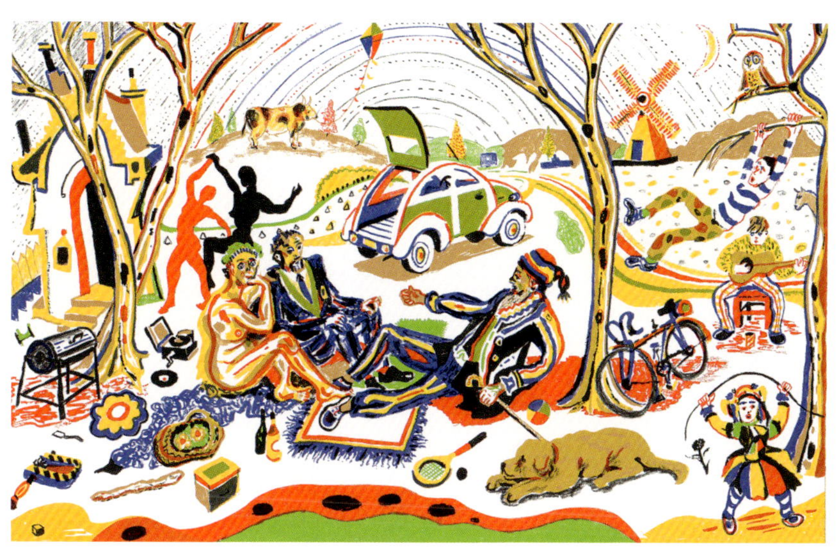

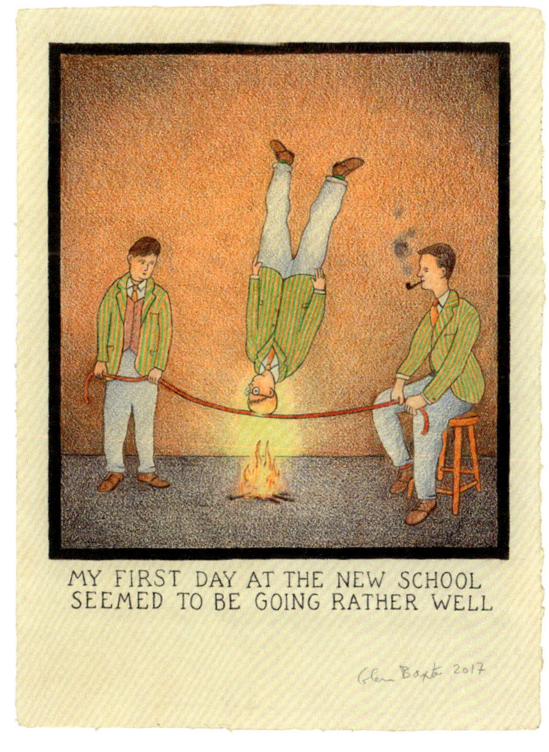

Dr Leonard McComb RA
Welsh Cottage
Oil
45 × 56 cm

Anthony Whishaw RA
Microparticles Moving Westwards
Acrylic
56 × 168 cm

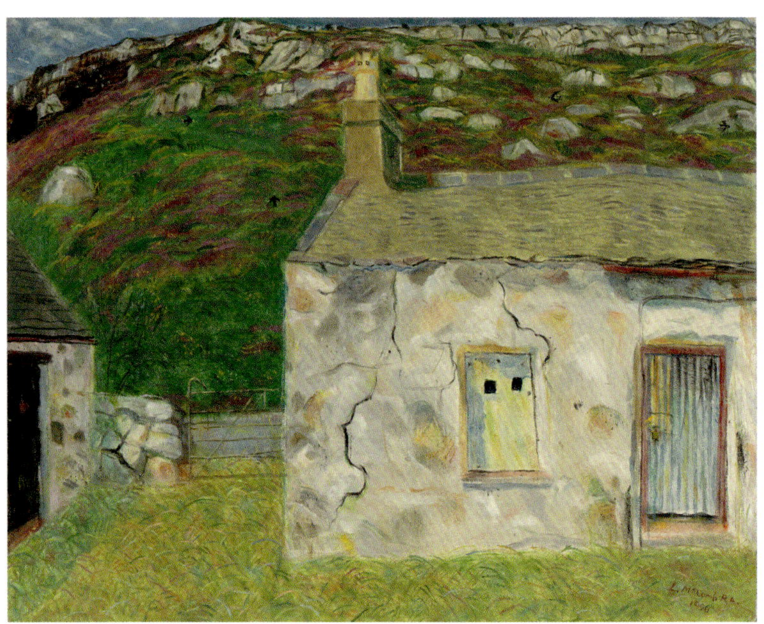

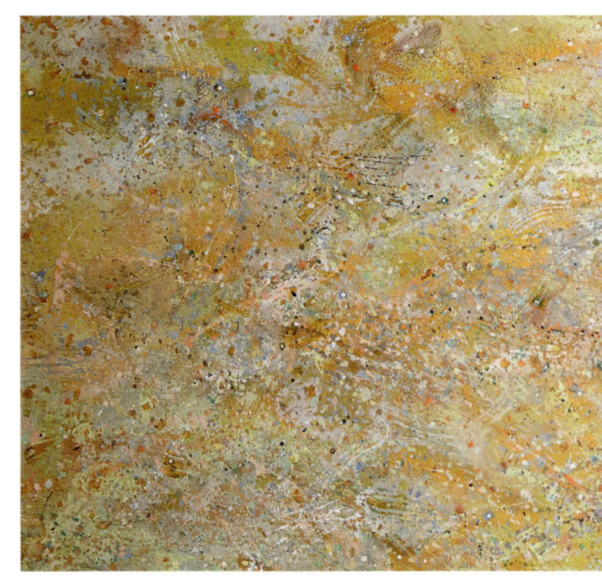

Dame Elizabeth Blackadder DBE RA
Four Poppies
Screenprint
62 × 50 cm

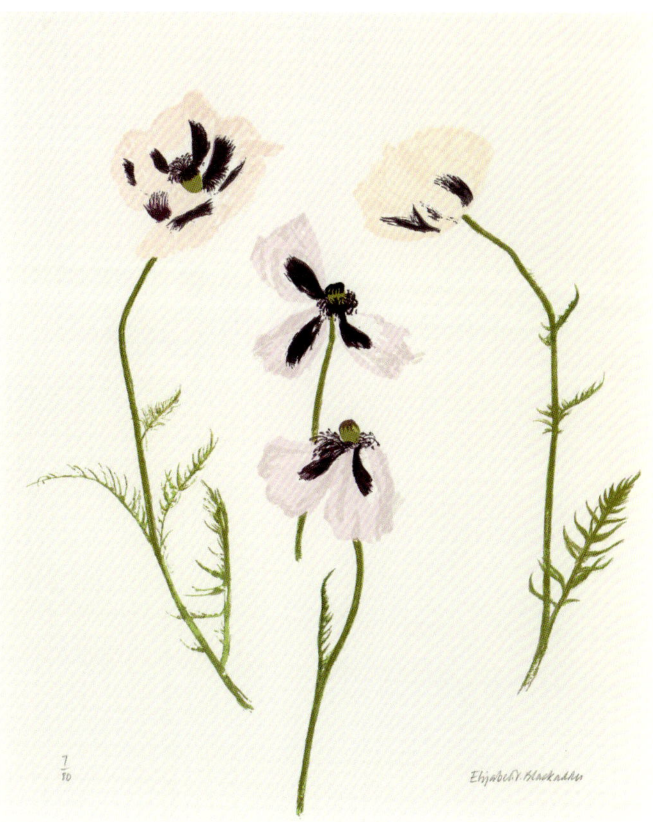

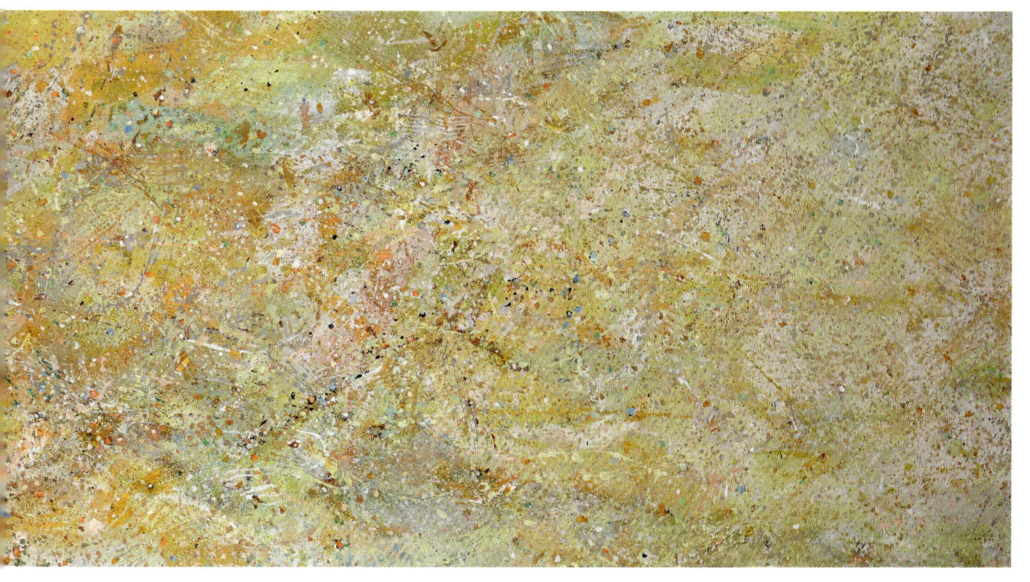

Hughie O'Donoghue RA
Blue Water
Hand-worked multiple
57 × 75 cm

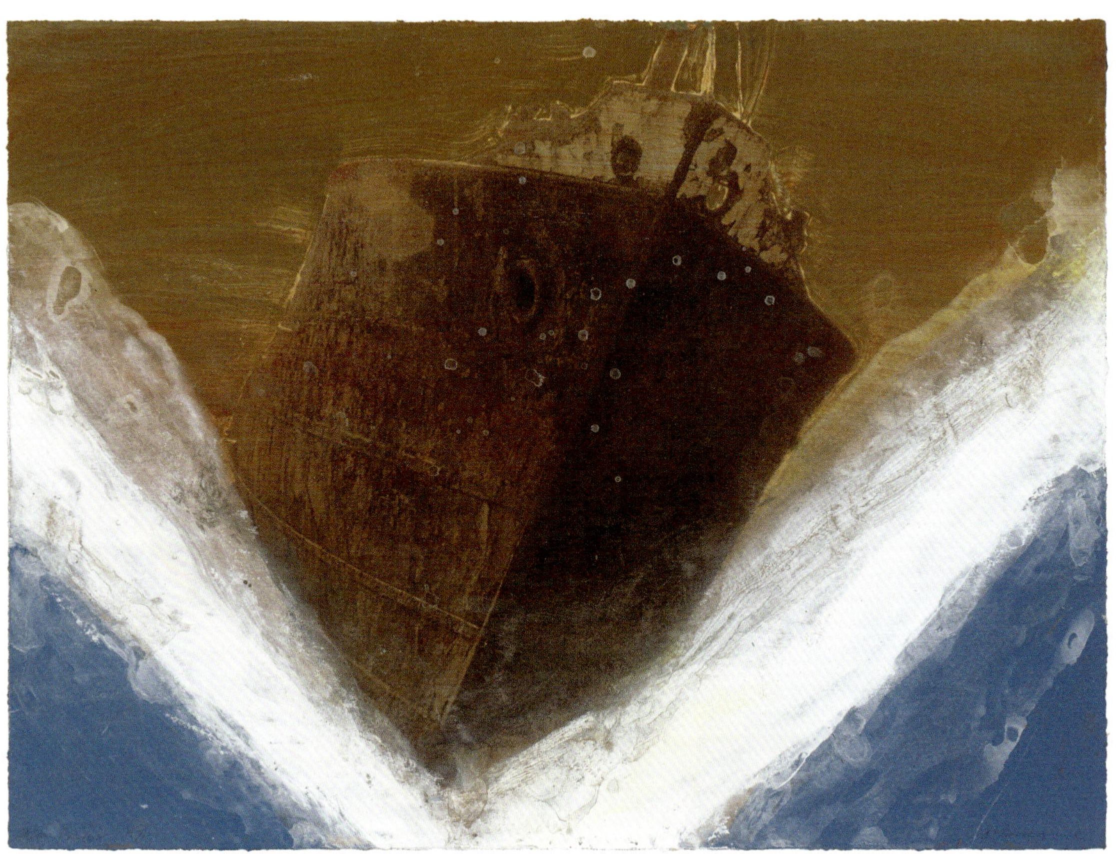

Terry Setch RA
She Moon
Encaustic wax and beach detritus
270 × 180 cm

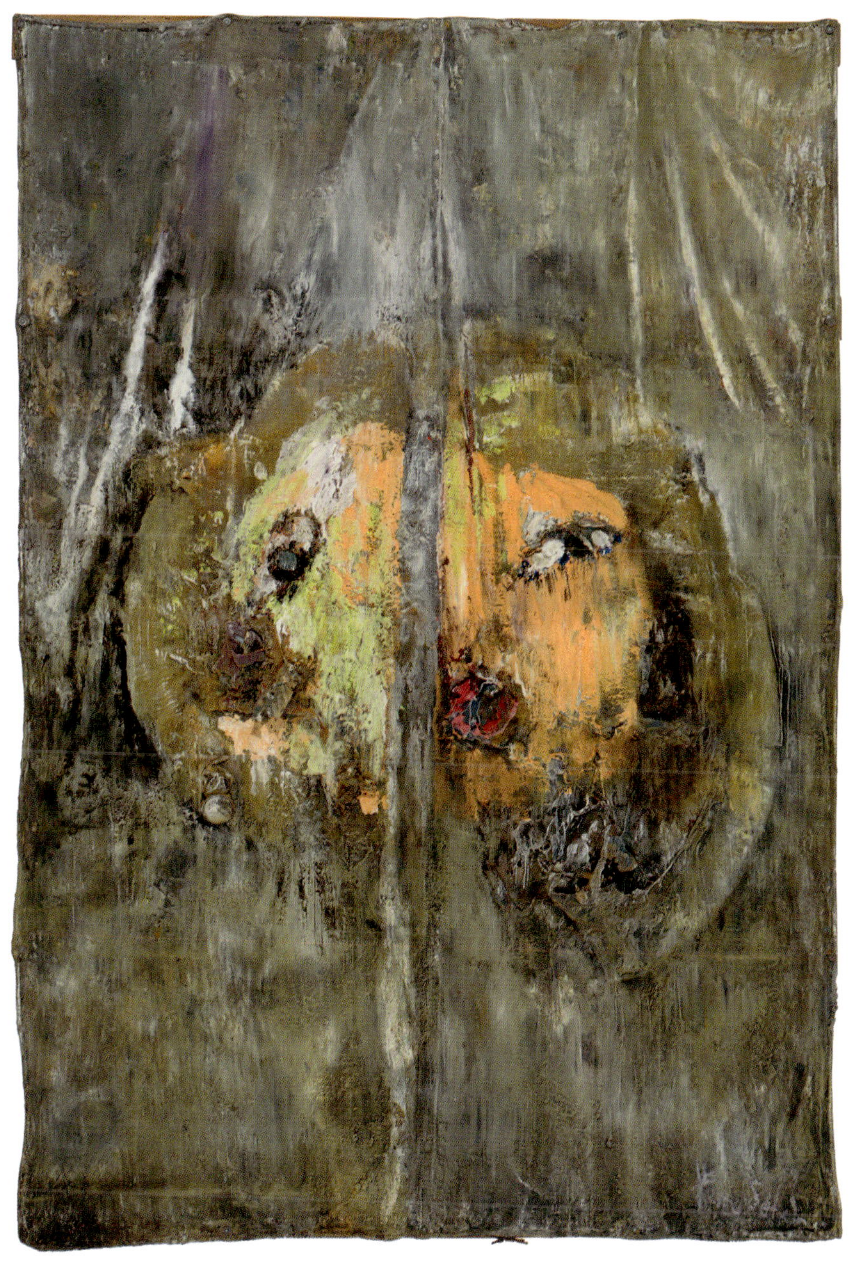

Prof Alison Wilding RA
X
Patinated brass
H 27 cm

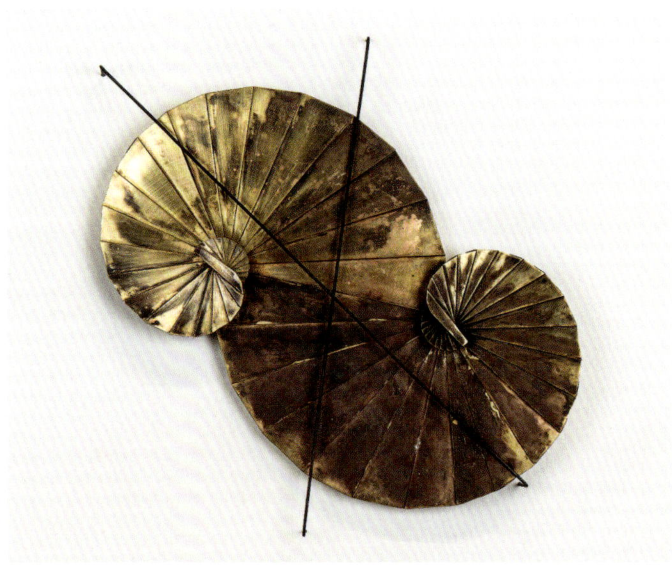

Antony Gormley RA
Open Perch
4mm Corten steel
59 × 132 × 50 cm

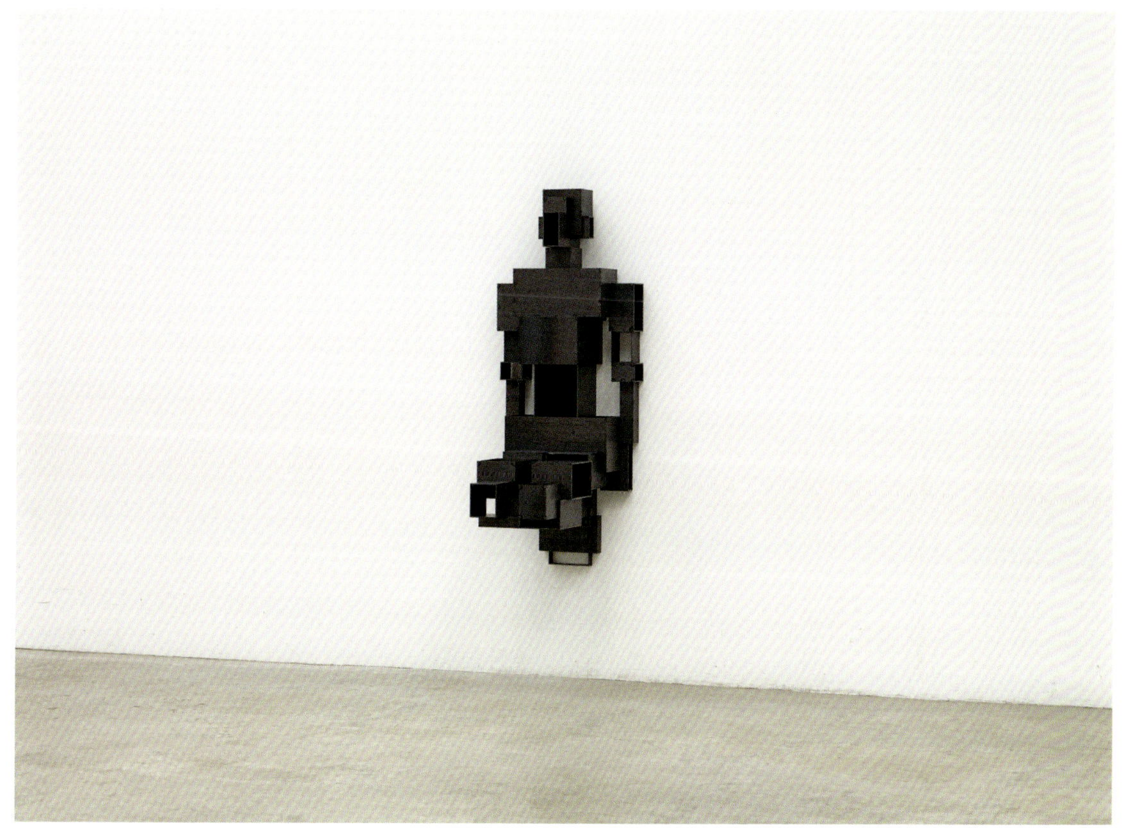

Prof Phillip King CBE PPRA
Green Leaf Gated
Painted PVC and Polyurethane foam
H 220 cm

Gary Hume RA
Water
Gloss paint
120 × 362 cm

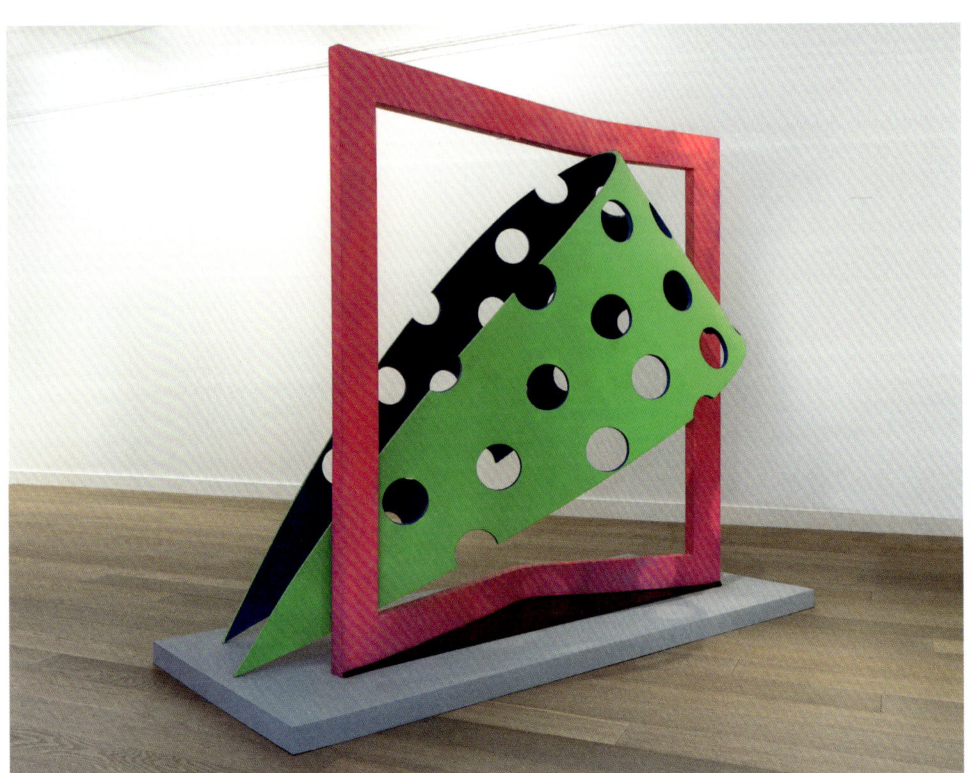

Neil Jeffries RA
Blue Oily Spokes and Worsened Saddles
Oil on metal
H 92 cm

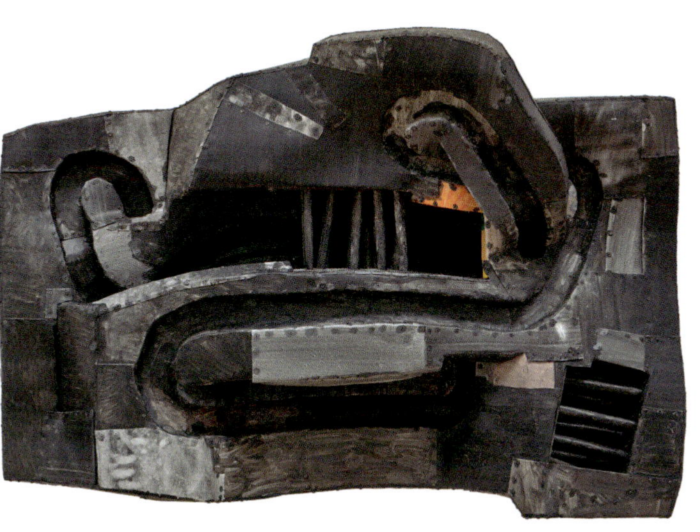

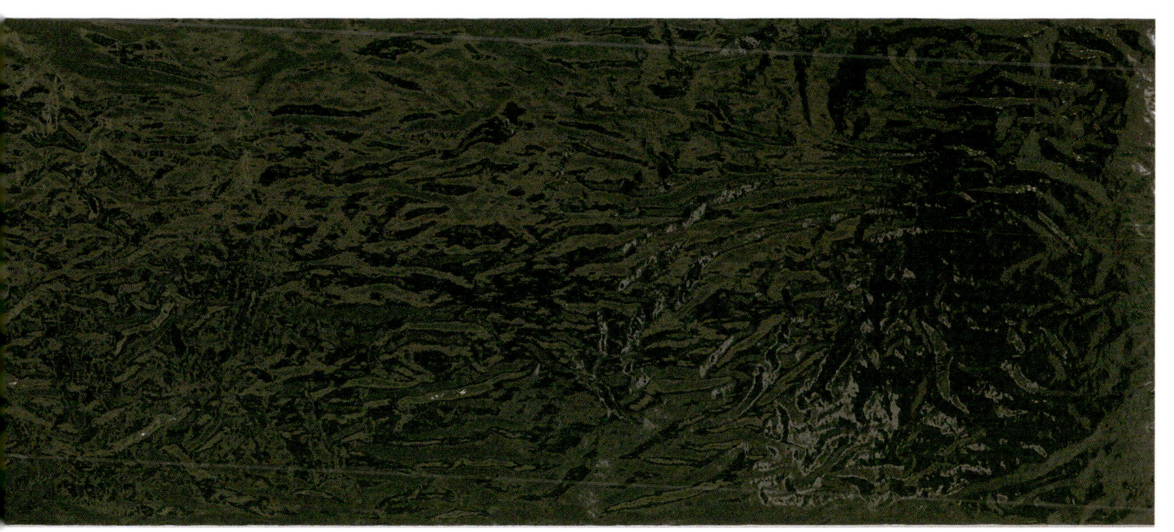

Sean Scully RA
Ghost Requiem
Oil and oil pastel
191 × 216 cm

William Tucker RA
Victory B
Charcoal
66 × 56 cm

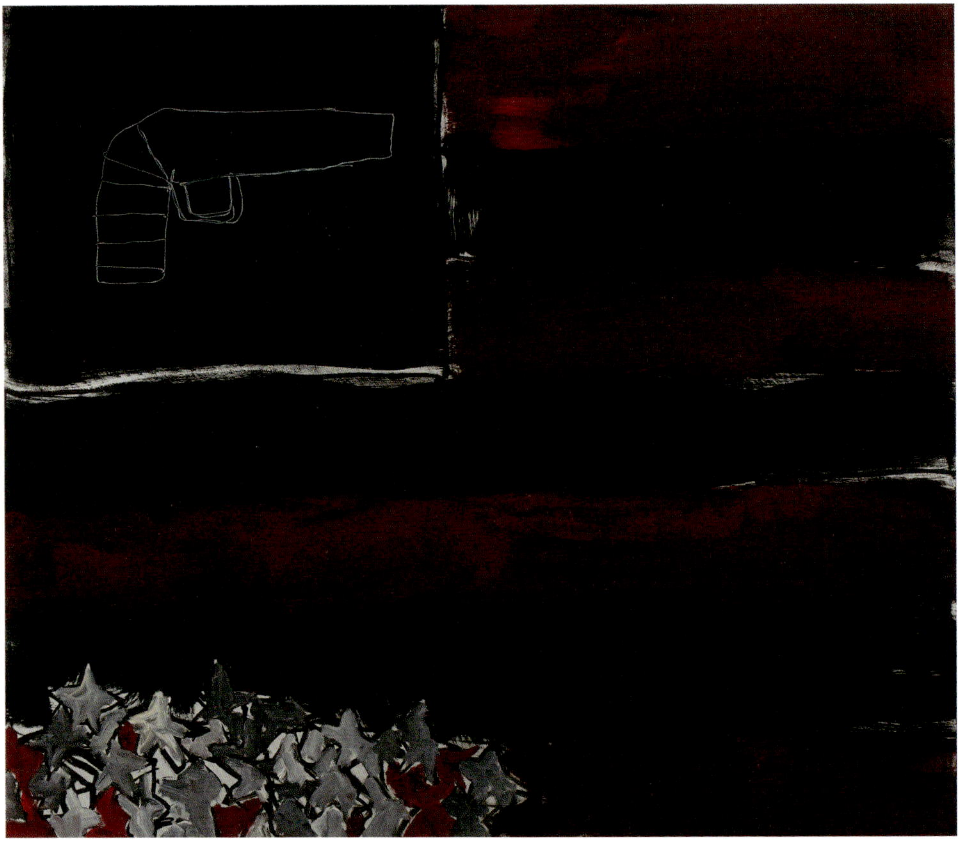

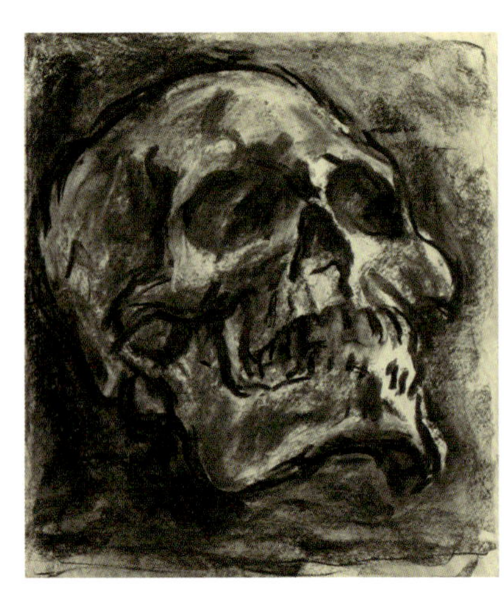

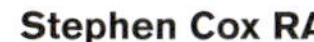

Prof Michael Sandle RA
The Joy of Melancholia
Ink
97 × 145 cm

Stephen Cox RA
Sword of St George
Porphyry, alabaster and basalt
H 111 cm

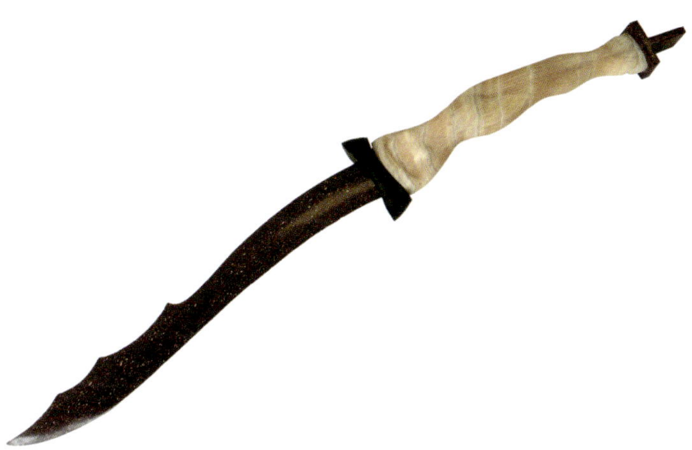

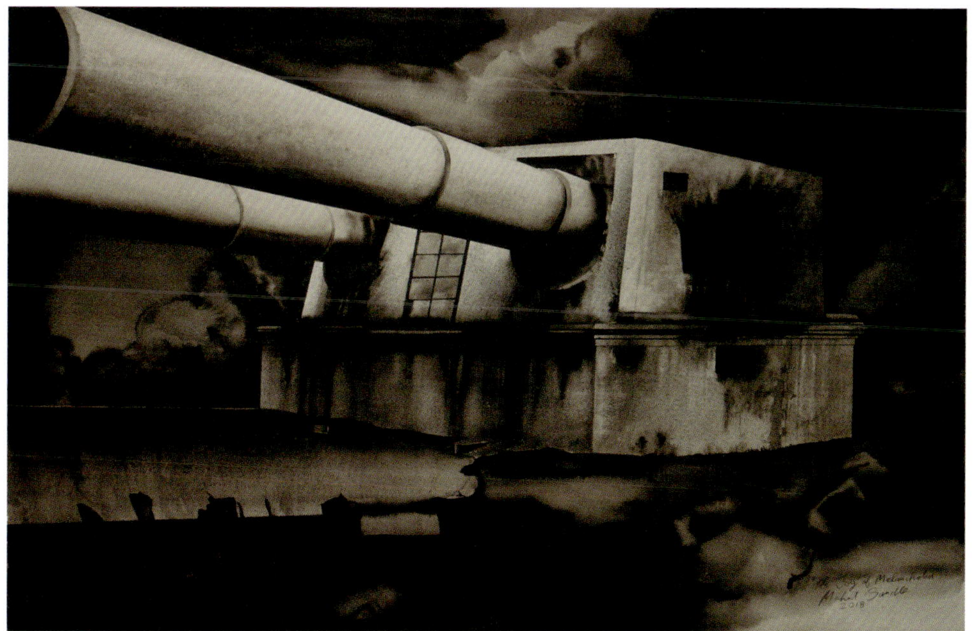

John Humphreys
The Queen
Painted fibreglass
H 64 cm

James Butler MBE RA
Her Majesty Queen Elizabeth, the Queen Mother
Bronze
H 61 cm

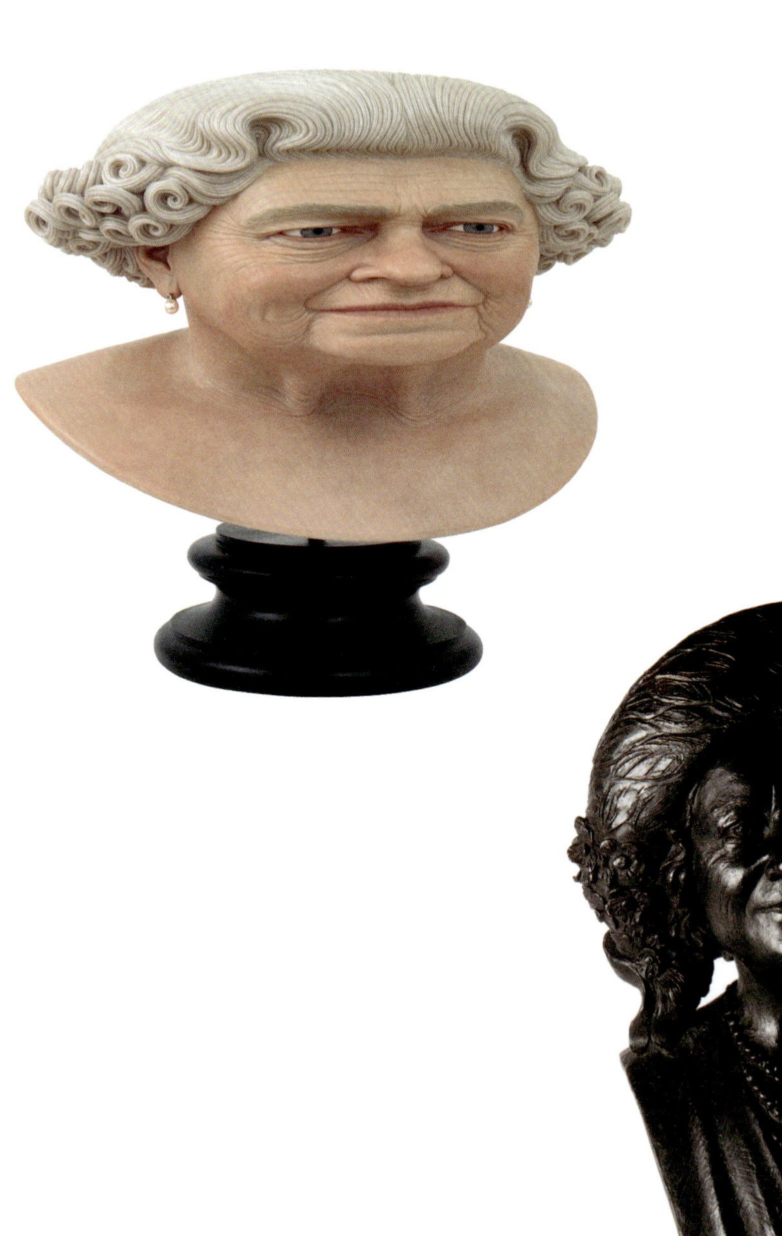

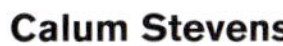

Lis Thomas
Cheater Cheetah
Acrylic
50 × 39 cm

Calum Stevens
Marlboro Man
Wool, waste pipe and plaster
H 95 cm

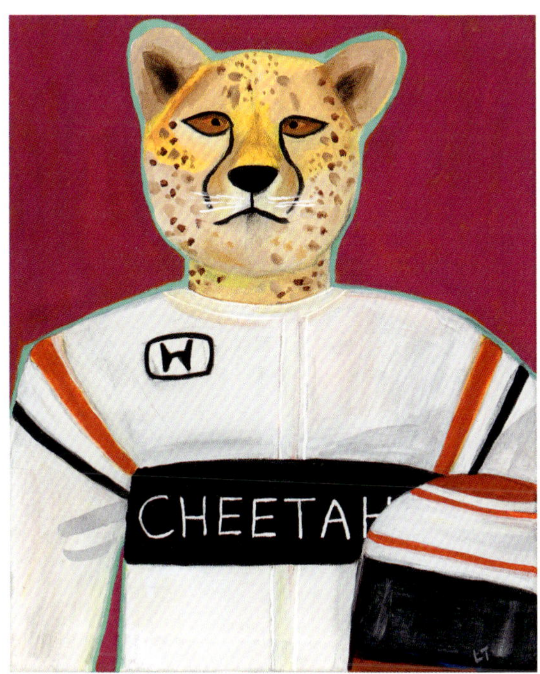

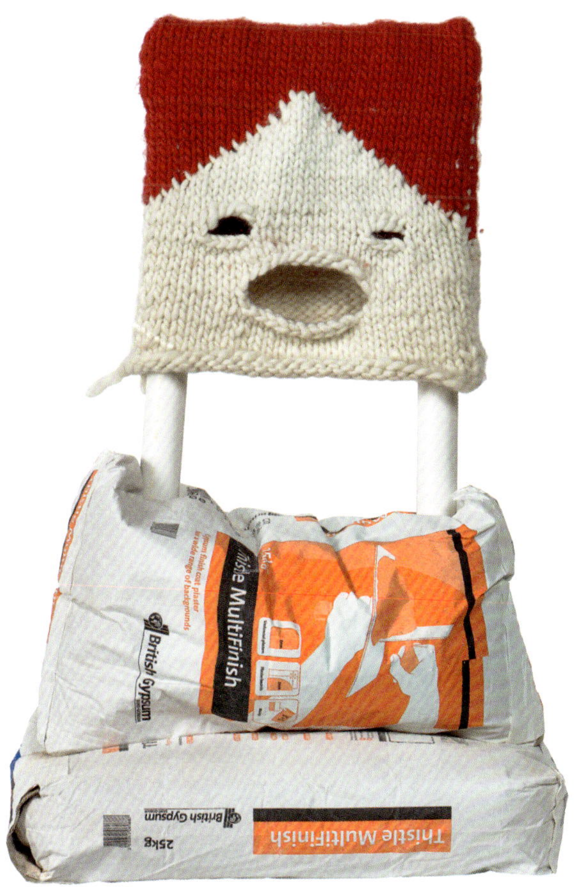

Eva Jiricna CBE RA
Cheer Up Our Cities
Photographic print
39 × 53 cm

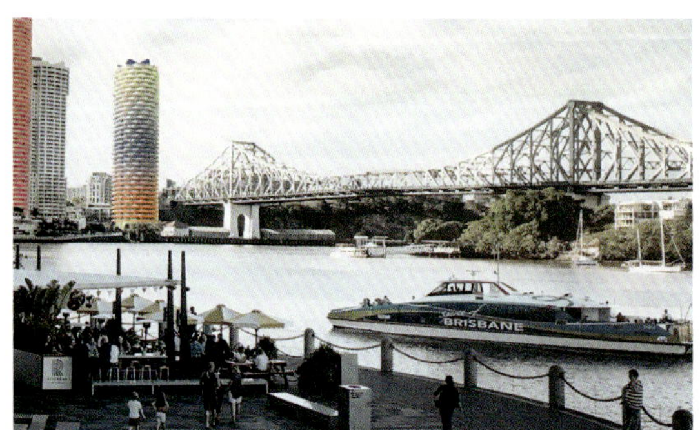

Sir Michael Hopkins CBE RA (Hopkins Architects)
ITV Headquarters – Site Context Models
Timber and 3D print
H 29 cm

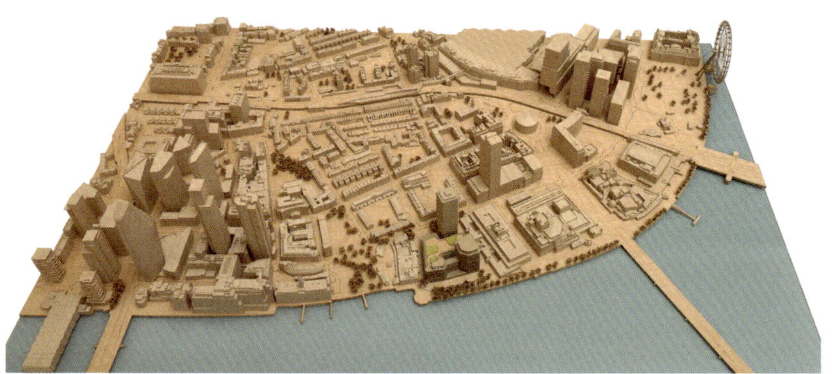

Senator Renzo Piano Hon RA
The Shard, London Bridge Tower
Marker, pastel and pencil
42 × 30 cm

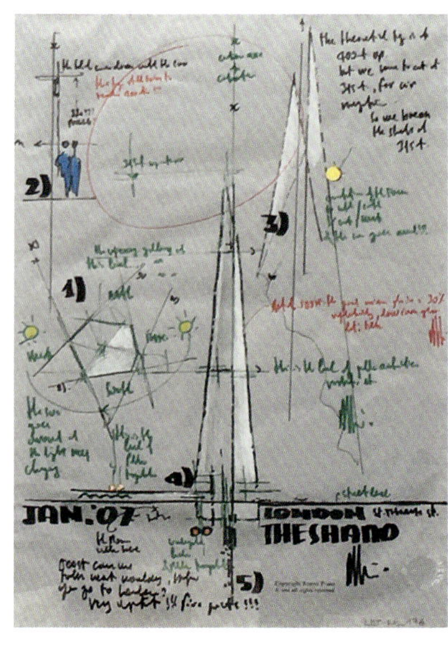

Prof Farshid Moussavi RA
130 Fenchurch Street
Cast resin
H 64 cm

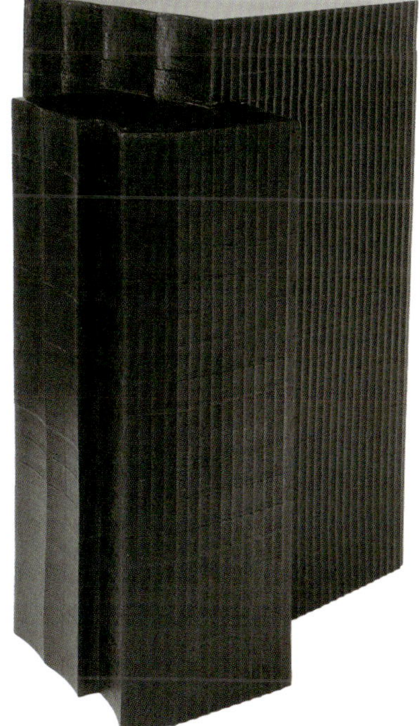

Louisa Hutton OBE RA and Matthias Sauerbruch (Sauerbruch Hutton)
Beehive
Mixed media
H 132 cm

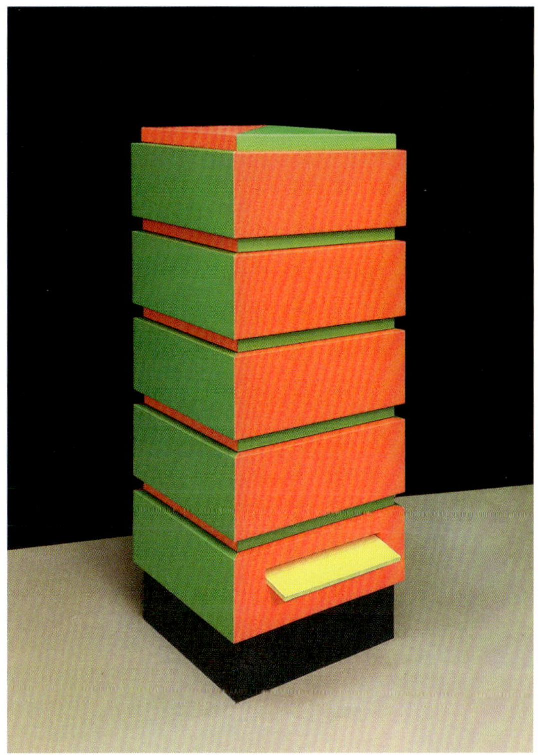

Prof Trevor Dannatt OBE RA
2CV 3816 OJ47
Pencil
14 × 21 cm

Paul Koralek CBE RA
Leaf Forms 3
Pencil
35 × 27 cm

Prof Ian Ritchie CBE RA
Snowoman and Snowboy
Etching
23 × 29 cm

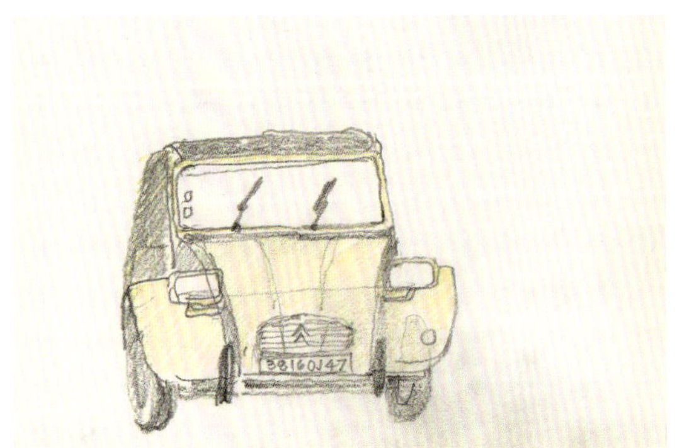

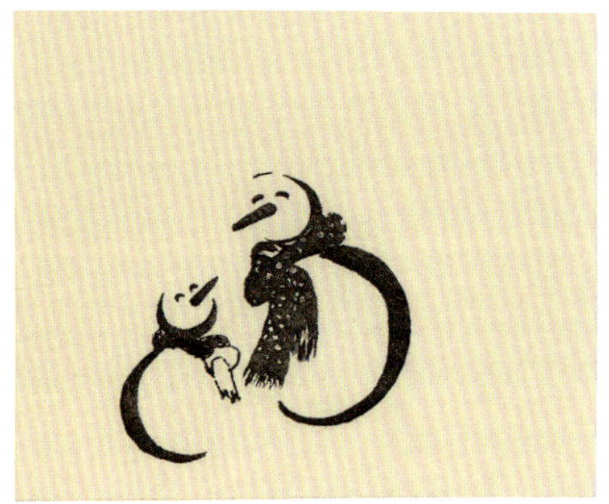

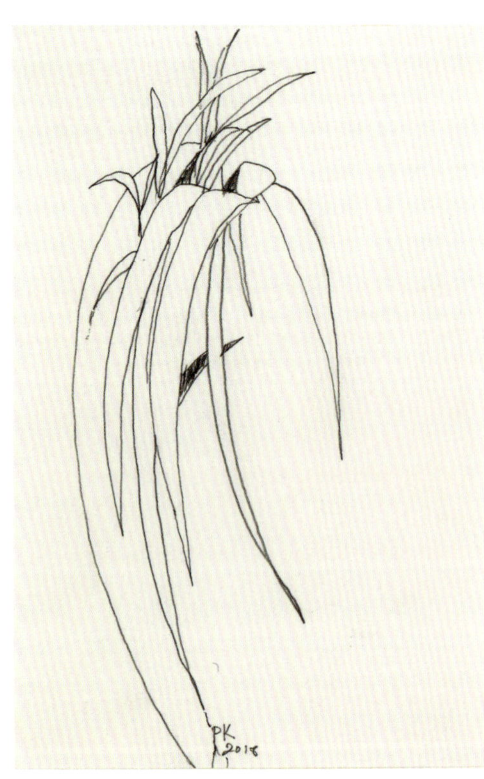

The late Prof William Alsop OBE RA and Jane Frere
A Kerfuffle of Collisions
Linocut and mixed media
41 × 41 cm

Prof Gordon Benson OBE RA
Rectangle
Hand-worked digital print
40 × 30 cm

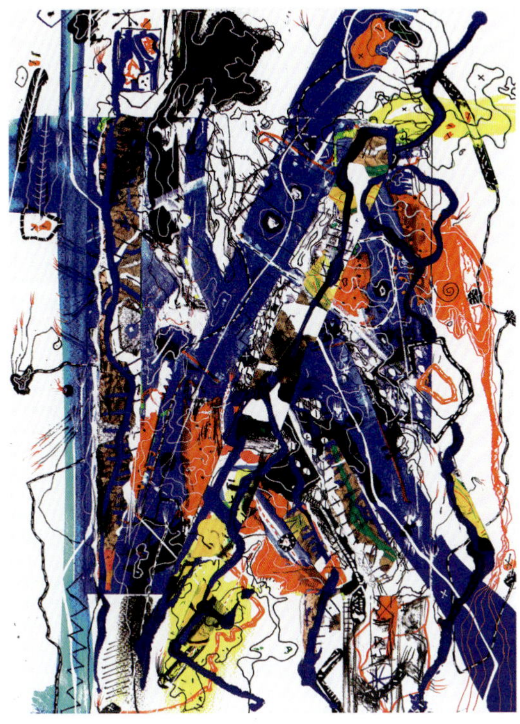

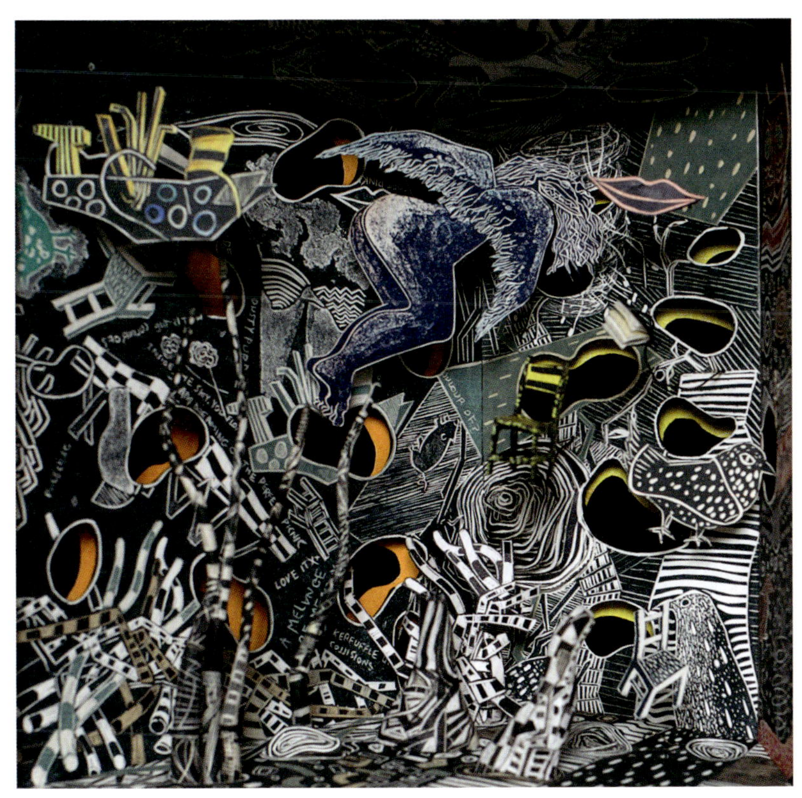

Lord Rogers of Riverside CH RA (Rogers Stirk Harbour + Partners)
Château La Coste
Acrylic and timber
H 20 cm

Chris Wilkinson OBE RA (WilkinsonEyre Model Making Workshop)
Student Housing at Dyson, Malmesbury
Mixed media
H 36 cm

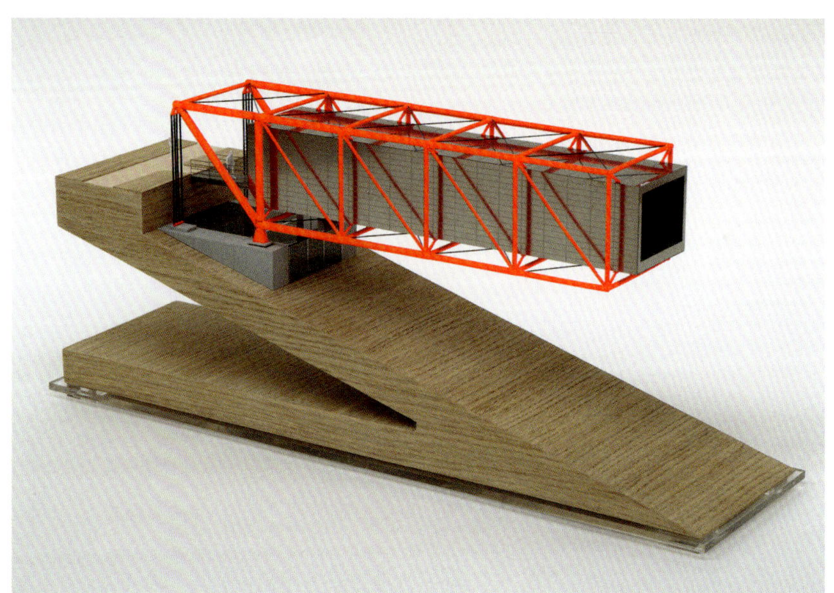

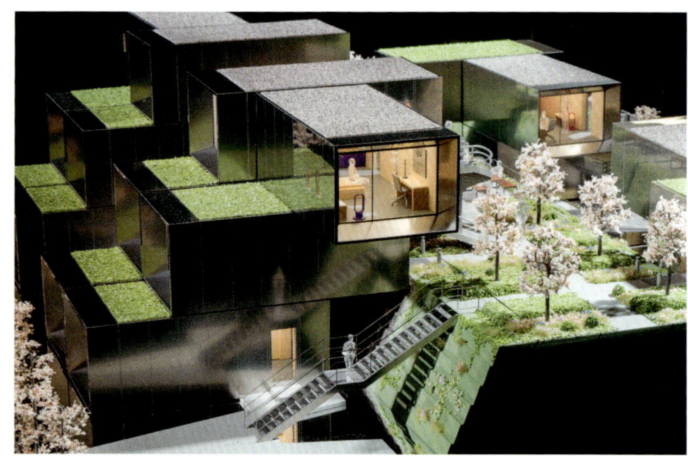

Prof Sir Peter Cook RA
Urban Retreat
Print from ink and watercolour
42 × 62 cm

Thomas Heatherwick CBE RA (Heatherwick Studio)
Google Mountain View
Mixed media
H 45 cm

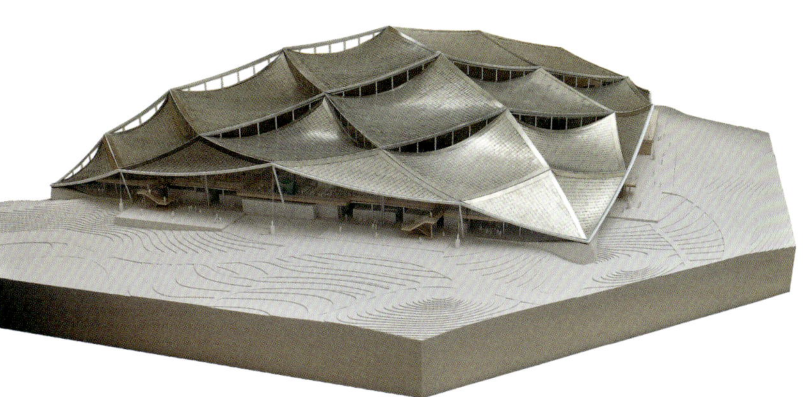

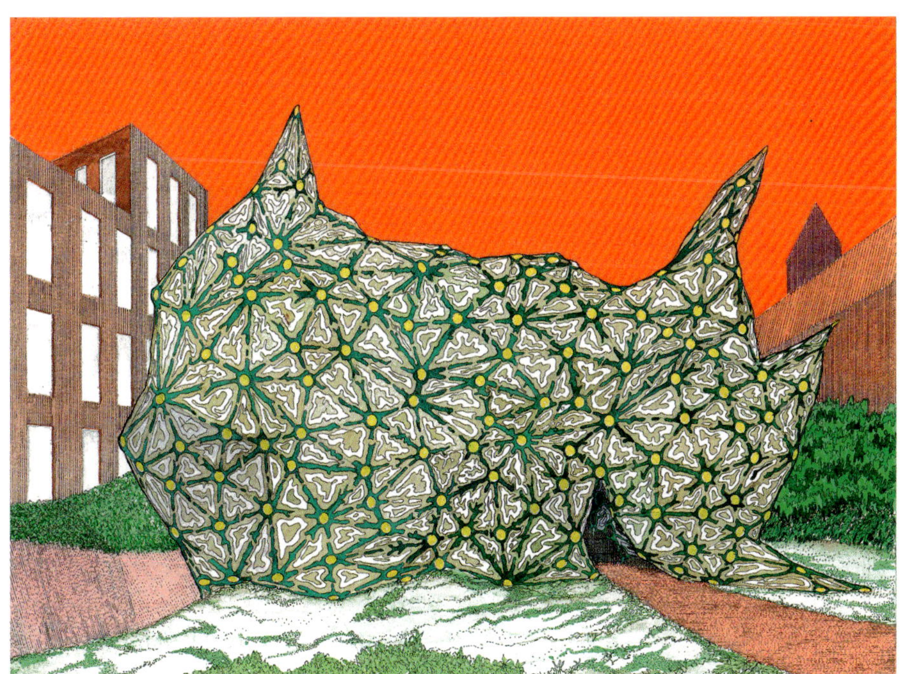

Eric Parry RA
Fenchurch Avenue
Mixed media
H 44 cm

Edward Cullinan CBE RA (Cullinan Studio)
Conkers Aerial Walkway
Cardboard and plastic
H 5 cm

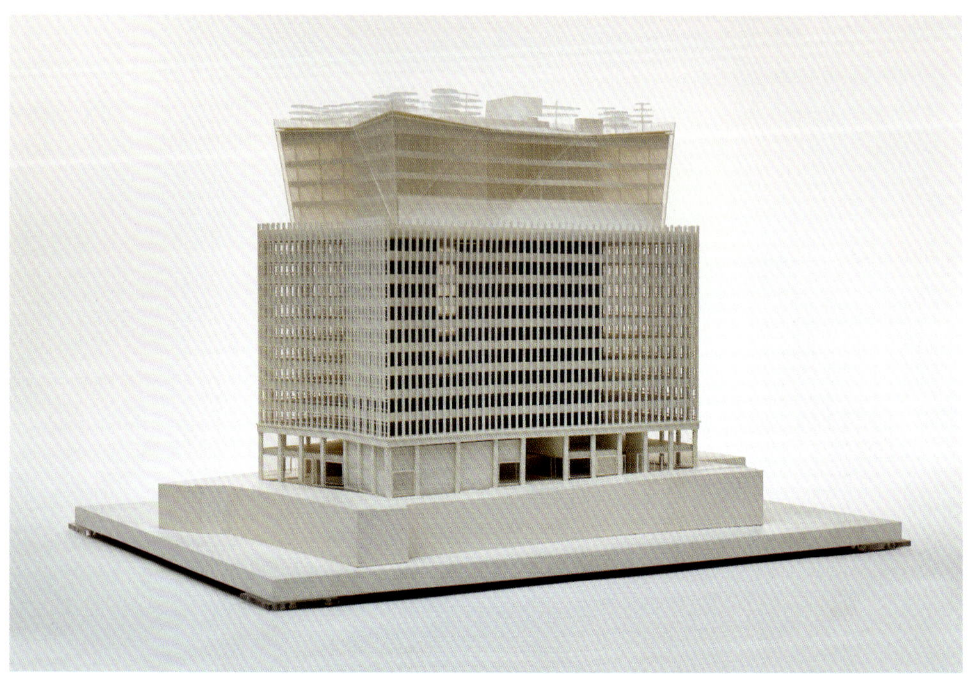

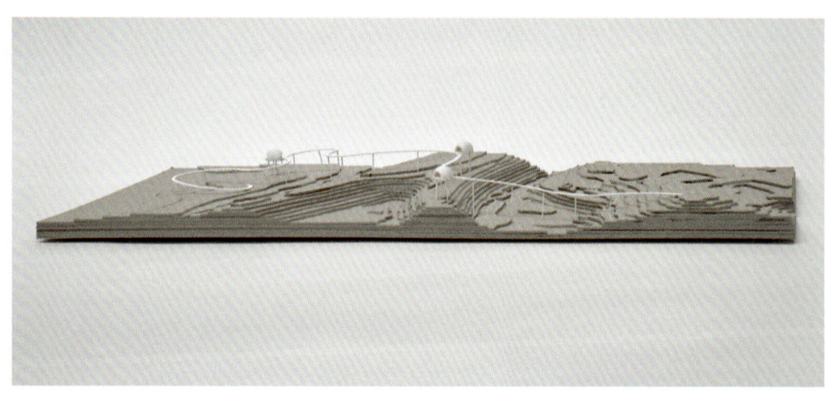

Kohn Pedersen Fox
China Resources Headquarters
Wood
H 104 cm

Brady Mallalieu Architects Ltd
Garden Pavilion
3D print on fused glass
H 20 cm

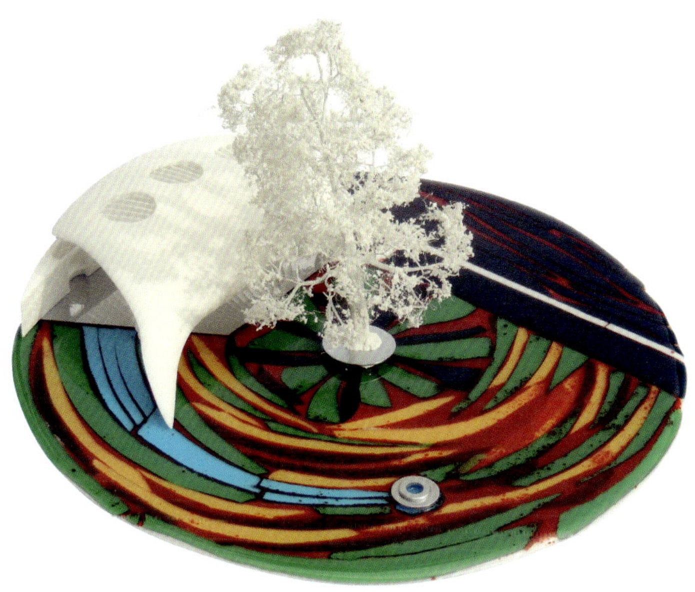

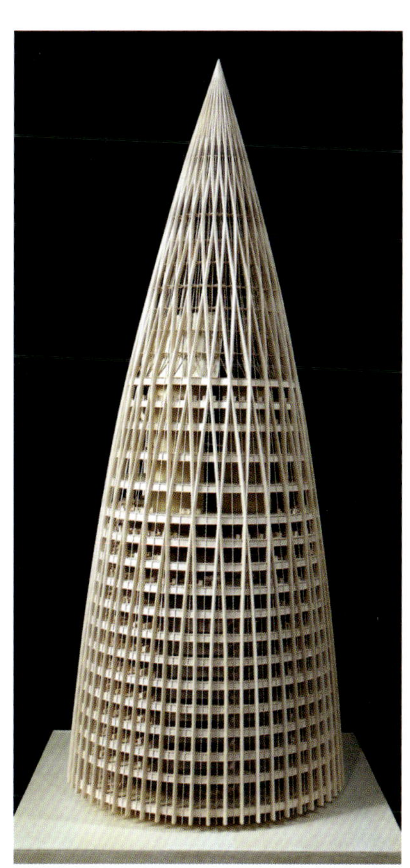

Sir David Adjaye OBE RA (Adjaye Associates)
Studio Museum Harlem, New York
Foamex and acrylic
H 100 cm

Spencer de Grey CBE RA (Foster + Partners)
Study Model for a Hotel in the Middle East
Timber and acrylic
H 80 cm

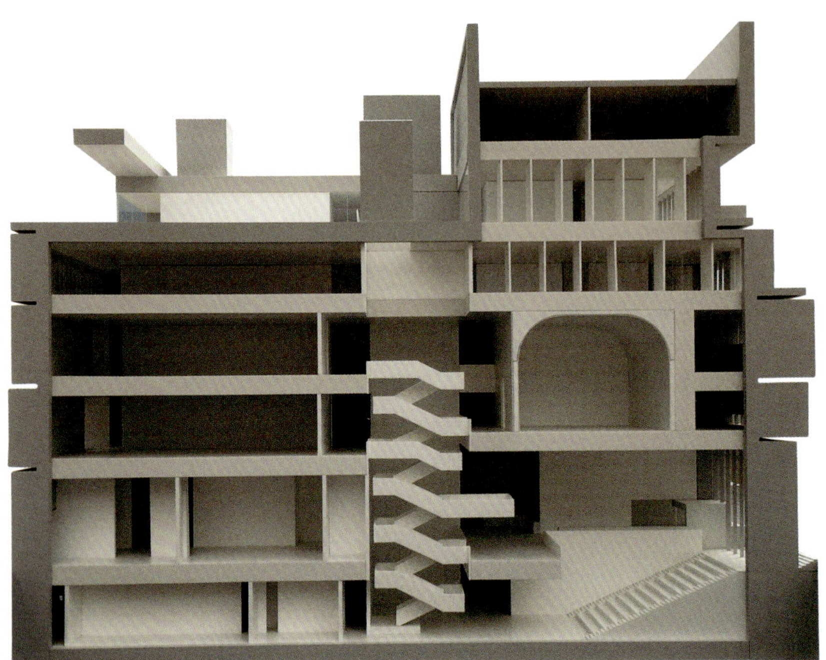

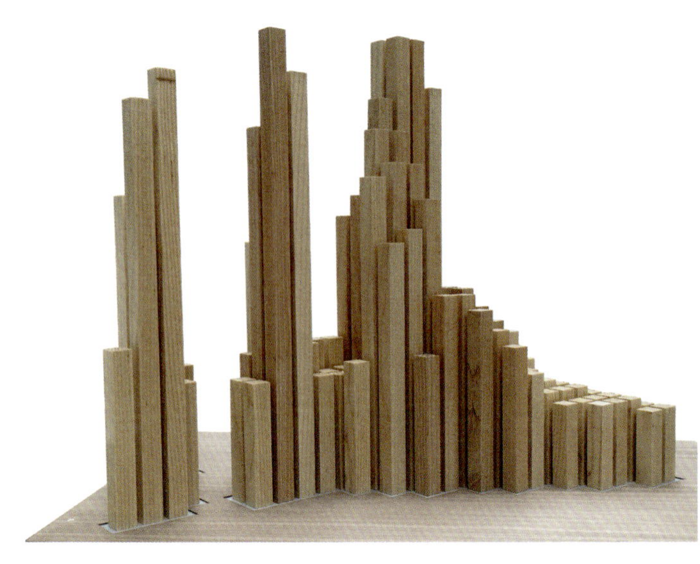

Lord Foster of Thames Bank OM RA (Foster + Partners)
Hall of Realms, Prado Museum, Madrid
Timber and acrylic
H 65 cm

Sir Nicholas Grimshaw CBE PPRA
Phillip and Patricia Frost Museum of Science Aquarium
Framed model
H 19 cm

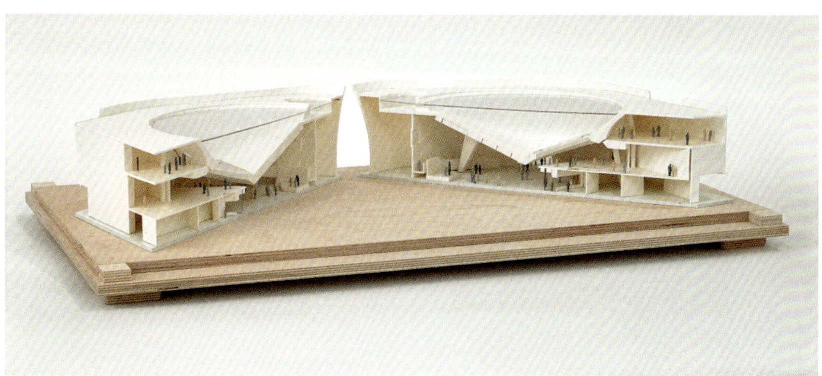

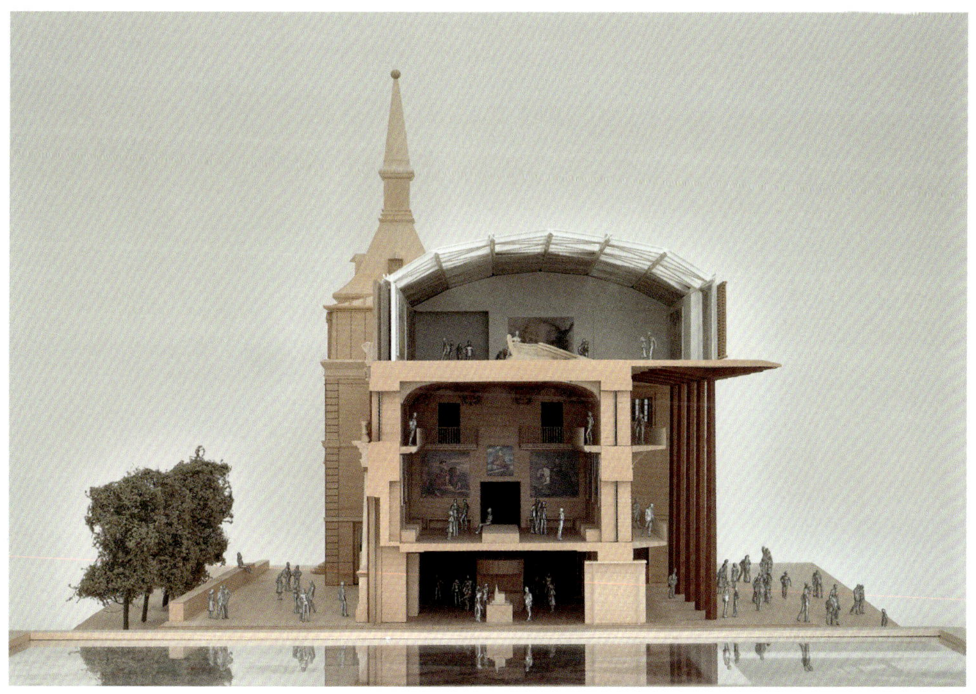

Dickon Drury
Double Bill
Oil
90 × 70 cm

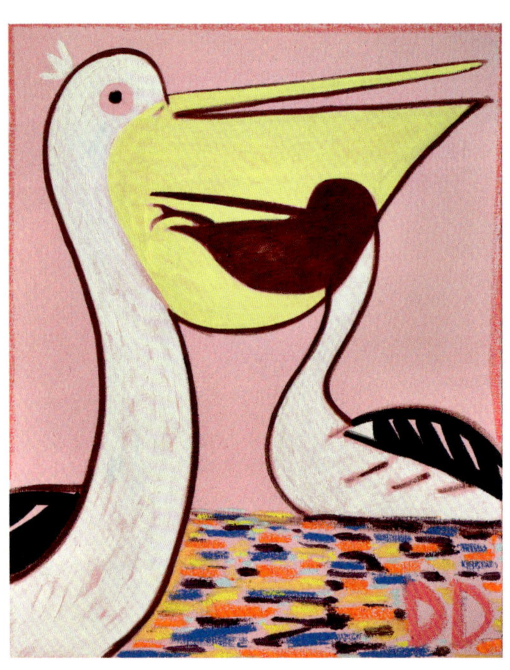

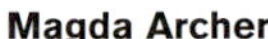

Magda Archer
Please Don't Talk to Me About Art
Acrylic
89 × 59 cm

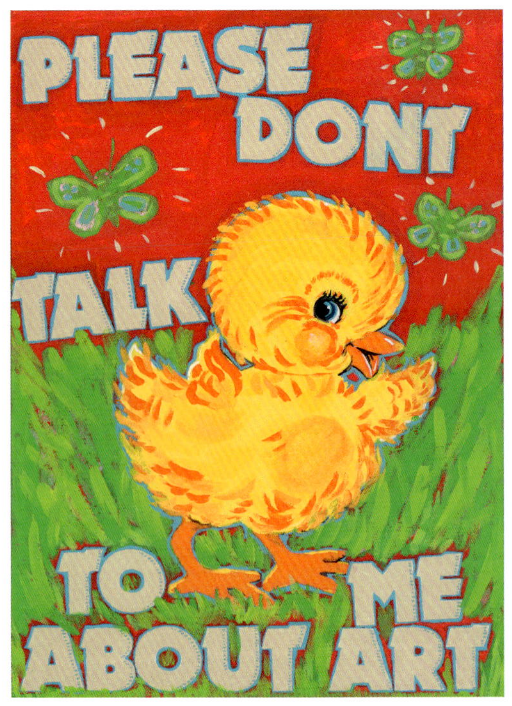

Prof Stephen Farthing RA
A Gallery of Gold Boxes:
The Gilbert Collection, South Kensington
Acrylic
70 × 100 cm

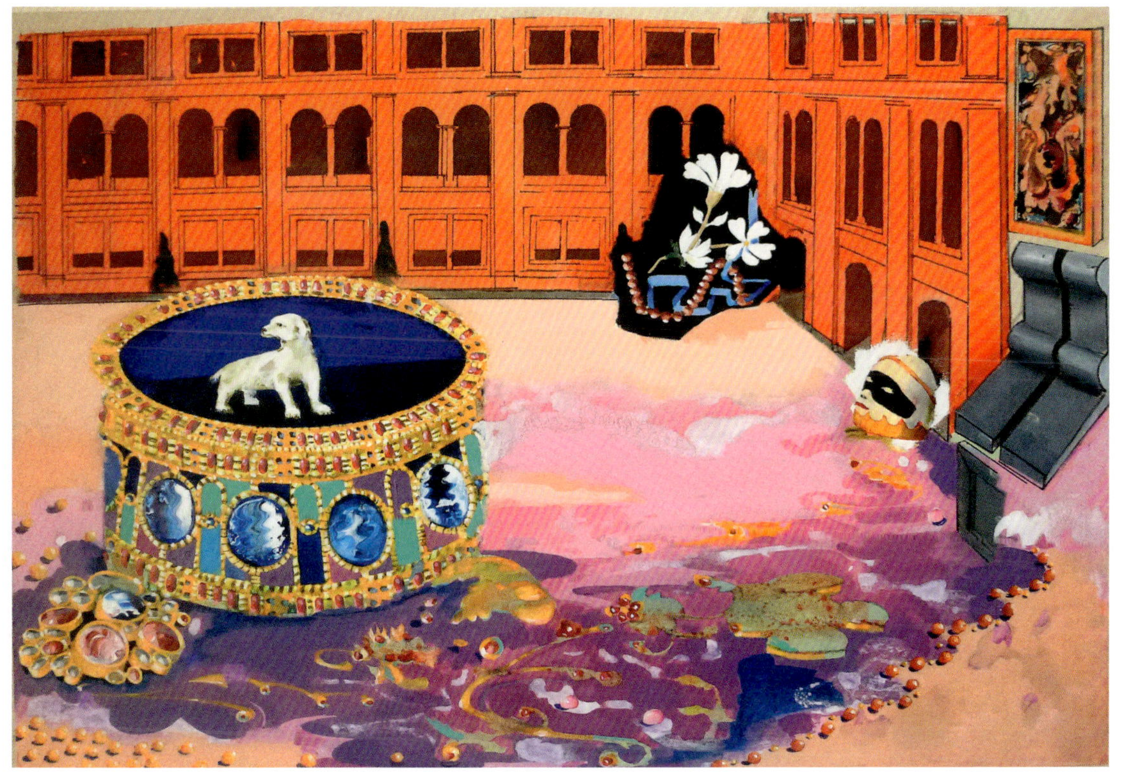

Sarah Maple
Snow White the Scientist
Archival inkjet print
50 × 70 cm

Rossanne Pellegrino
Strange New World
Embroidery on giclée print
30 × 30 cm

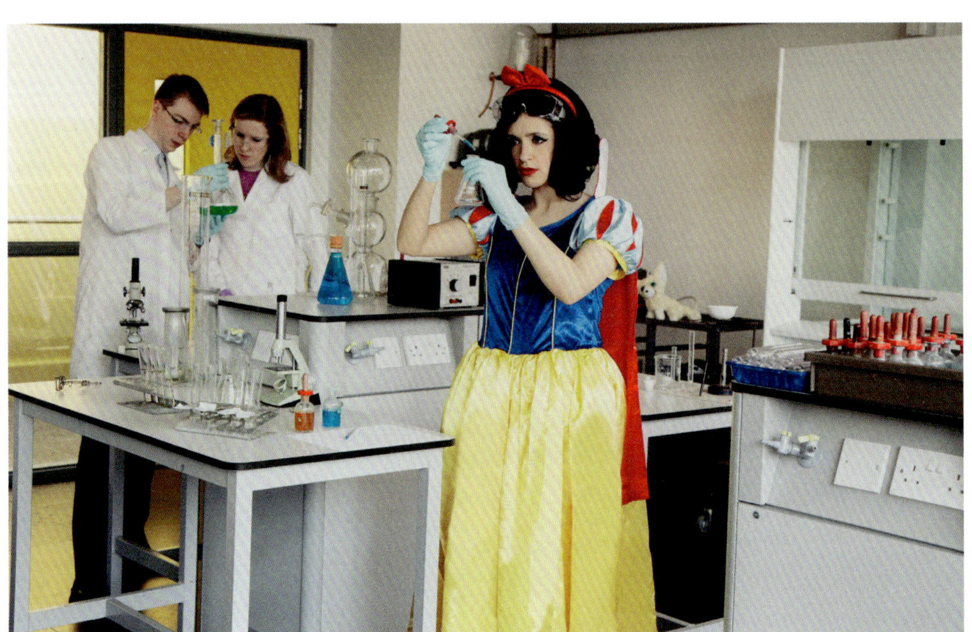

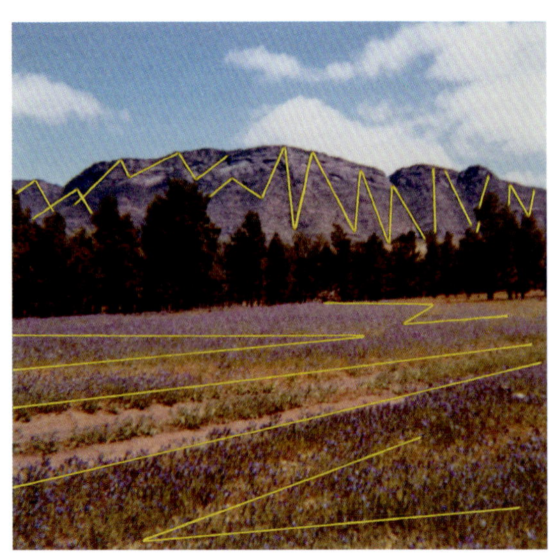

Martin Parr
Botanical Gardens, Ooty, India
Pigment print
61 × 86 cm

Tom Broadbent
Syrrus, a Fox and Lupestripe, a Wolf Having a Barbecue at Home in Leeds (from the series 'At Home with the Furries')
Giclée print
50 × 75 cm

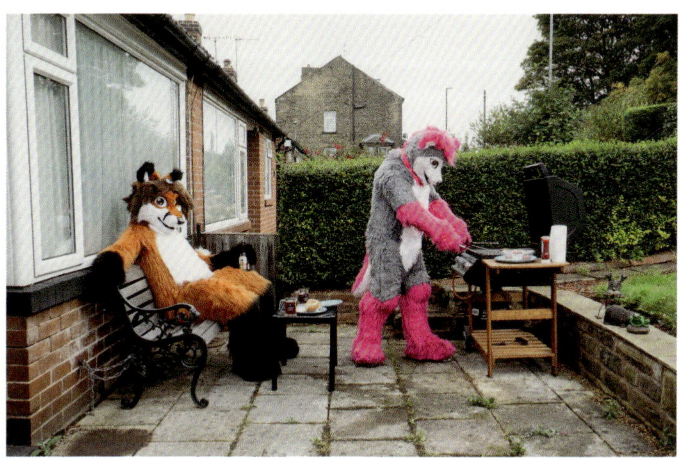

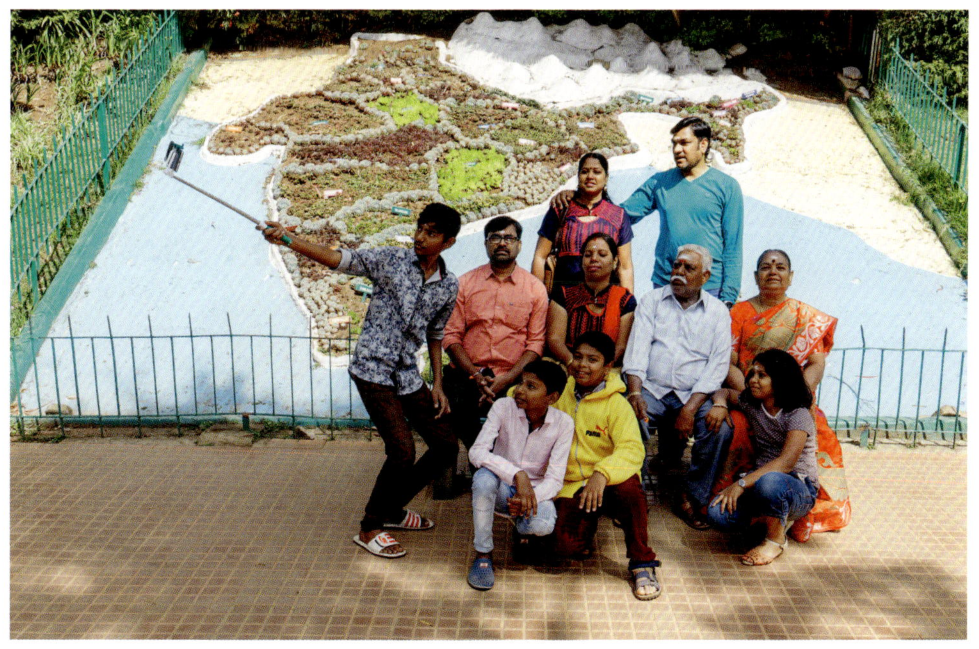

Sasha Okun
A Woman and a Man
Oil
183 × 301 cm

Graeme Miller
TV with Dad
Mixed media
H 45 cm

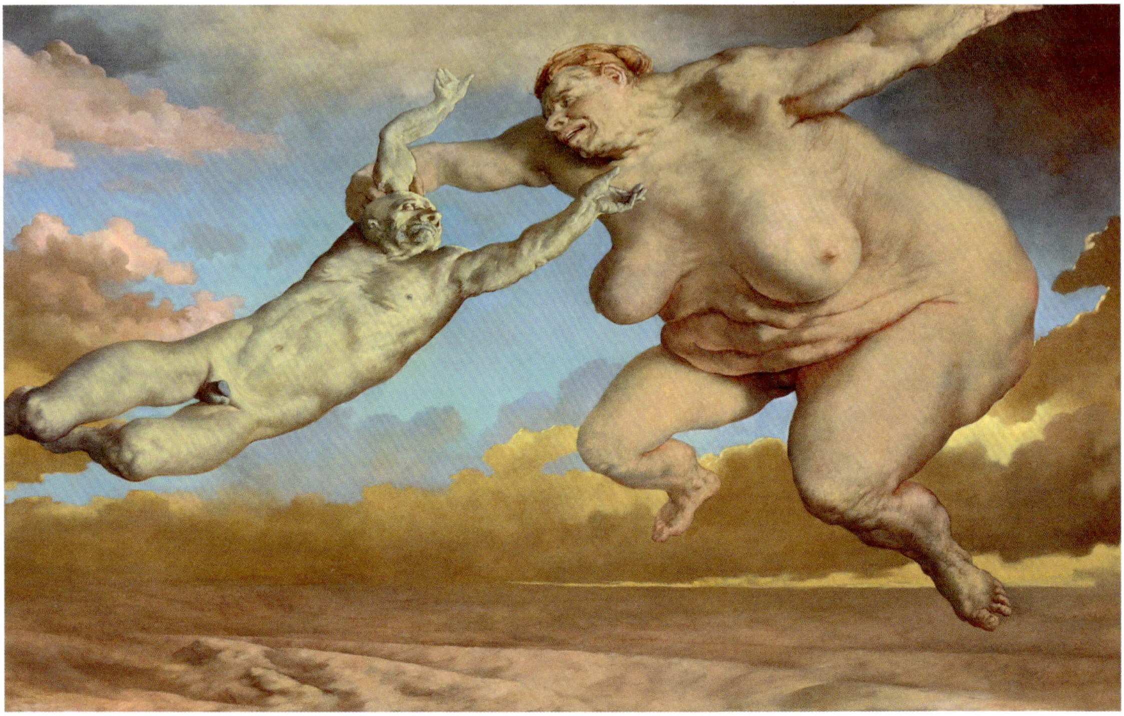

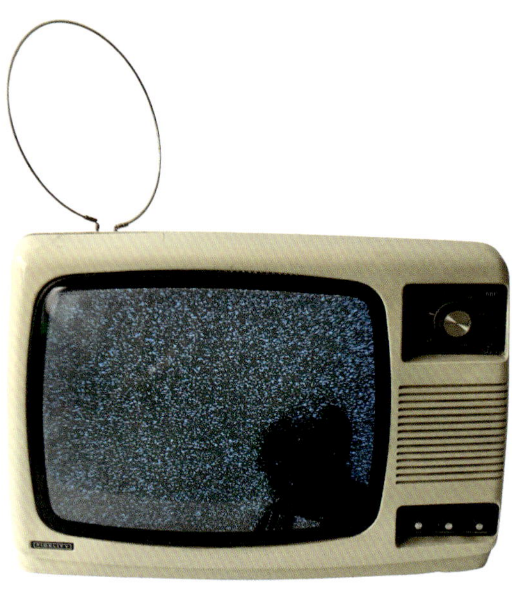

Mick O'Dea
William Joyce and Friends
Acrylic and charcoal
120 × 150 cm

Gavin Turk
Tulips
Painted bronze
H 14 cm

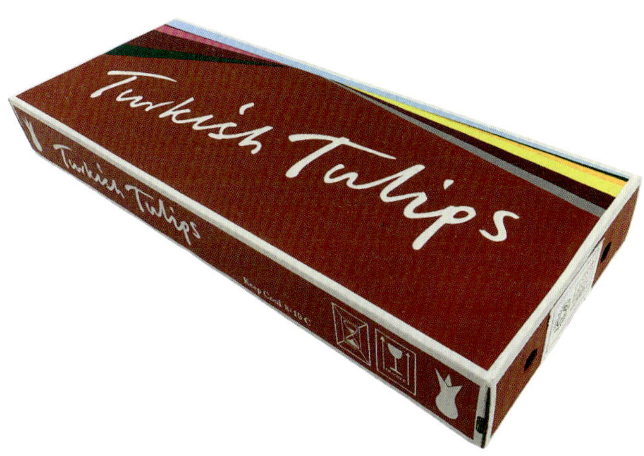

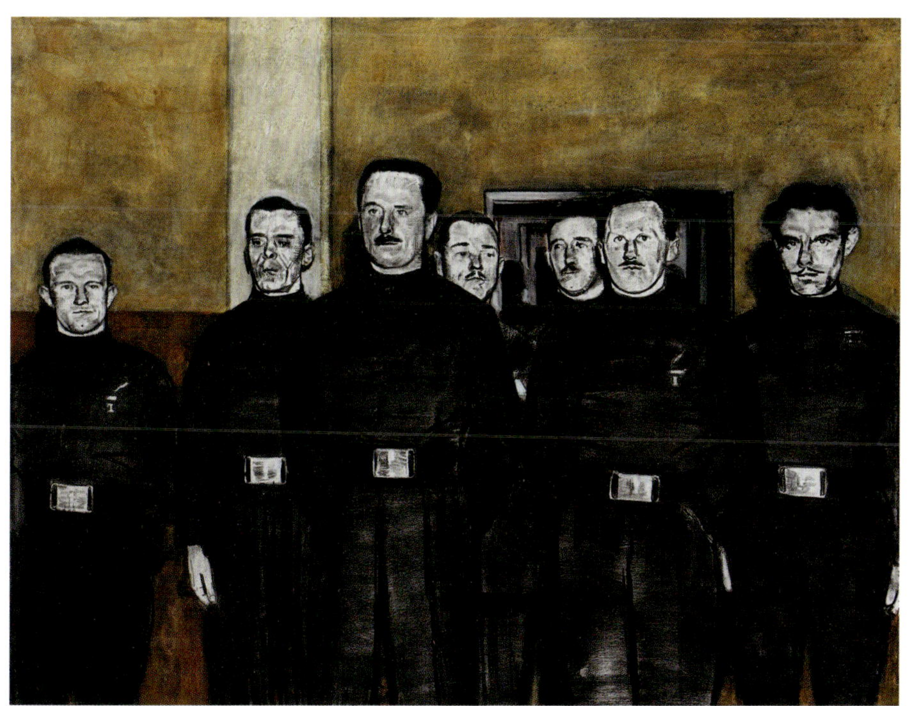

Clancy Gebler Davies
Hersuit 13/02/2018 17.01
Digital print
52 × 34 cm

Katy Wix
A Little Trump
Acrylic
50 × 42 cm

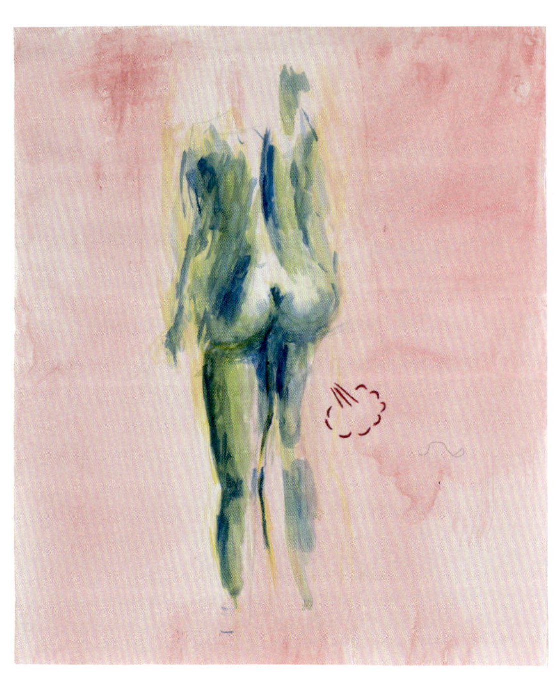

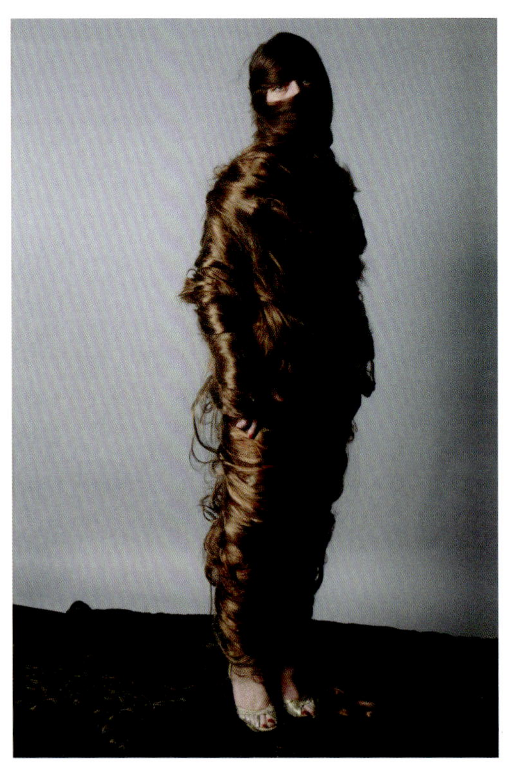

Isaac Julien CBE RA
Before Paradise
Pigment ink print
100 × 100 cm each

Samantha Parkhouse
Fortitude
Oil
220 × 190 cm

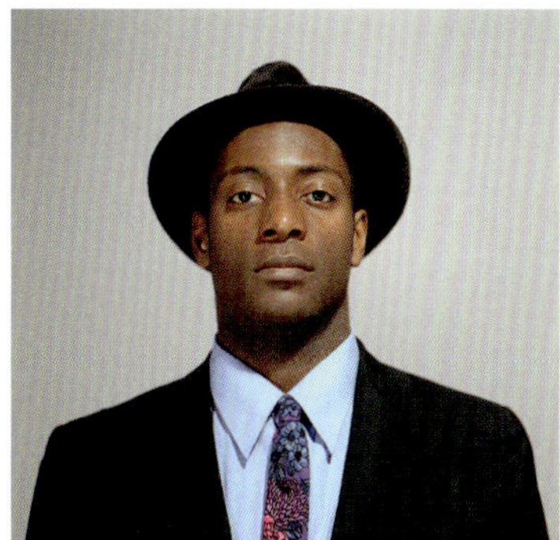

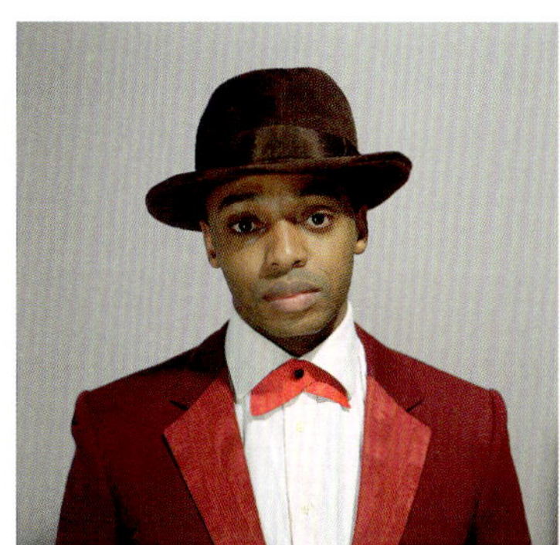

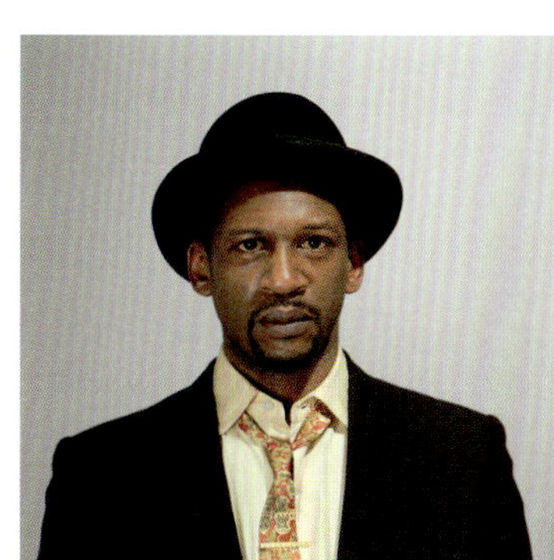

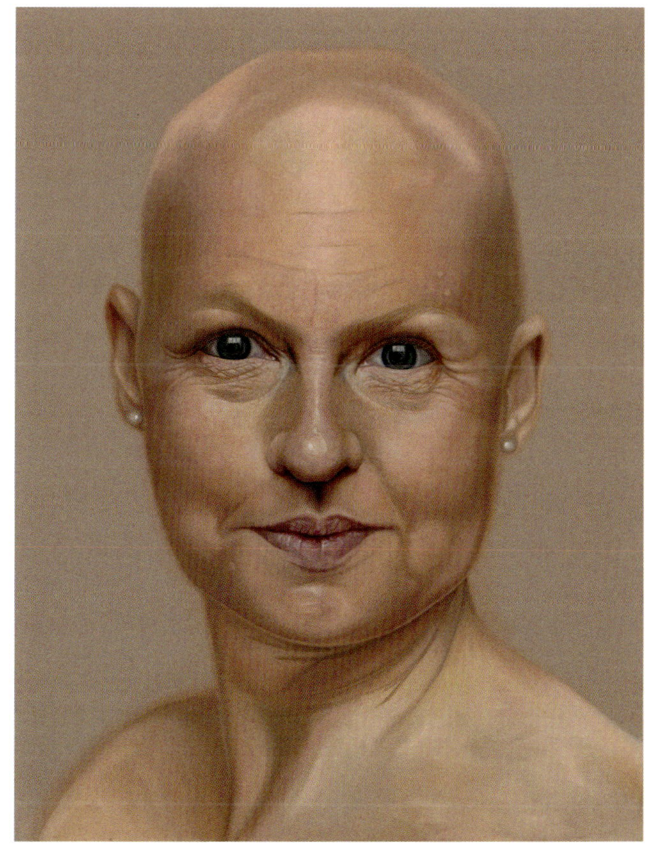

Timothy Blewitt
Gnasher
Wood, metal objects and nails
H 113 cm

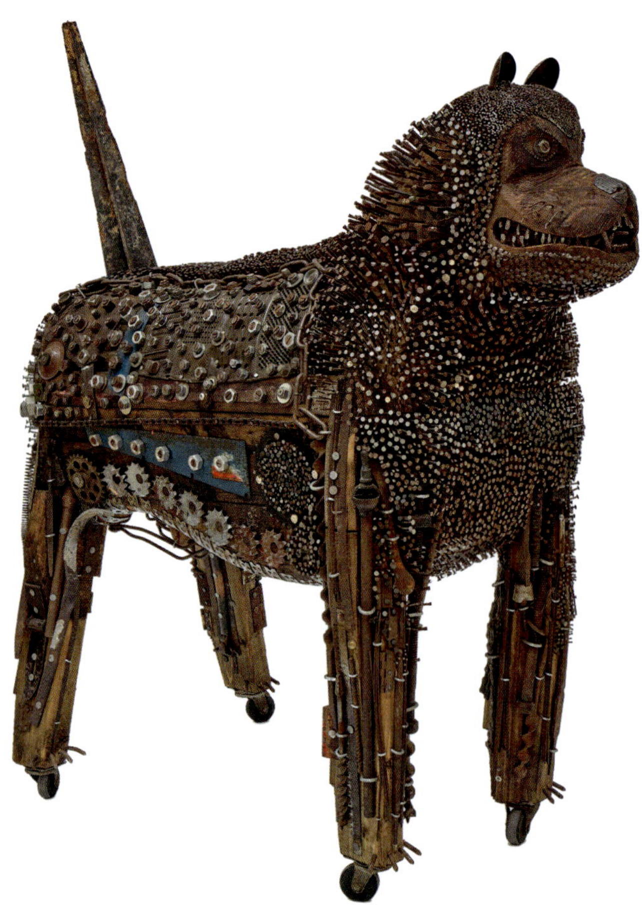

James Prosek
A Tyger for William Blake
Oil and acrylic
114 × 284 cm

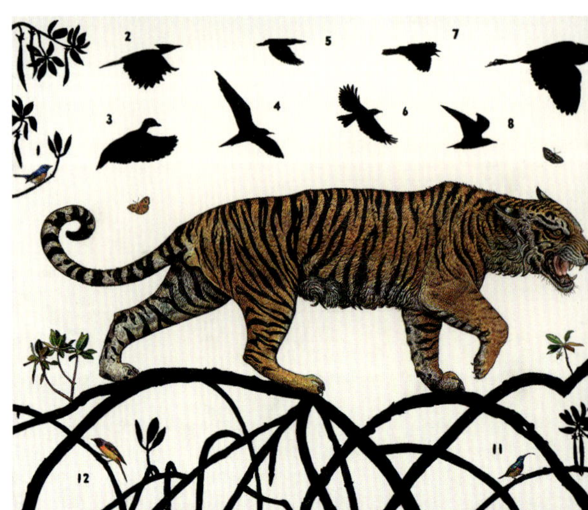

Tal R
House 44
Pigment and rabbit glue
254 × 254 cm

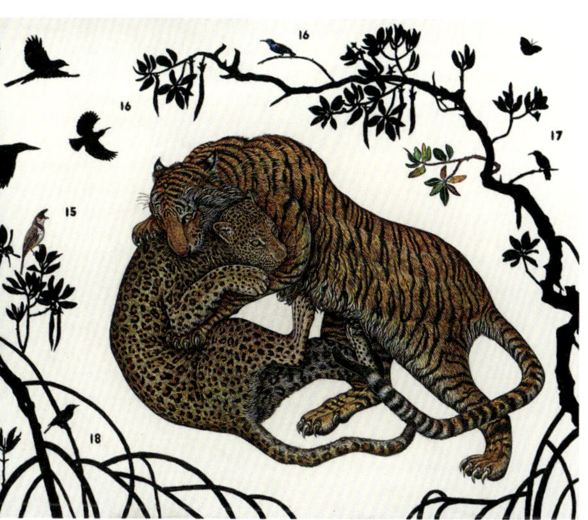

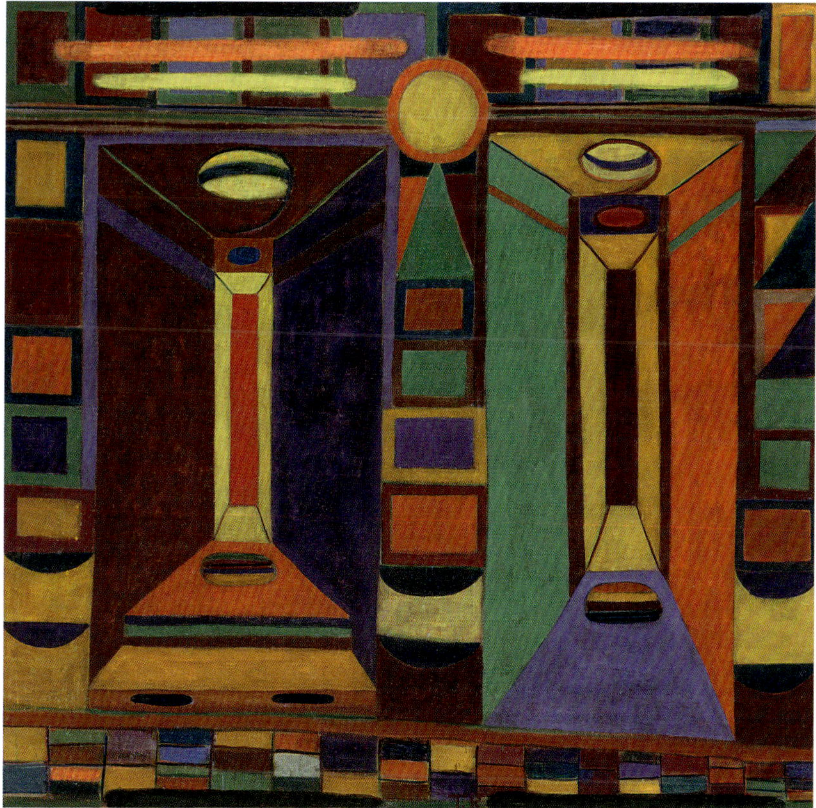

Andrew Lee
Gangland Caff
Menu board
62 × 46 cm

John Smith
Veneer on Board
Mixed media
H 32 cm

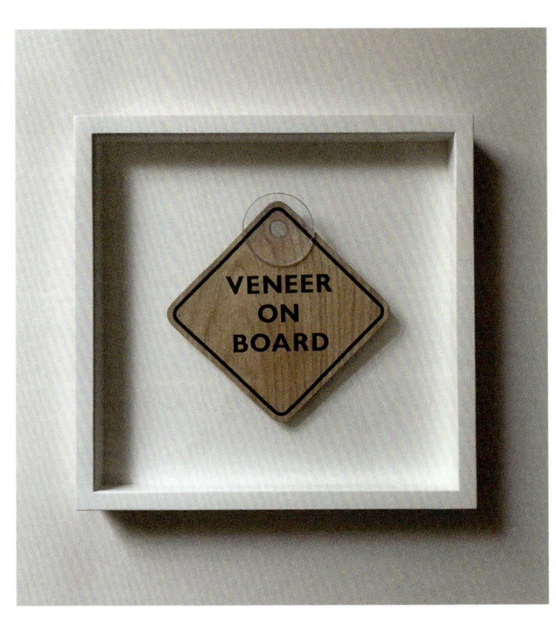

GANGLAND CAFF

SLAP – UP MENU

BRAWN	1/6
KNUCKLE SANDWICH	2/6
PRESSED TONGUE	3 S
BATTERED COD	5 S
KRAY FISH	7/6
MINCEMEAT	2 S
BLACK EYED BEANS	3 d
CAULIFLOWER EARS	5 d
BUNCH OF FIVES	9 d
MASHED SWEDE	6 d
PORRIDGE	1/6
SAUCY TARTS	2 S
CAKE WITH SAW	10/6
JAM SANDWICH	1 S
MARS BAR	2 S
ICE SCREAM	2/6
COKE	2/6
GINGER BEER	2 S
TEA LEAF	1/6

▶ USED £ NOTES ONLY

Rosie Raven
Younger, Hipper, Cooler
Mixed media
H 45 cm

Ronald Henry
Go Go Chicks
Pen and pencil
29 × 41 cm

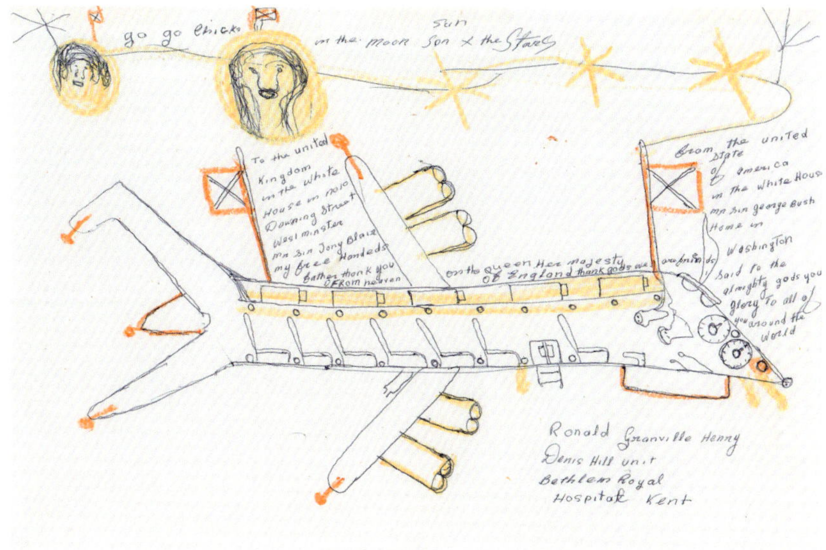

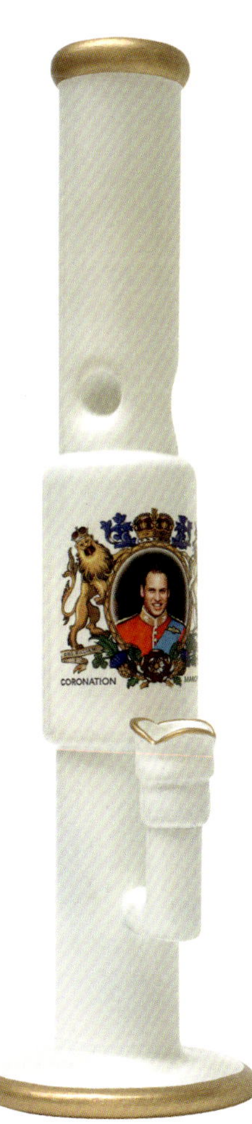

Jeff McMillan
Western Union
Gloss paint
82 × 89 cm

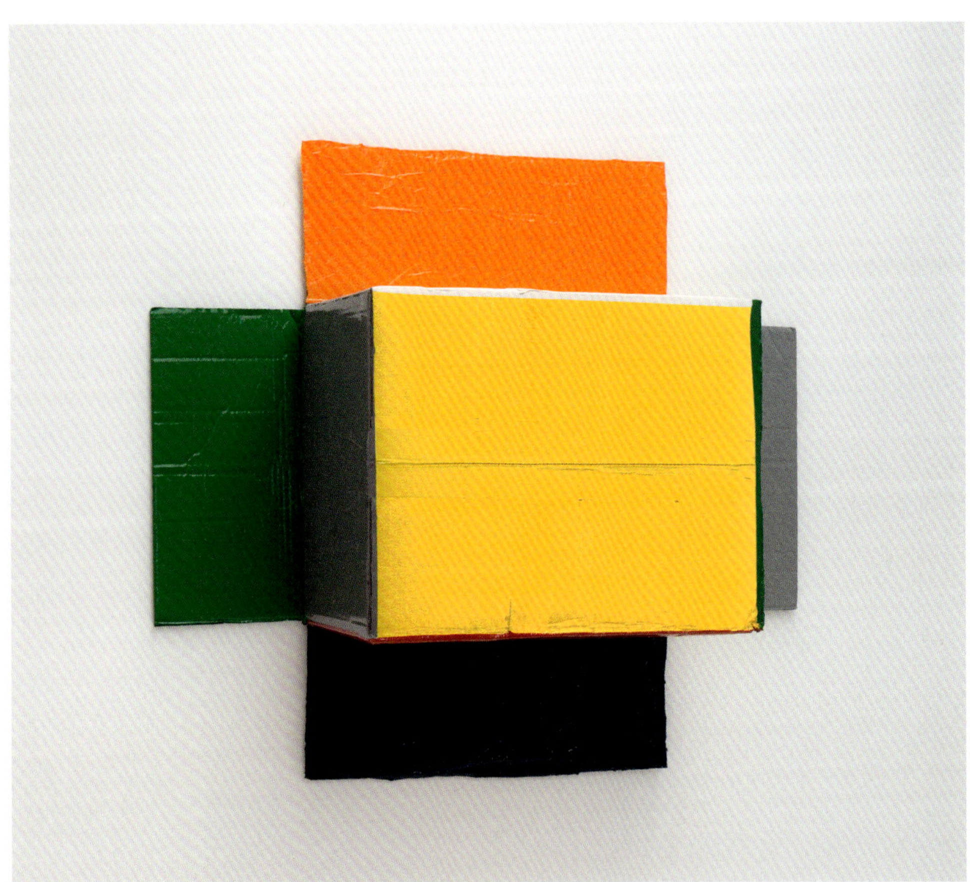

Tim Balaam
Untitled
Oil and varnish
76 × 61 cm

Zsofia Schweger
Charger
Screenprint
57 × 50 cm

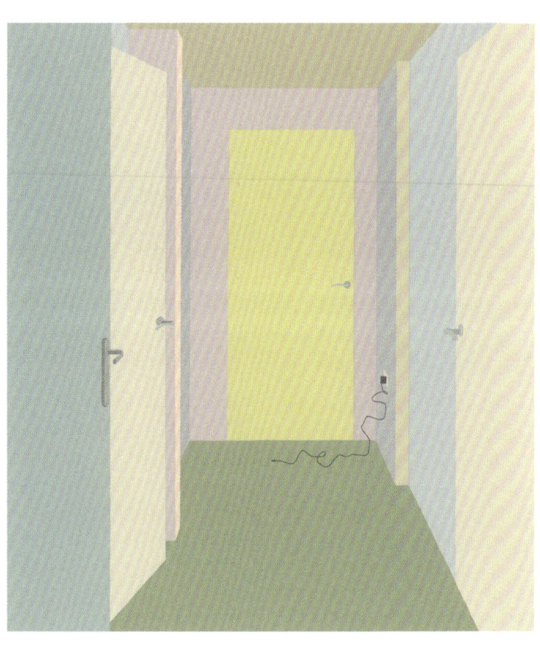

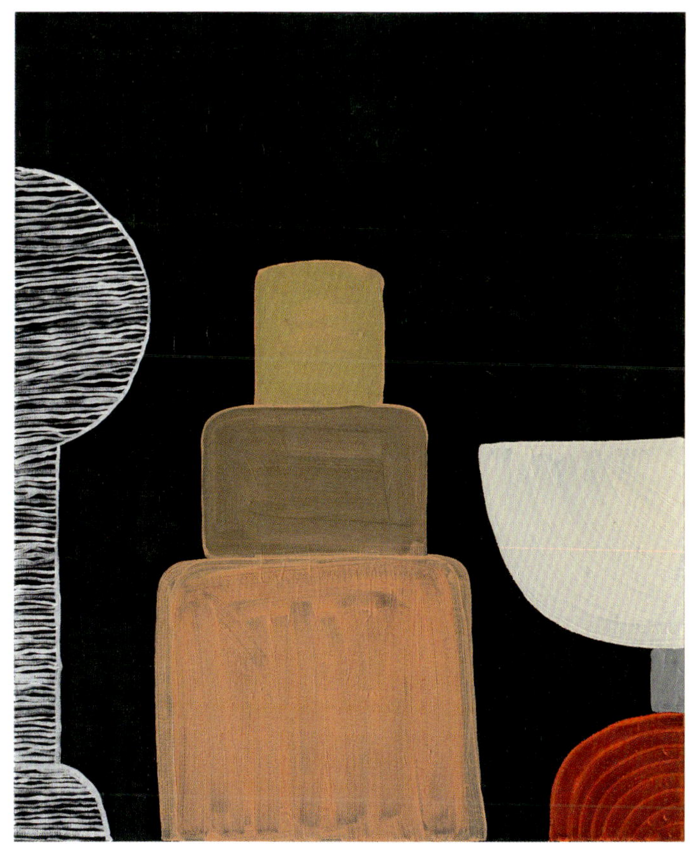

Conrad Shawcross RA
Paradigm – B (Structural)
Weathered steel
H 141 cm

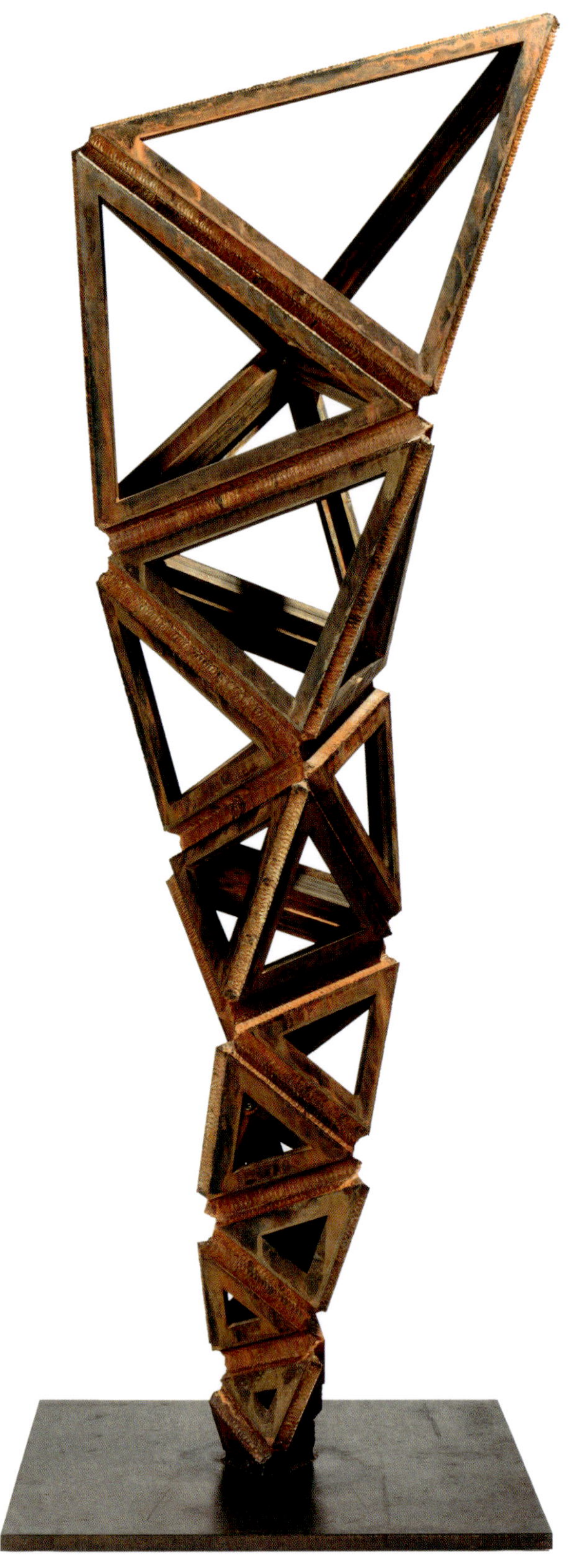

Prof Sir Tony Cragg CBE RA
Lost in Thought
Wood
H 340 cm

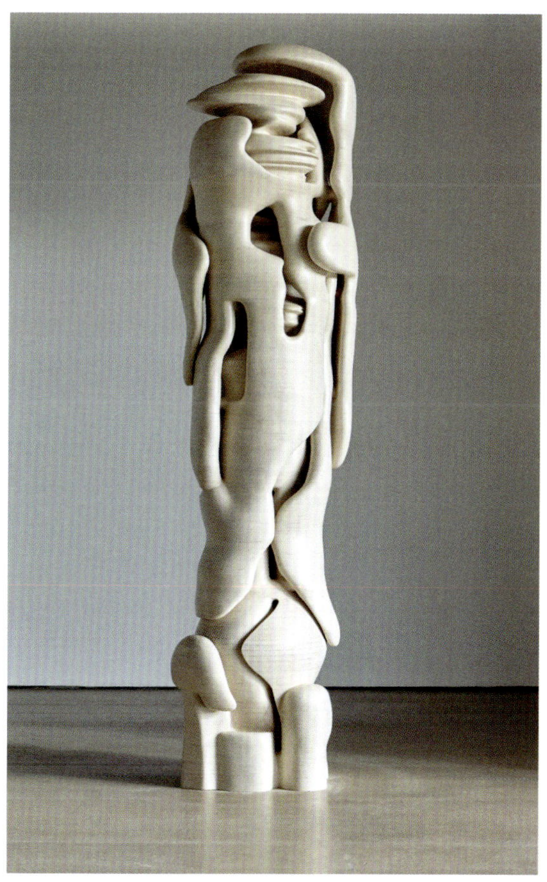

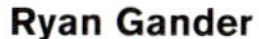

Ryan Gander
Overturned Rietveld Chair after a Snow Flurry
Ash and marble resin
H 60 cm

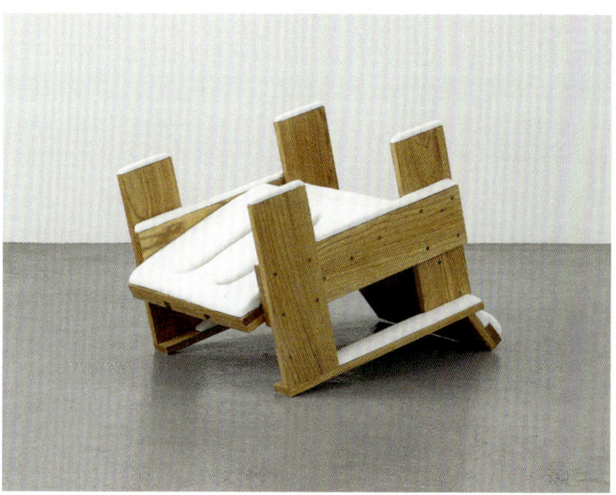

Prof El Anatsui Hon RA
Change in Fortune
Aluminium and copper
294 × 290 cm

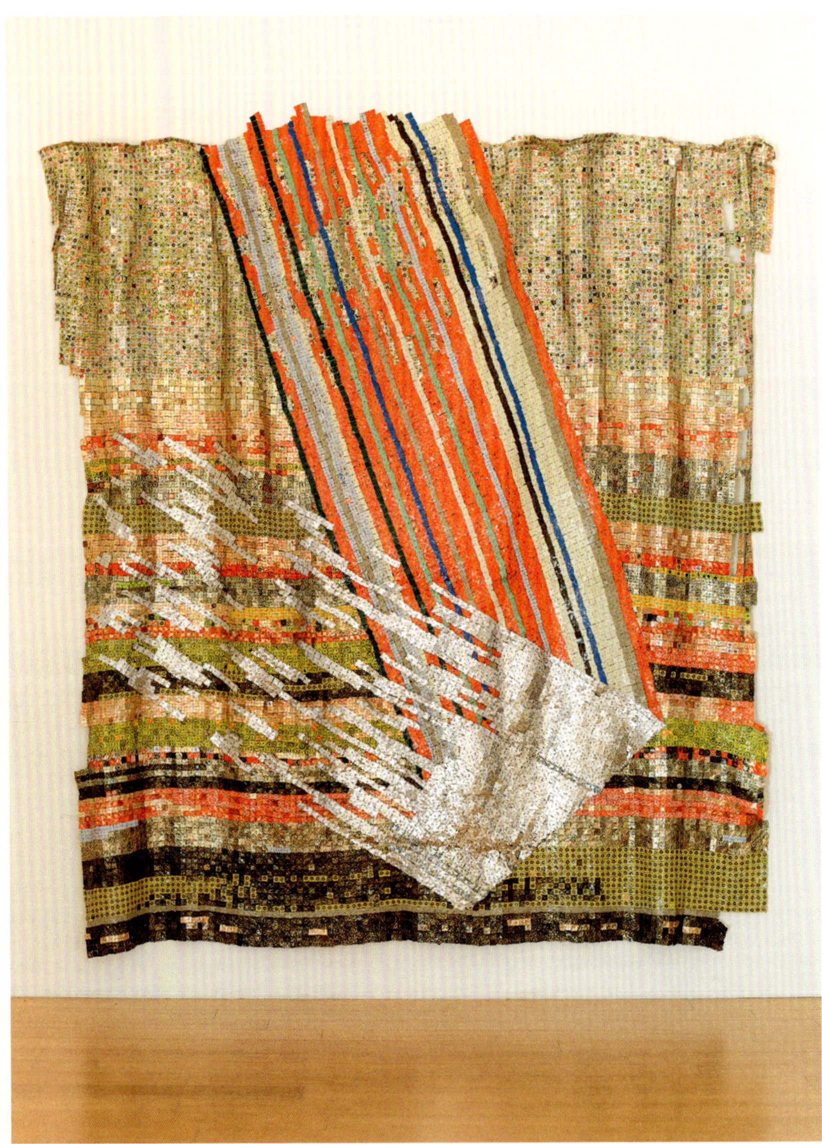

Sean Cavanaugh
Humbug Brothers
Watercolour and gouache
117 × 84 cm

Her Majesty Queen Sonja of Norway
Surprising Angles
Intaglio
54 × 39 cm

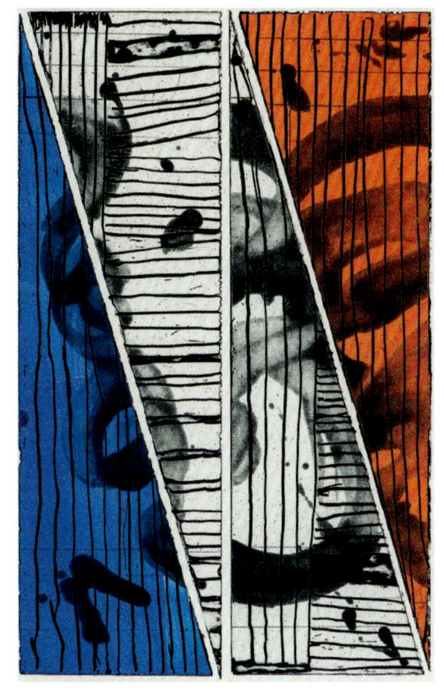

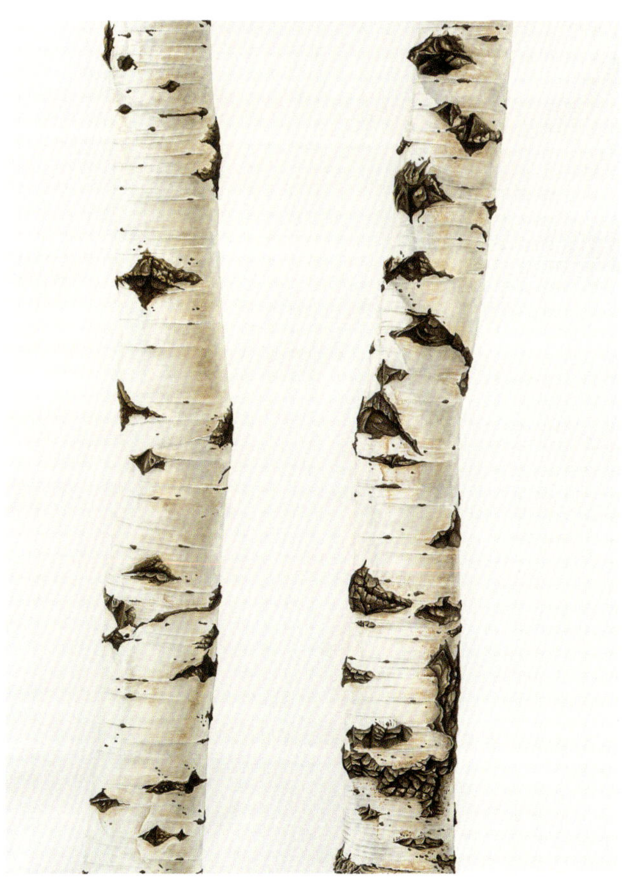

Wolfgang Tillmans RA
Paint Spill
Inkjet print
208 × 138 cm

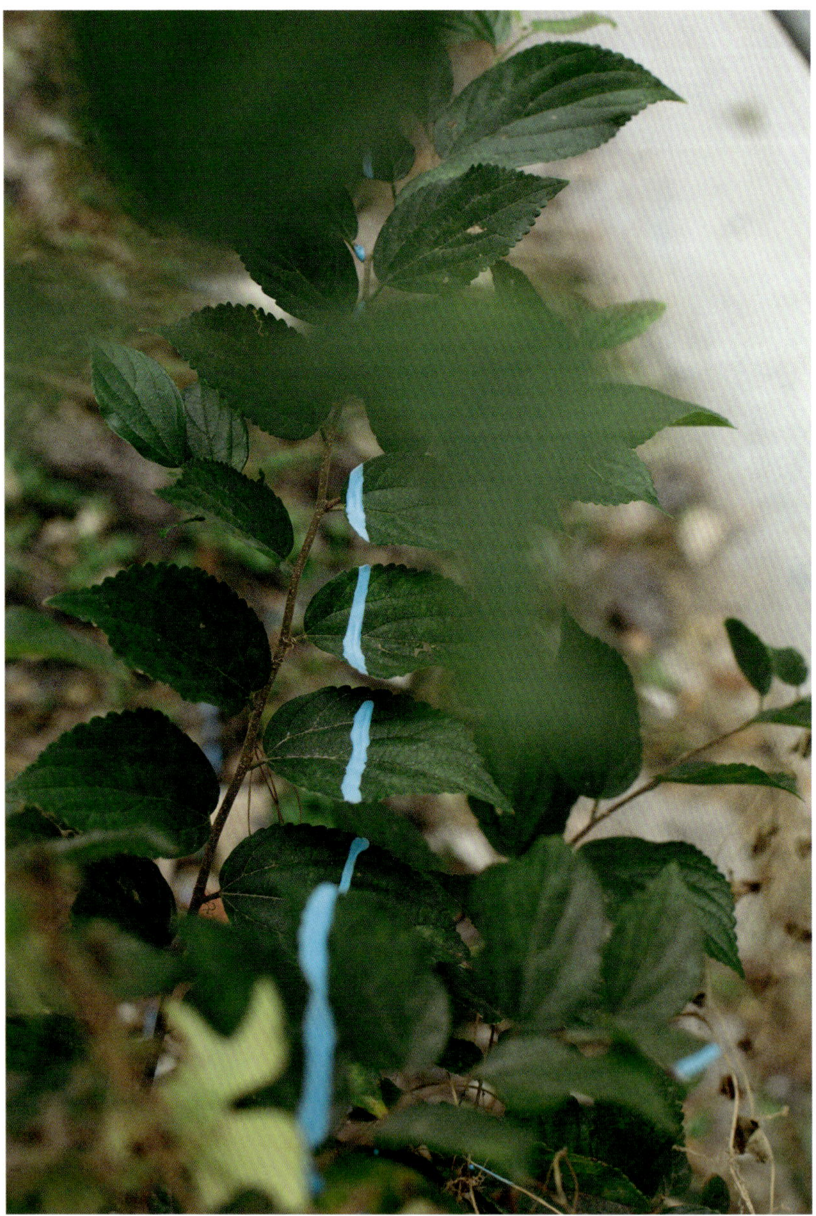

Juergen Teller
Leg, Snails and Peaches, No. 72
Giclée print
102 × 76 cm

Jane and Louise Wilson RA
Blind Landing, Lab 5, H-bomb Test Facility, Orford Ness, Suffolk
C-type print
180 × 225 cm

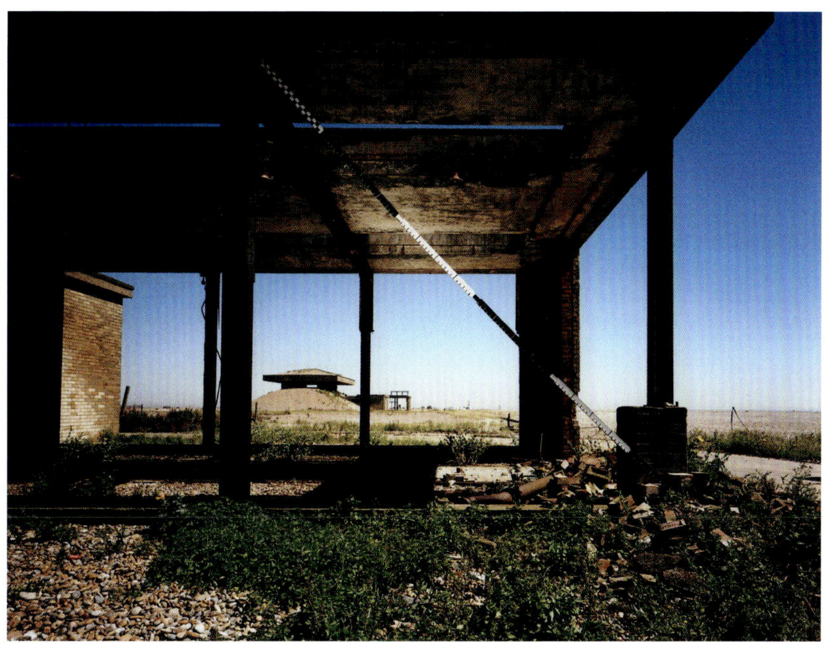

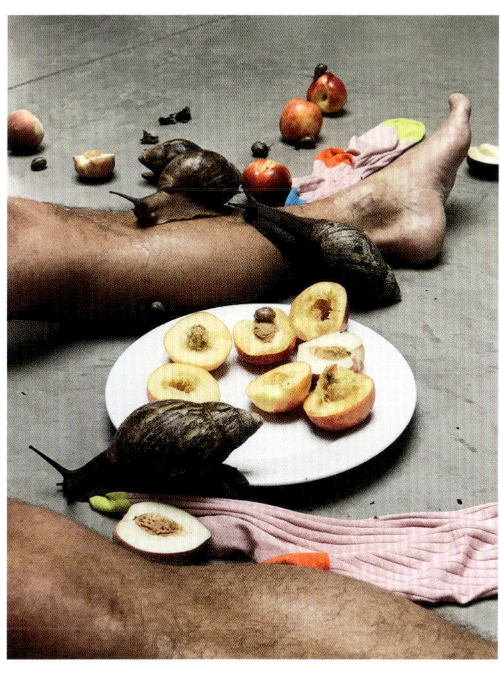

Bill Viola Hon RA
Lifespans
Video installation

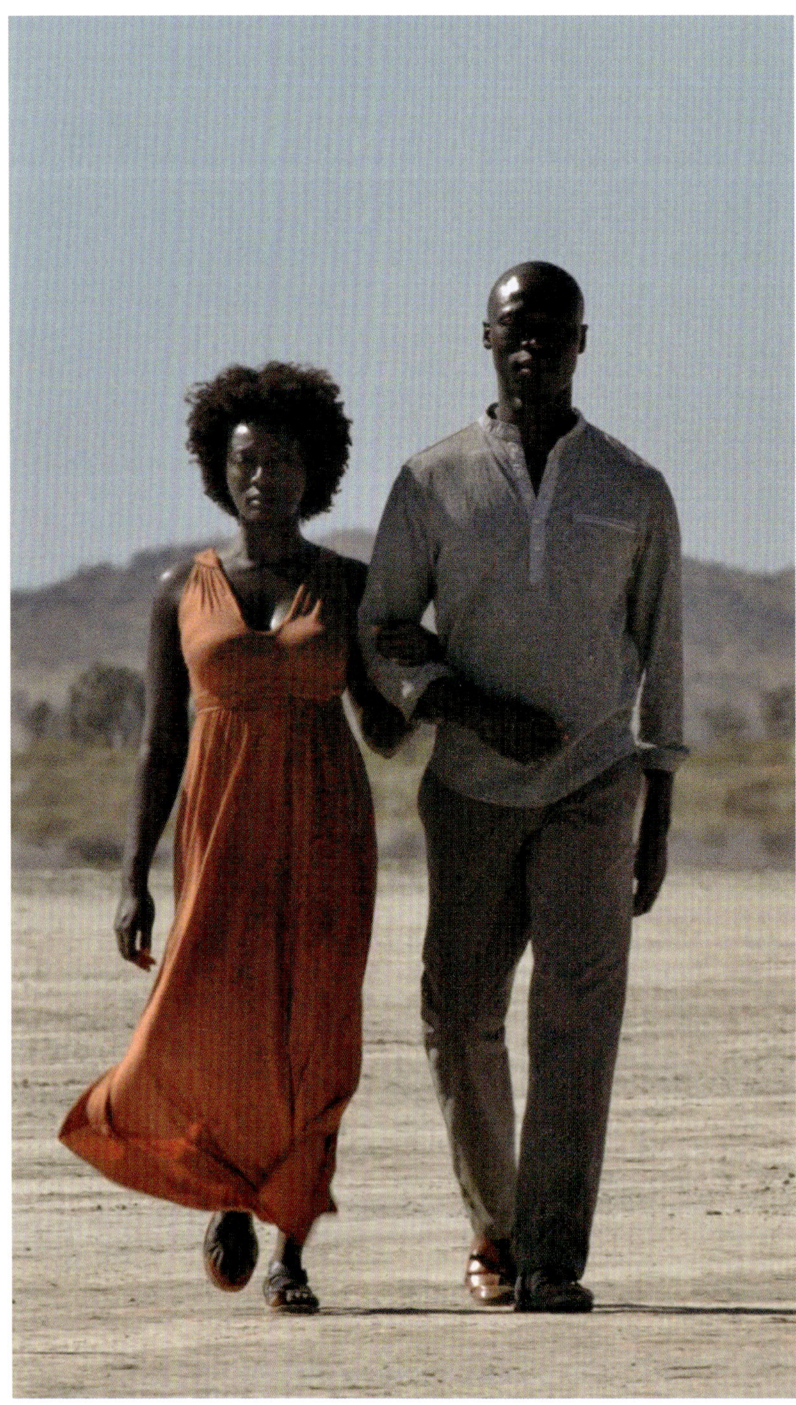

Fiona Banner RA
Self-portrait as a Book, Cyan
Screenprint
90 × 64 cm

Marina Abramović Hon RA
Freeing the Body
Silver gelatin prints
208 × 244 cm

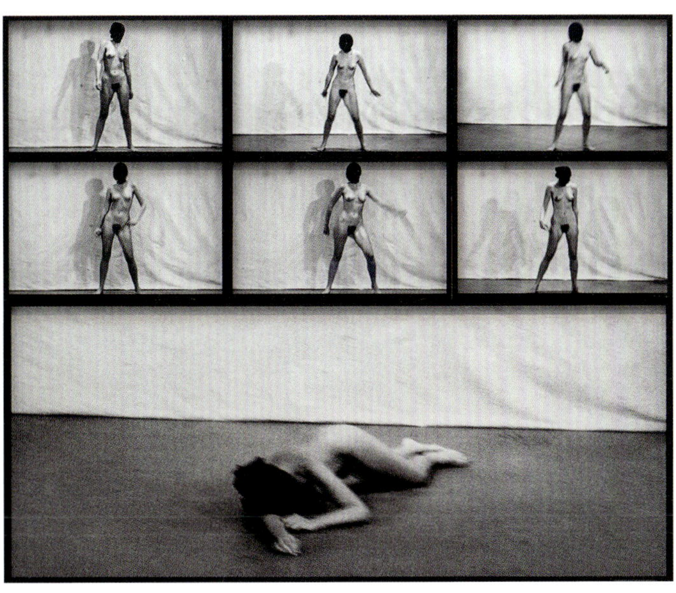

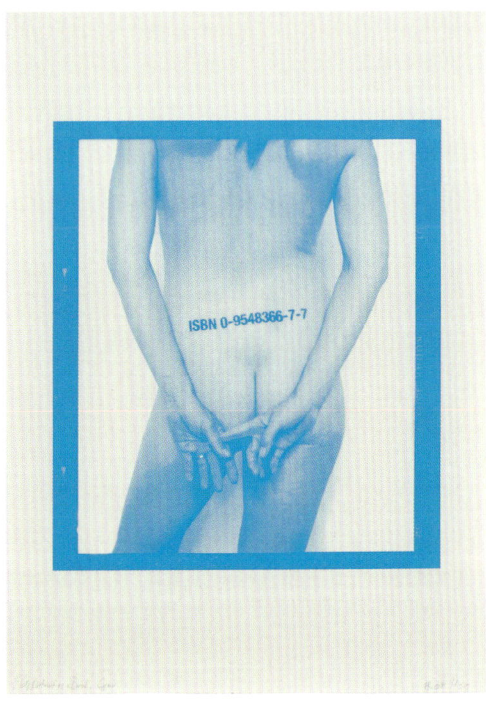

Bruce Nauman Hon RA
4th Finger Start
Video installation

Dr Jennifer Dickson RA
The Palace of the Favourite, Marrakech
Archival inkjet print
43 × 56 cm

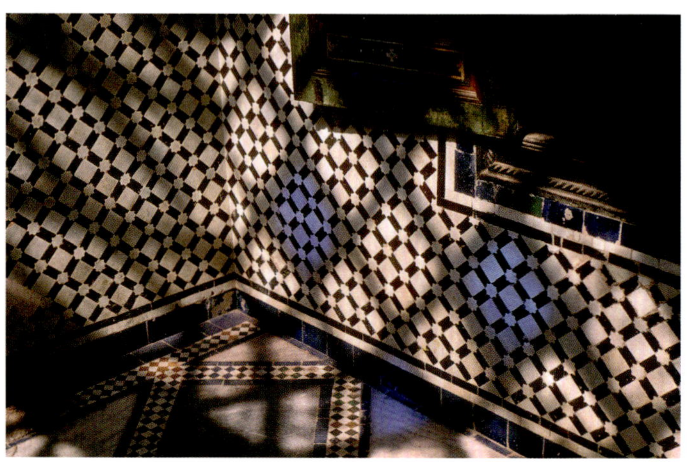

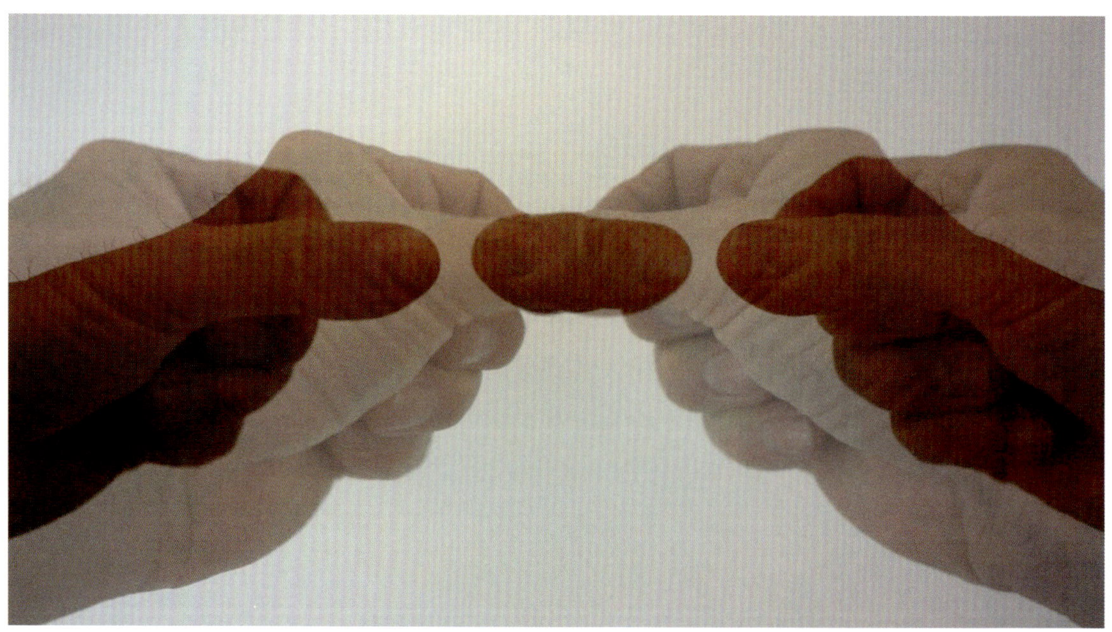

Jim Dine Hon RA
Tools in a Puzzled Vessel (from a series of 8)
Mixed media
194 × 133 cm

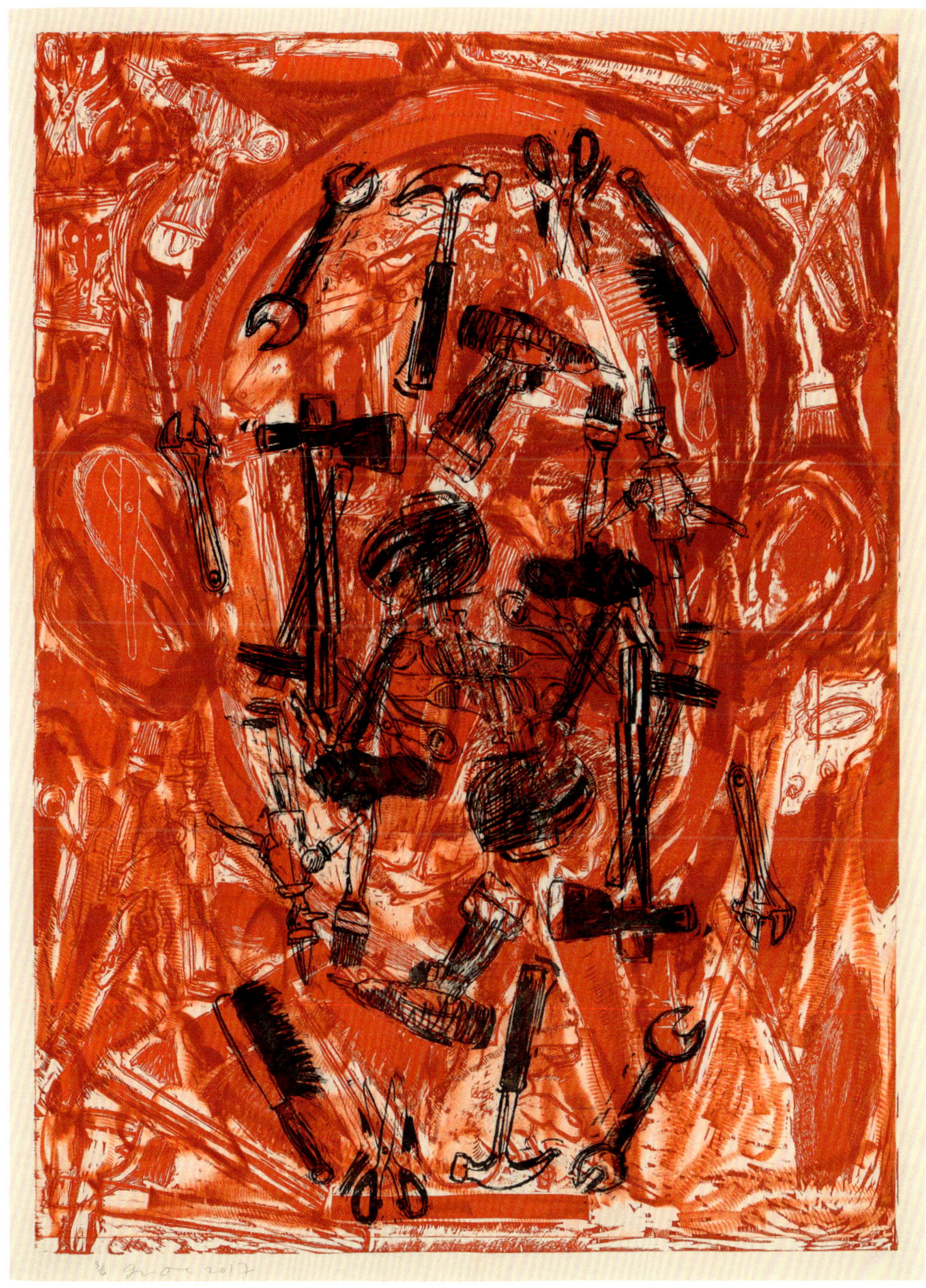

Oli Kellett
Cross Road Blues (Houston)
C-type print
153 × 191 cm

Patrick Dalton
Sellfridges
C-type print
30 × 42 cm

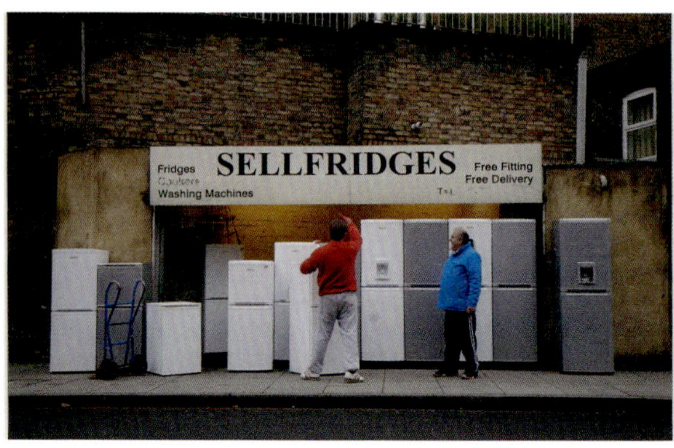

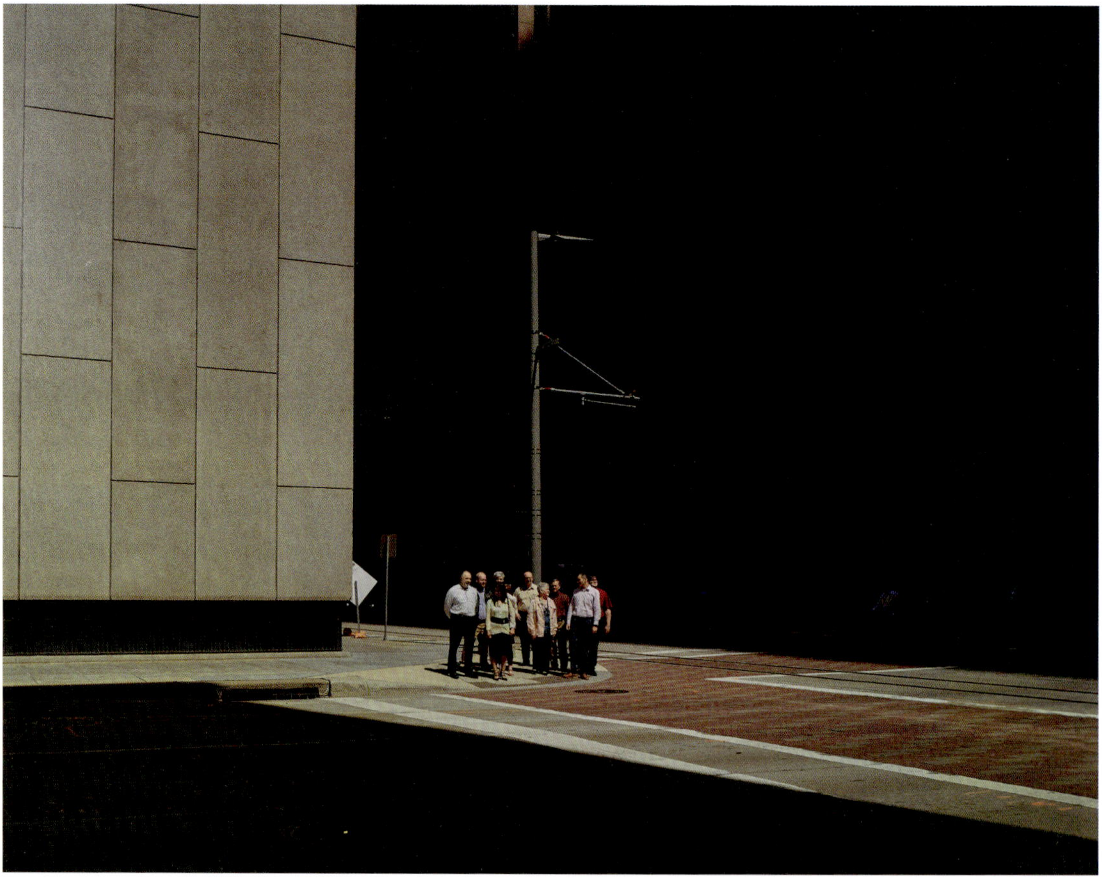

Dominic Greyer
Uncouth Road, Milnrow
Giclée print
30 × 42 cm

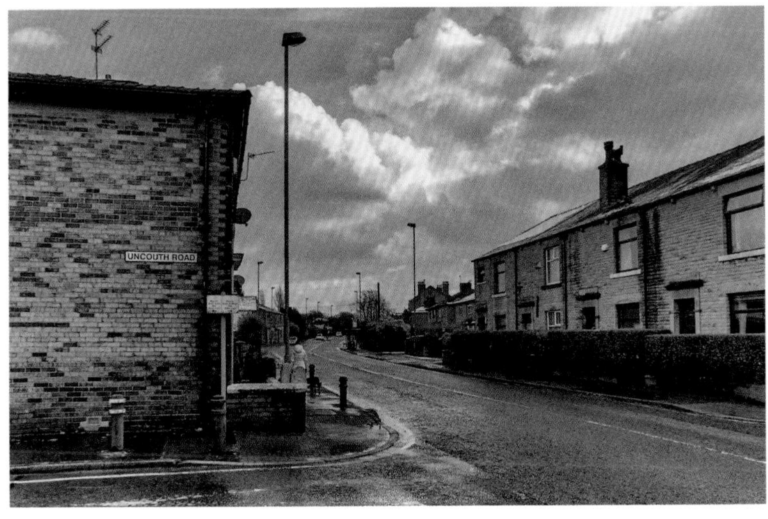

Kathy Prendergast
AF House 3
Giclée print
59 × 42 cm

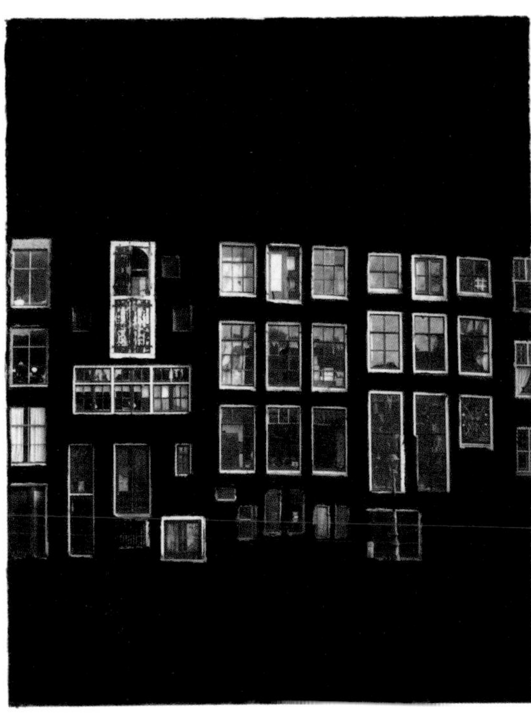

Toby Jury Morgan
I'm Not Lost, I'm Just Exploring
Screenprint
75 × 56 cm

Jo Kitchen
Untitled
Mixed media
H 120 cm

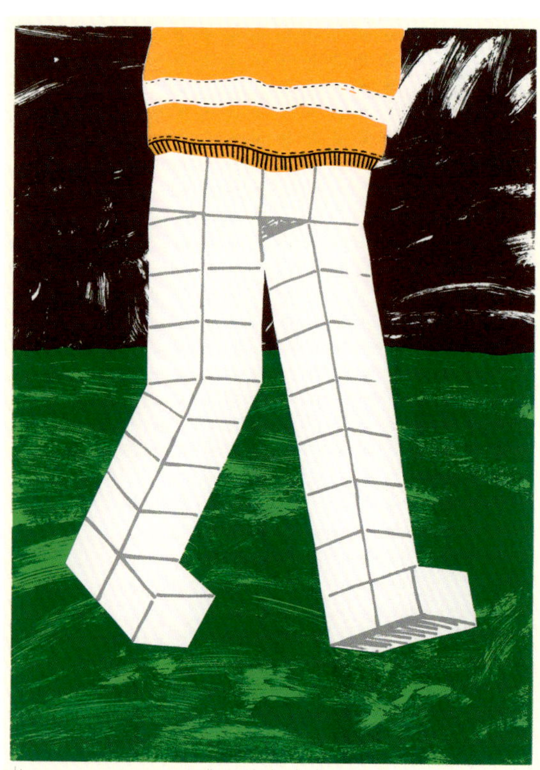

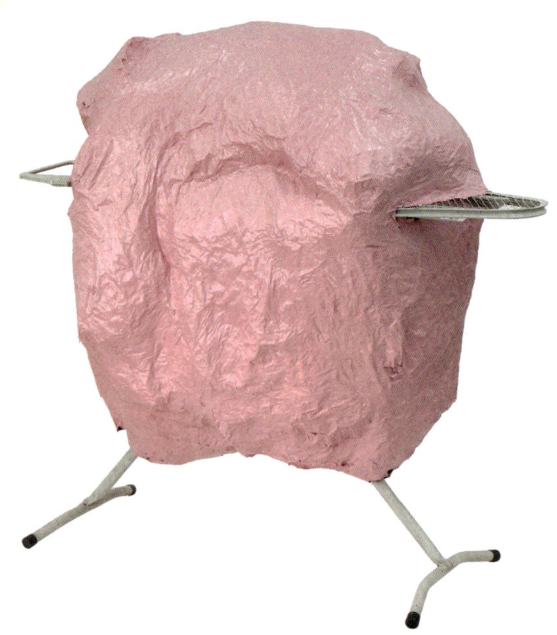

Lorsen Camps
Two Masks (Pollux and Castor)
Painted bronze
H 38 cm

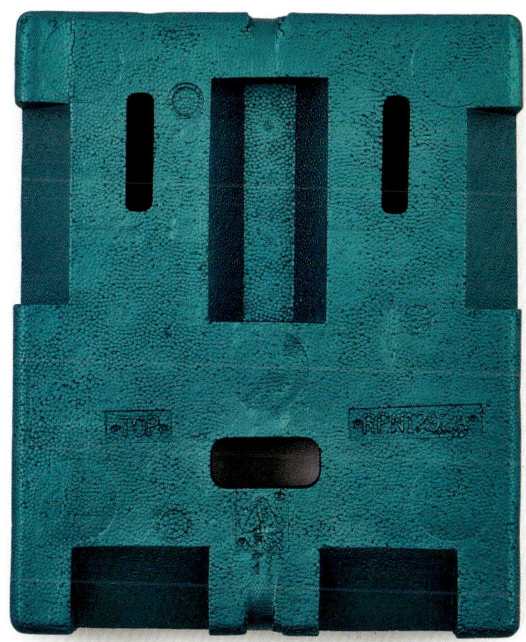

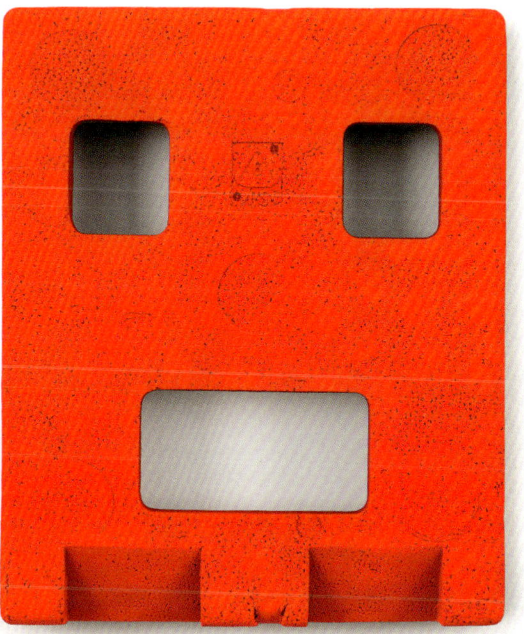

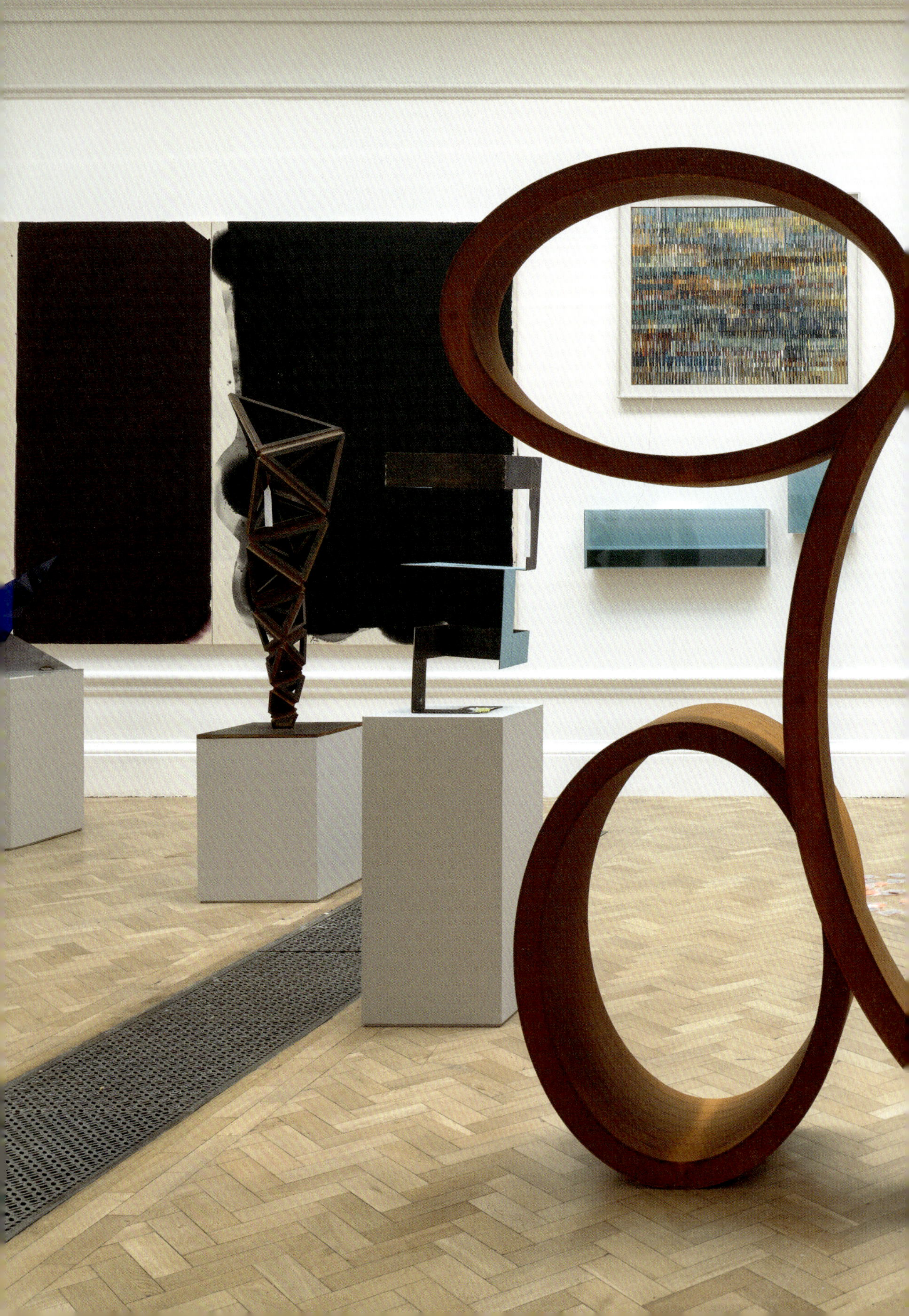

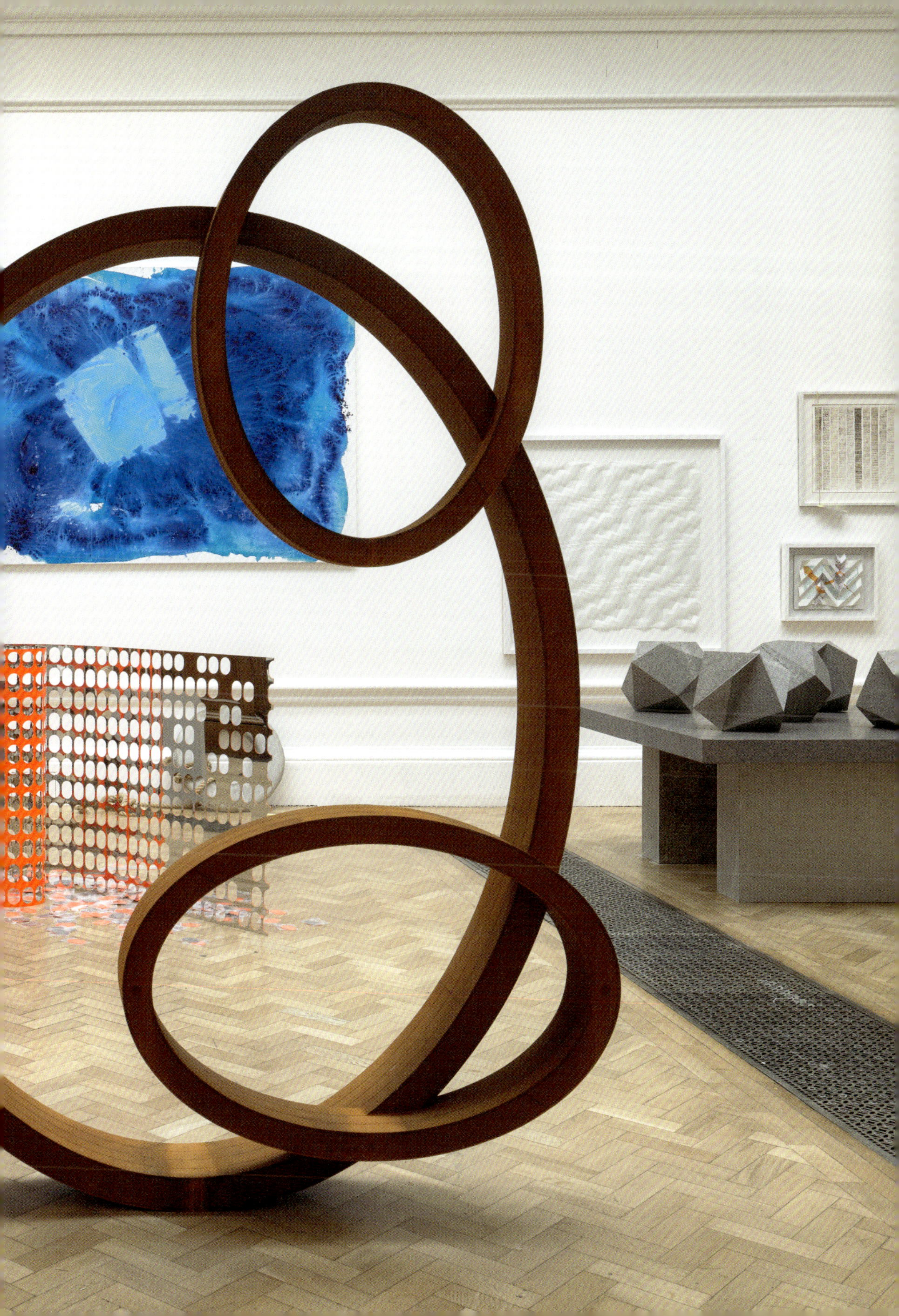

Richard Wilson RA
Slick Work 1
Archival pigment print
75 × 86 cm

Prof Brian Catling RA
Hugh Crane's Prayer Book
Engraving and ink
30 × 40 cm

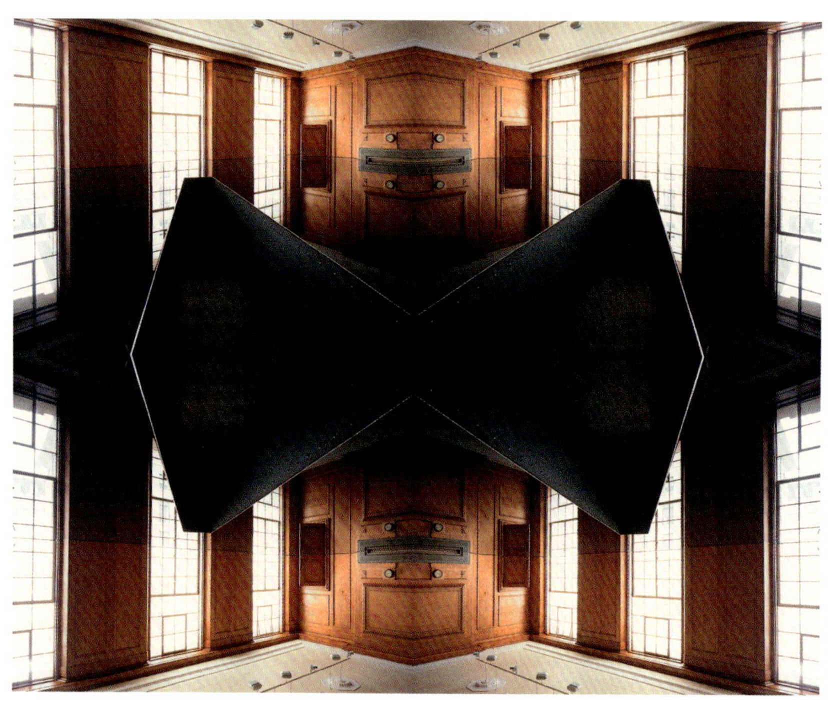

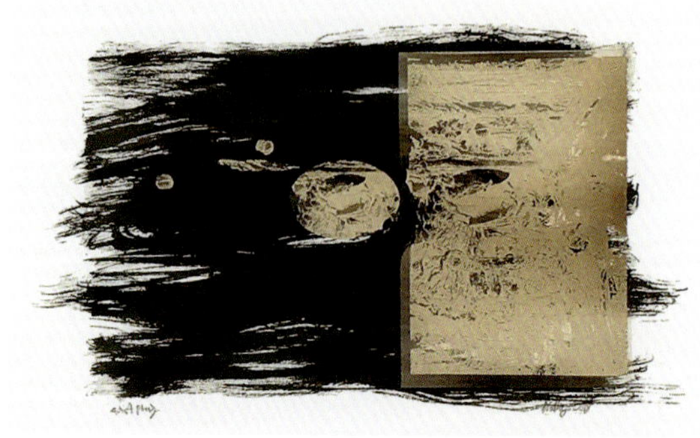

Güler Ates
Eton College Library and She IV
Archival pigment print
69 × 85 cm

Stanton Williams
Untitled
Giclée print
31 × 26 cm

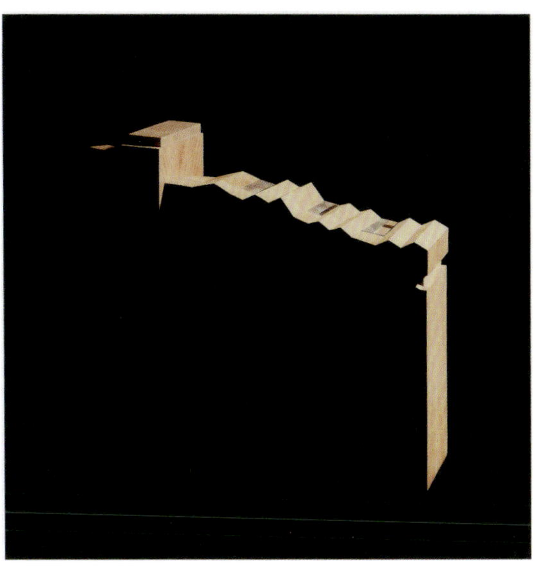

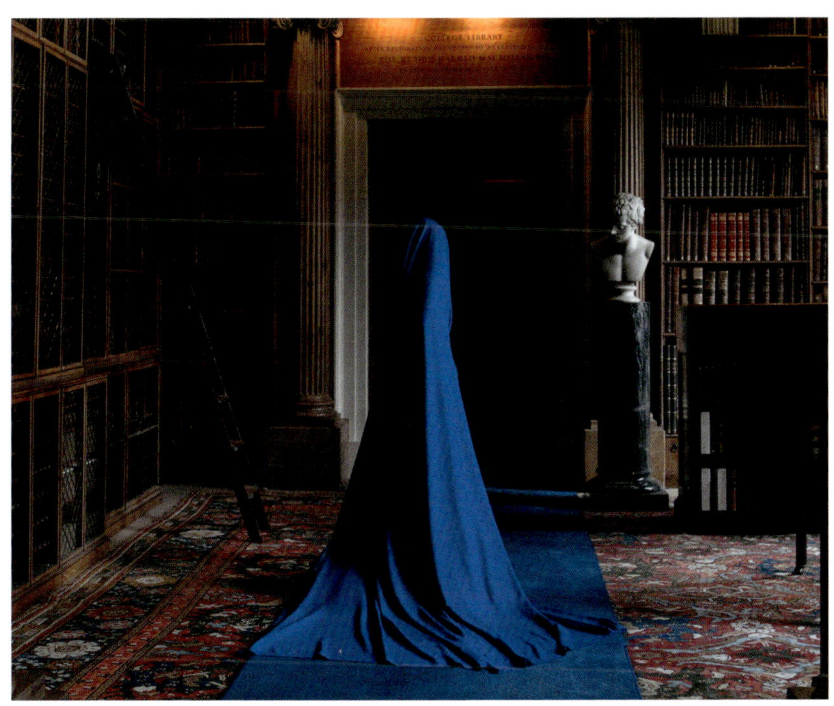

Milena ZeVu
Artwalks 139 Belgrade
Giclée print
80 × 120 cm

Tom Barker
French Fancies, a Young Toby's Dilemma
Giclée print
50 × 70 cm

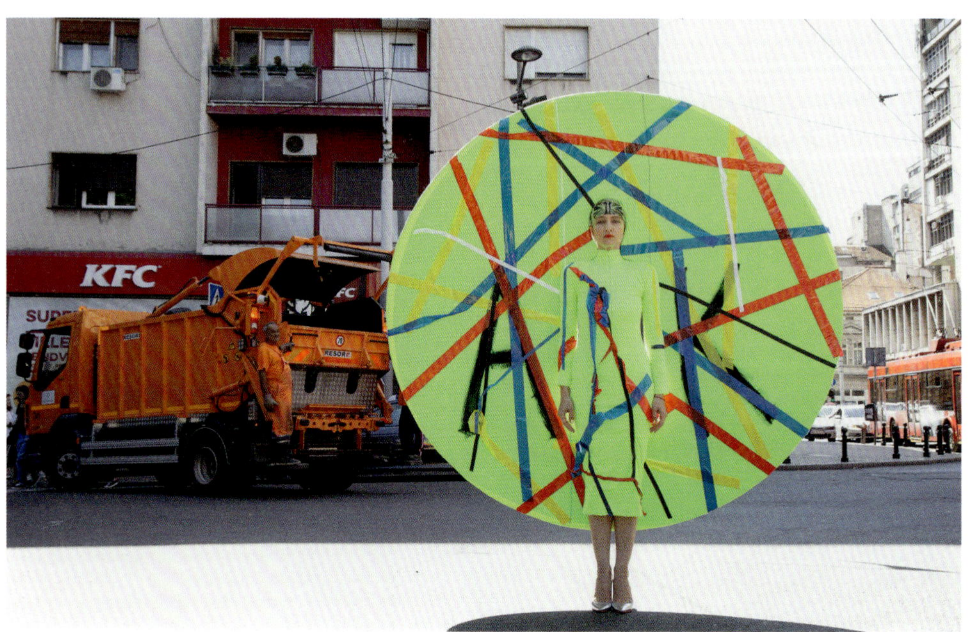

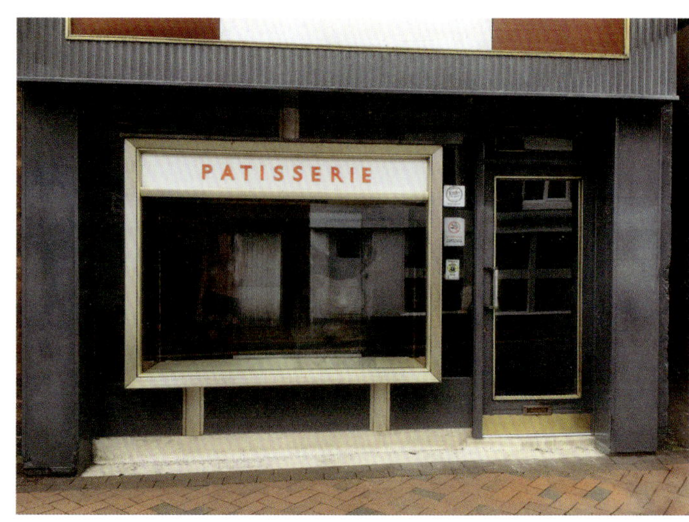

Jess Wilson
Lightswitch (Two)
Light switch and wallpaper
31 × 31 cm

Alice Mara
Sink 1
Digital print and oil on ceramic
H 27 cm

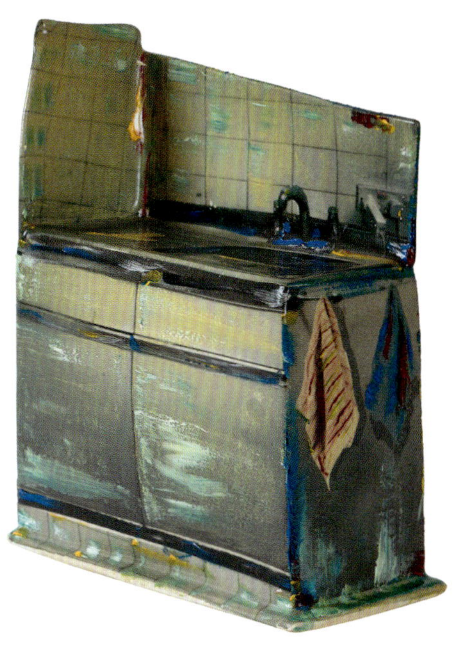

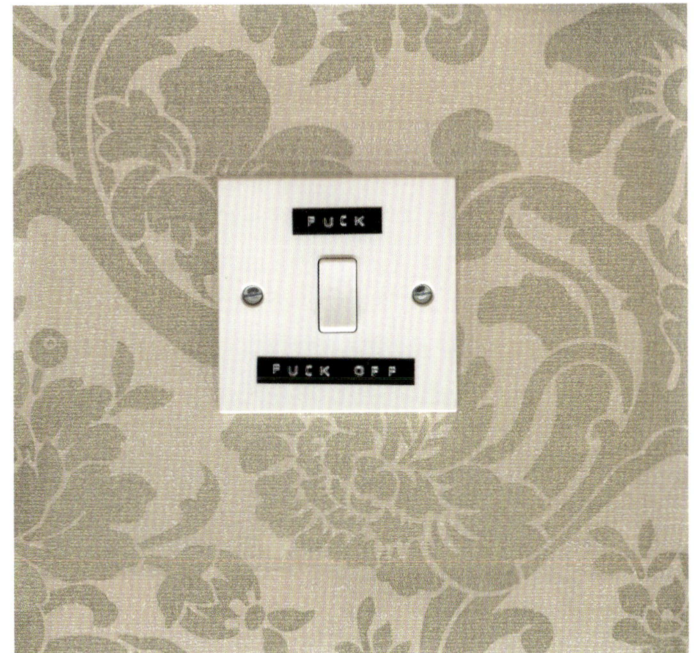

David Hockney OM CH RA

Seven Trollies, Six and a Half Stools, Six Portraits, Eleven Paintings and Two Curtains
Photographic drawing
278 × 760 cm

Inside It Opens Up As Well
Photographic drawing
278 × 760 cm

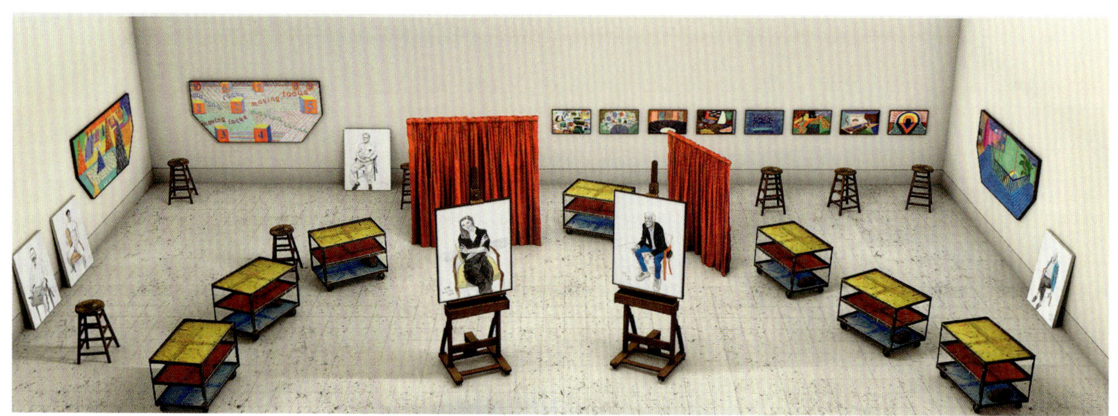

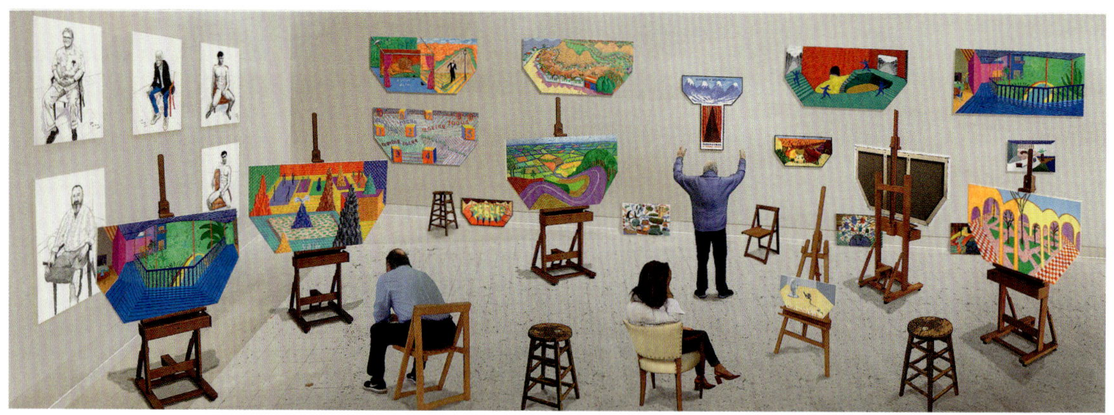

Mimmo Paladino Hon RA
Untitled
Mixed media
200 × 200 cm

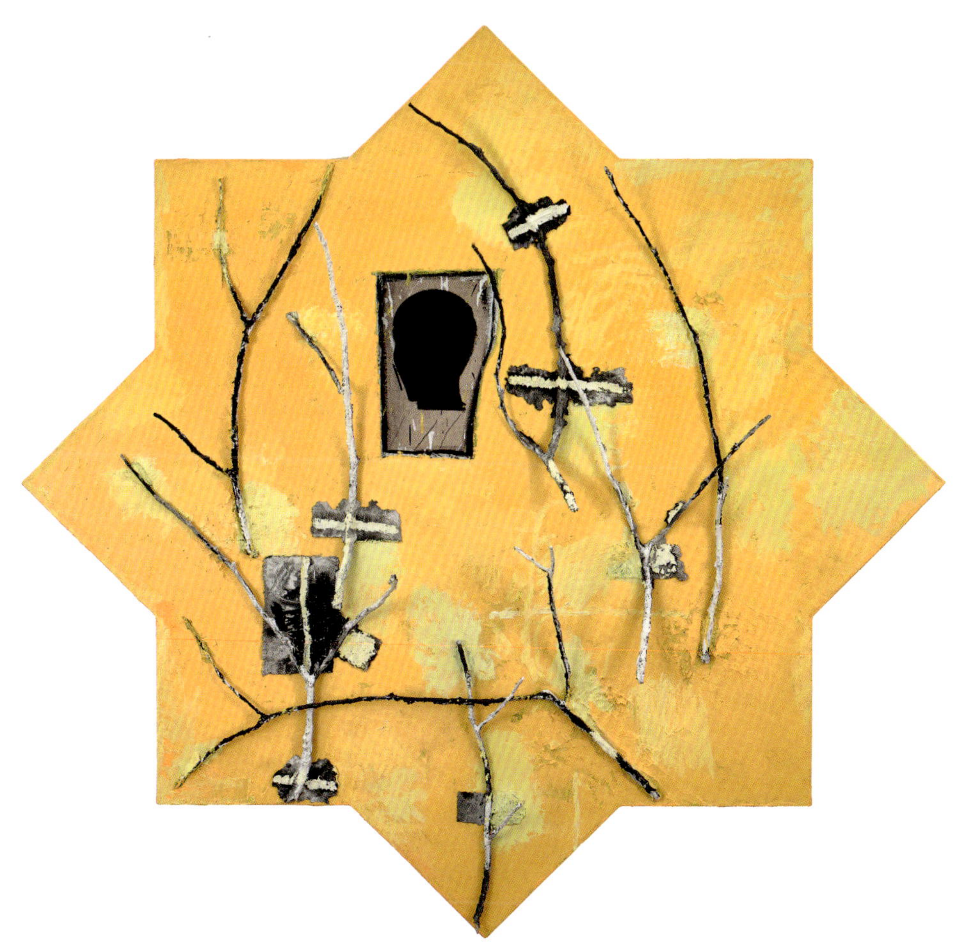

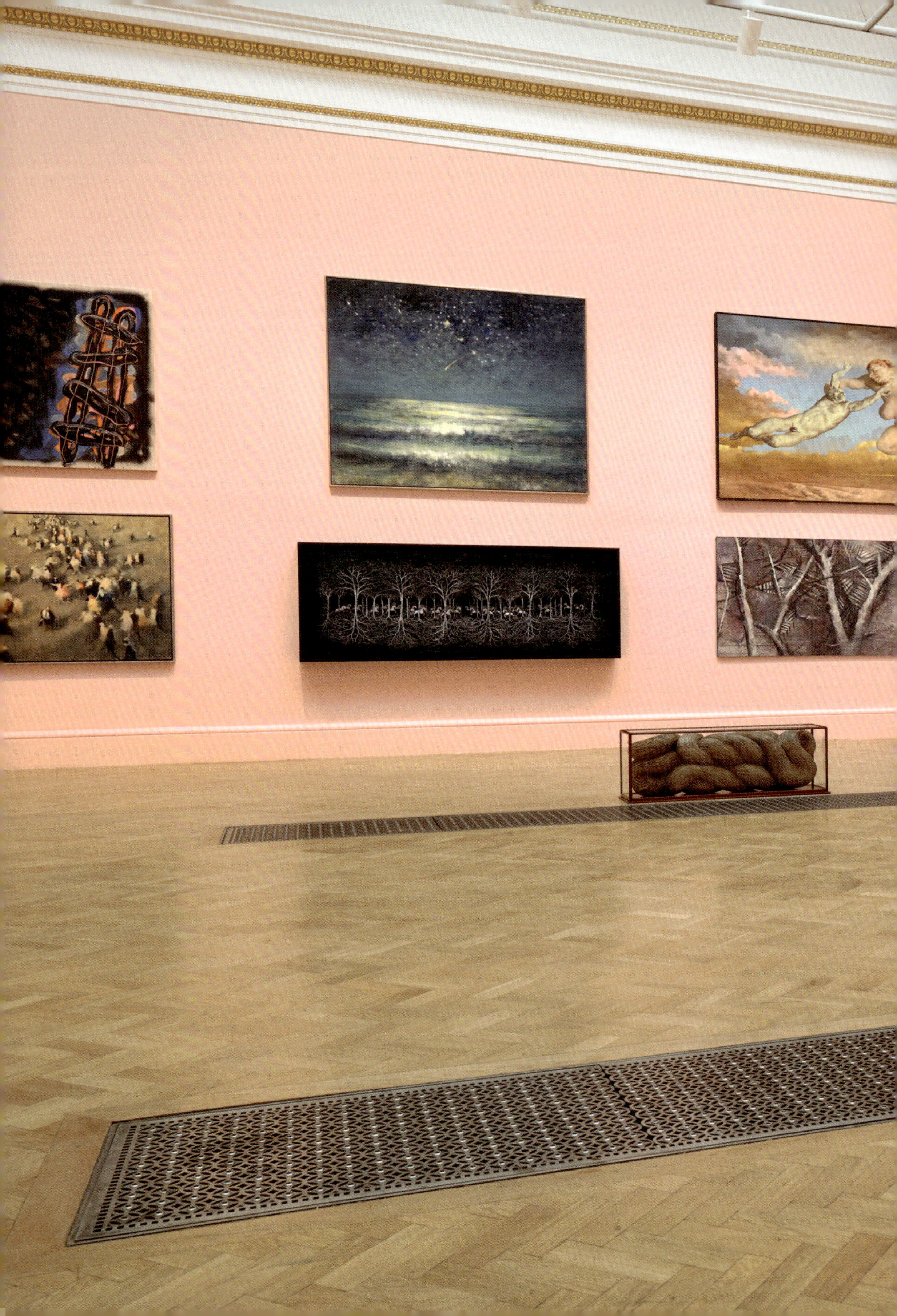

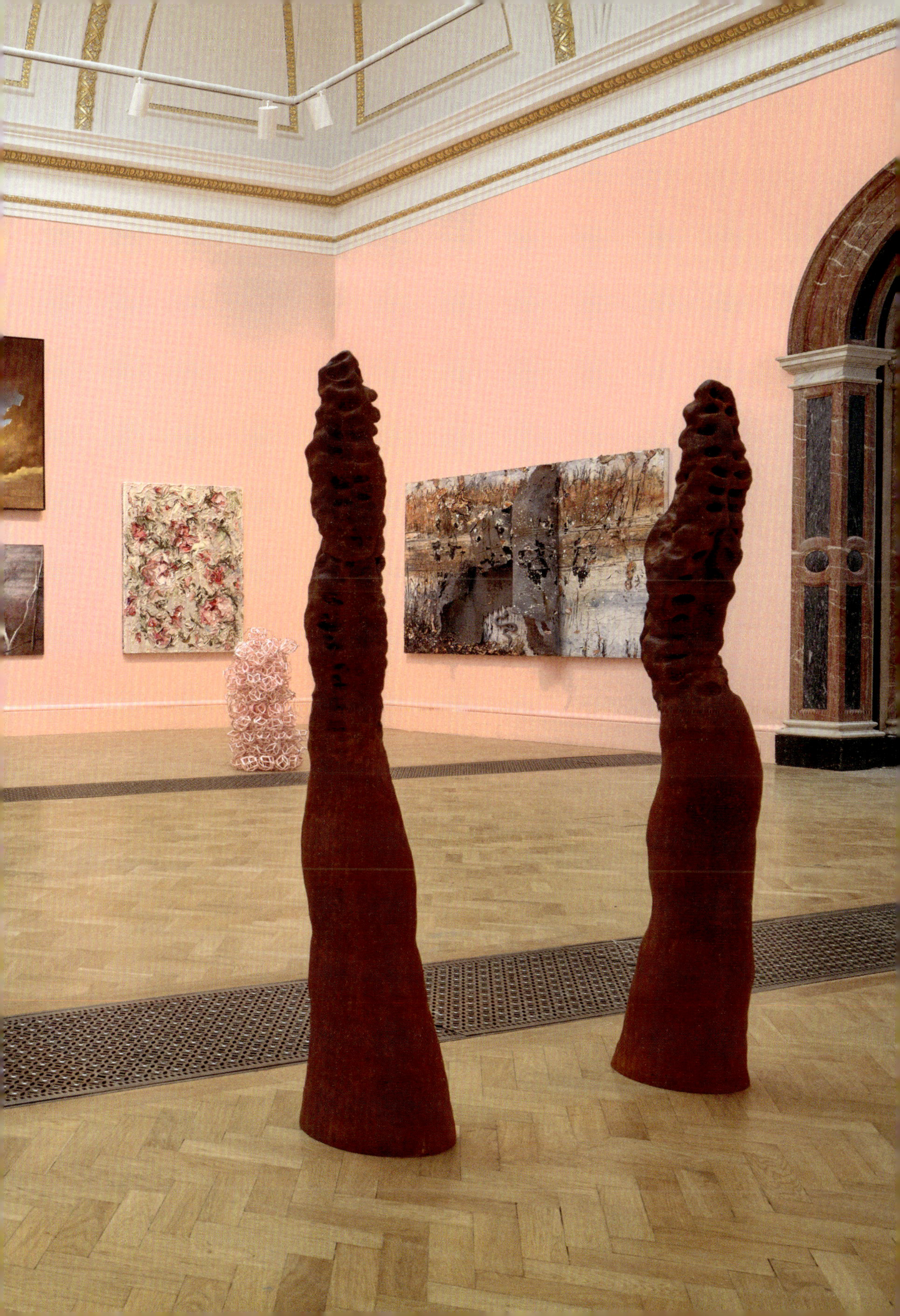

Ed Ruscha Hon RA
WEN OUT FOR CIGRETS N NEVER CAME BACK
Cast bronze with hand applied patina
H 50 cm

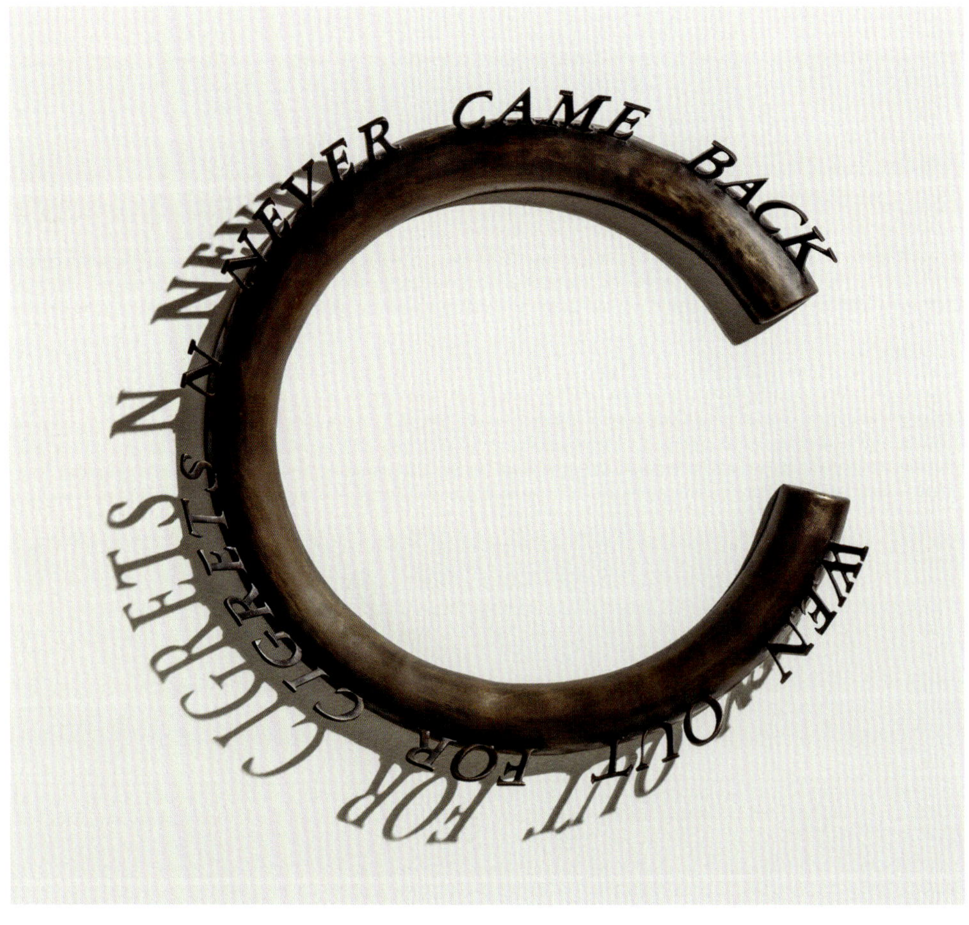

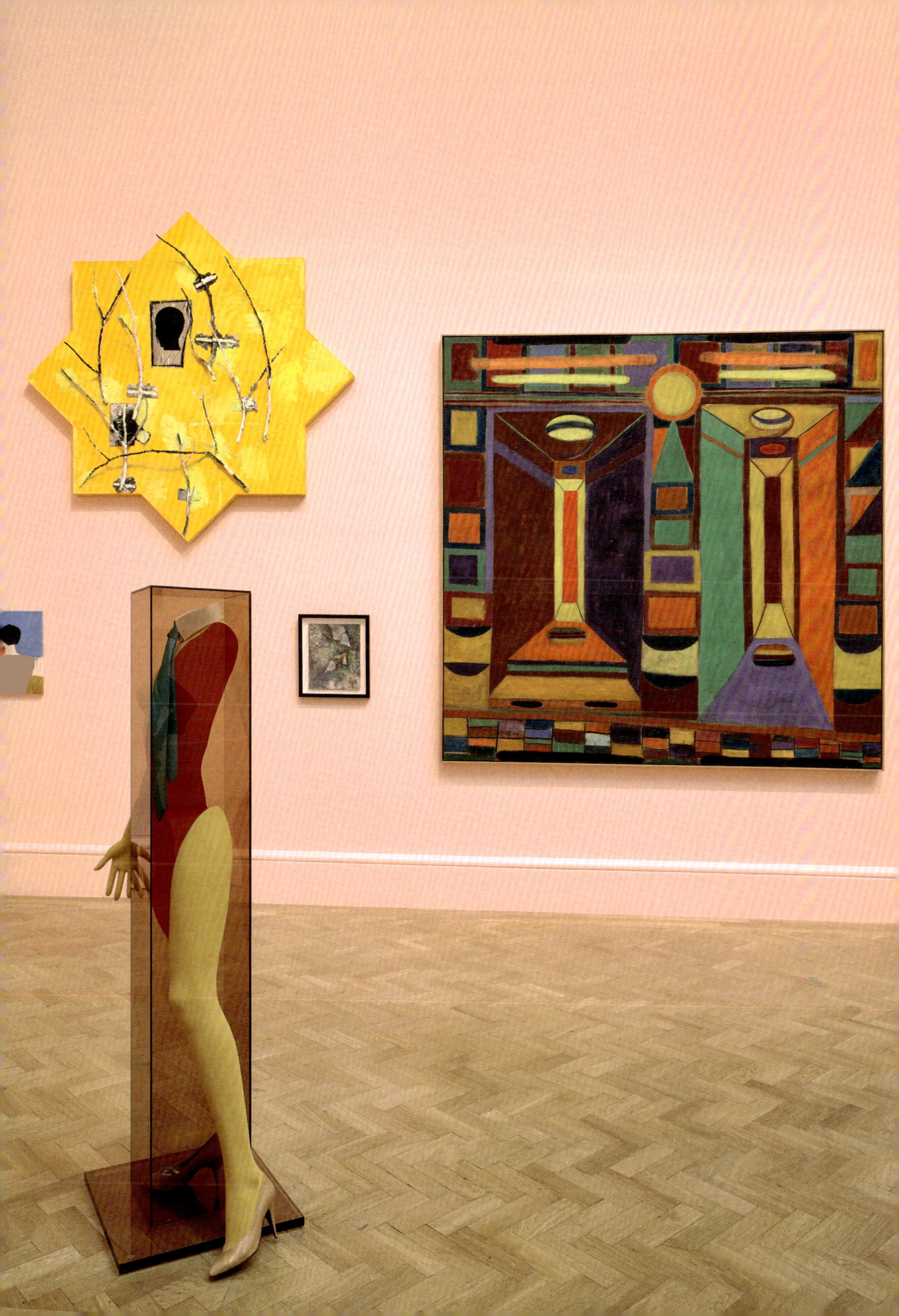

Ann Christopher RA
Following Lines – 3
Mixed media
62 × 98 cm

Yinka Shonibare MBE RA
Young Academician
Mixed media
H 203 cm

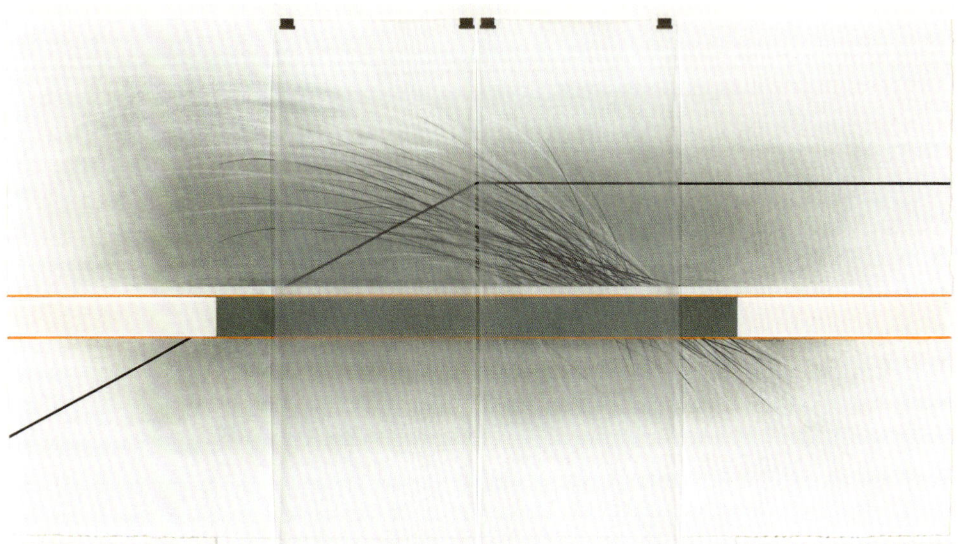

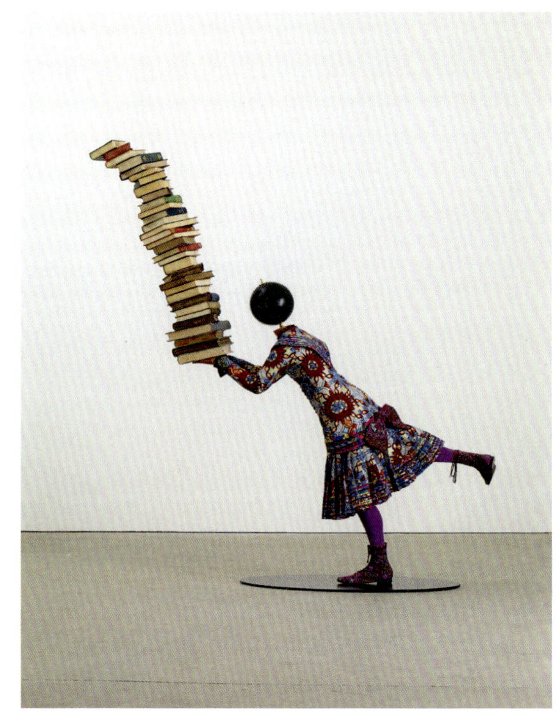

Allen Jones RA
Move It
Inkjet and silkscreen
100 × 70 cm

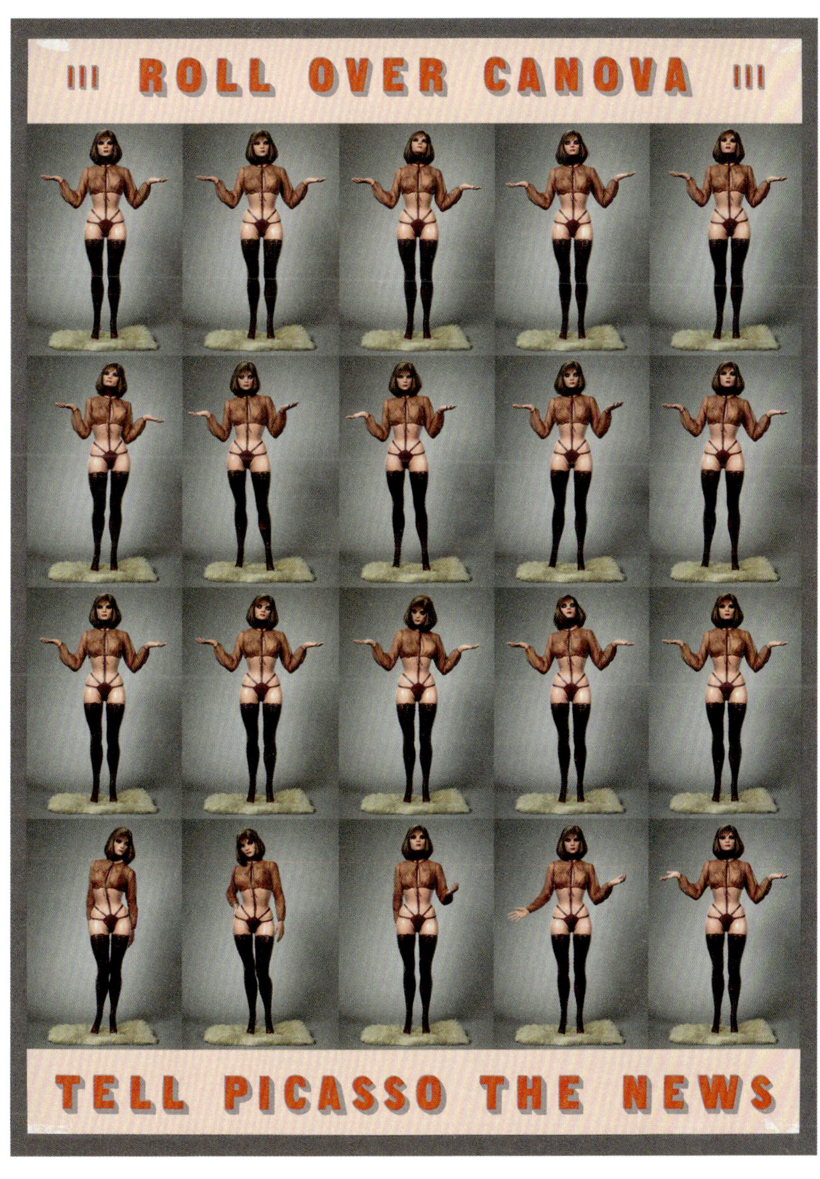

Rebecca Salter RA
Tabula Series 3
Japanese woodblock
35 × 27 cm

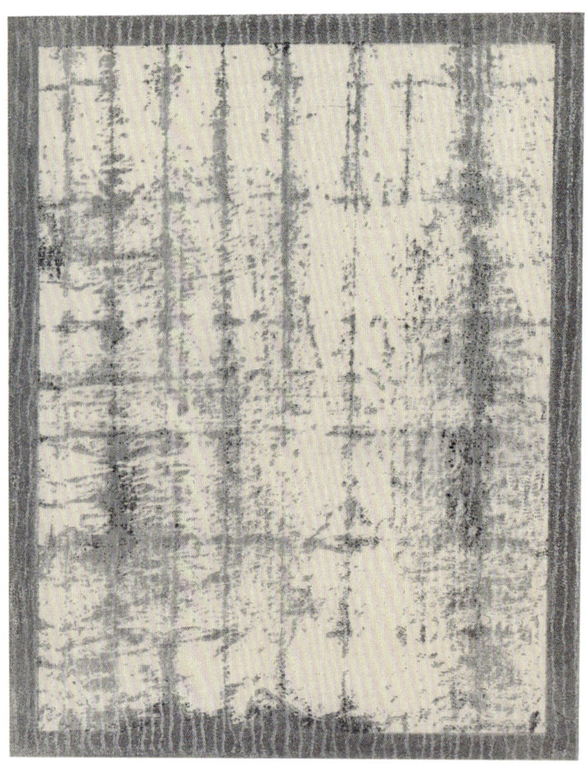

Jo Gorner
Diminish 2
Etching
55 × 77 cm

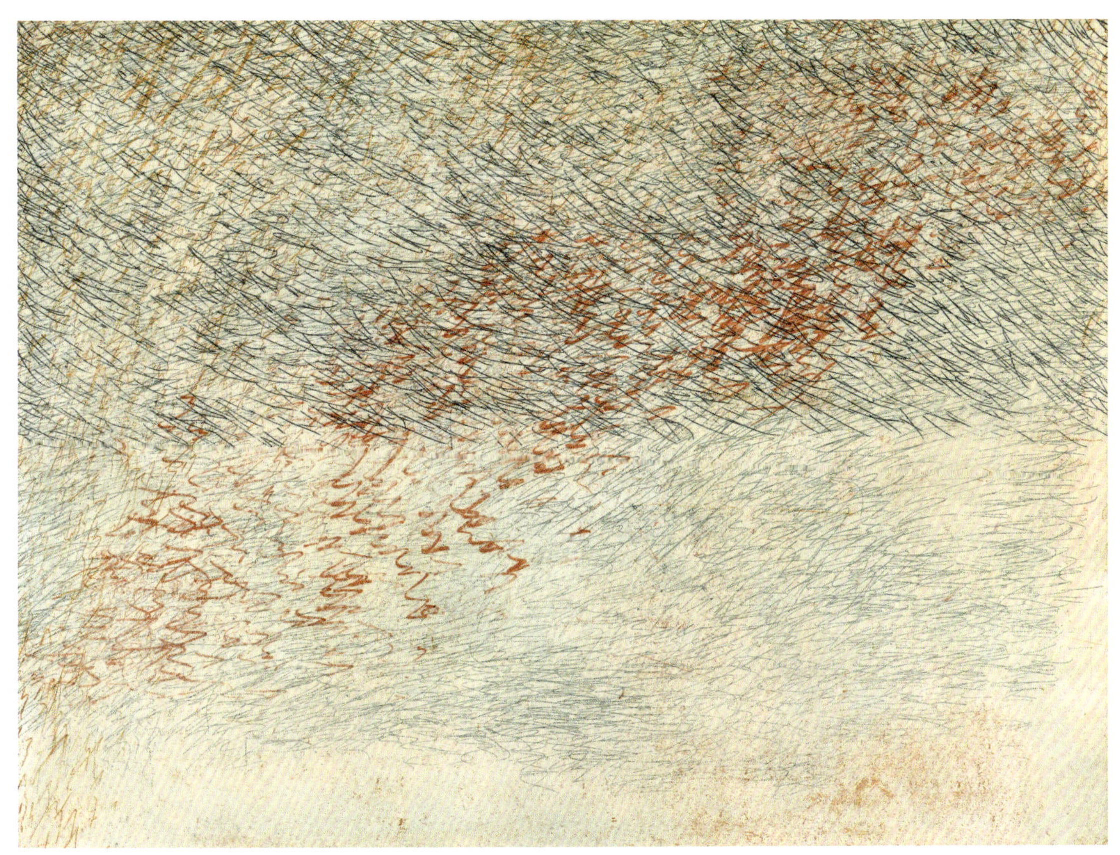

Prof Norman Ackroyd CBE RA
At Oranmore Castle, County Galway
Etching
20 × 27 cm

Peter Freeth RA
River Bank
Aquatint etching
28 × 26 cm

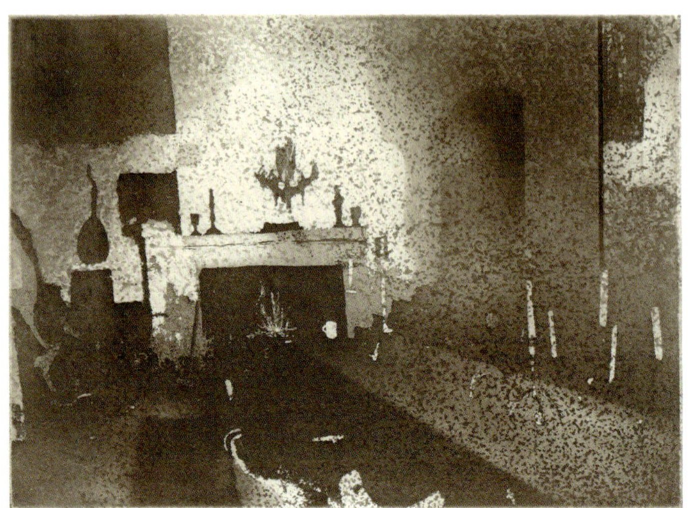

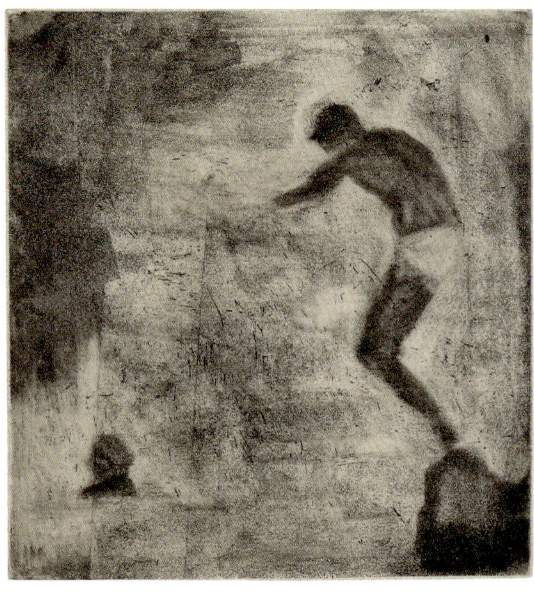

Cornelia Parker OBE RA
Fox Talbot's Articles of Glass (All Together Now)
Photogravure etching
77 × 56 cm

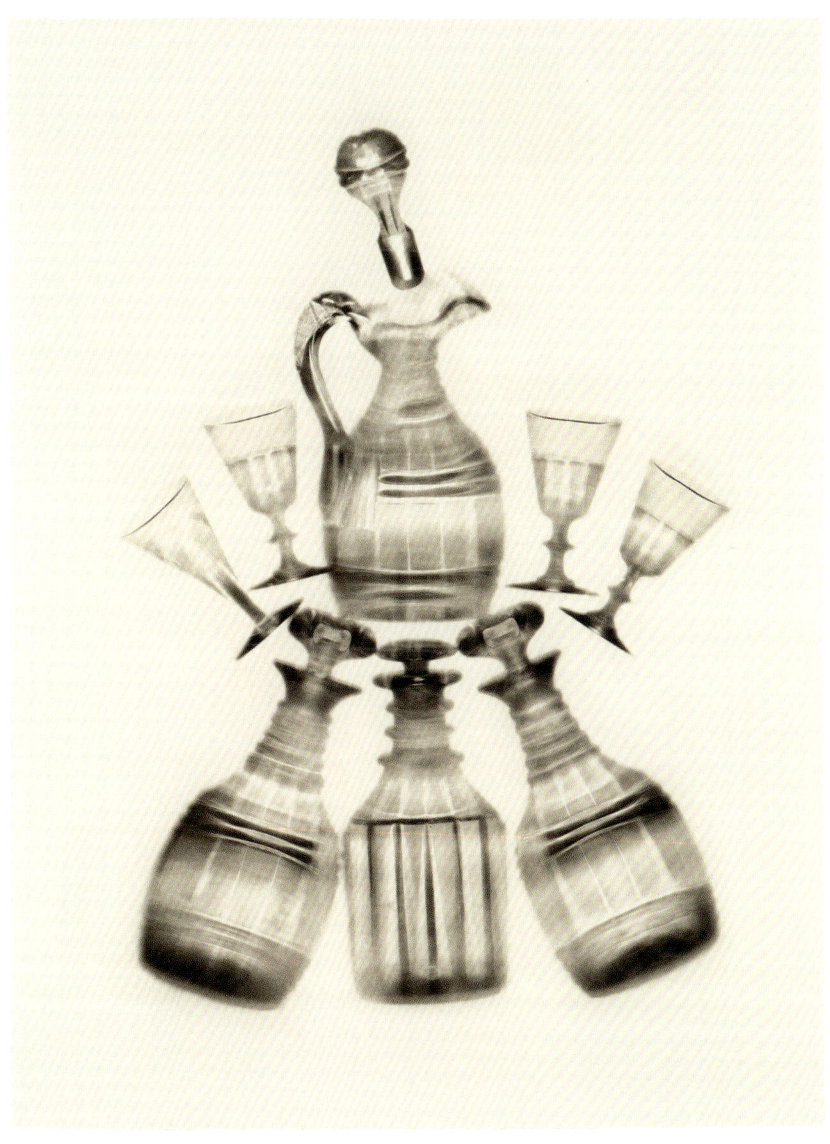

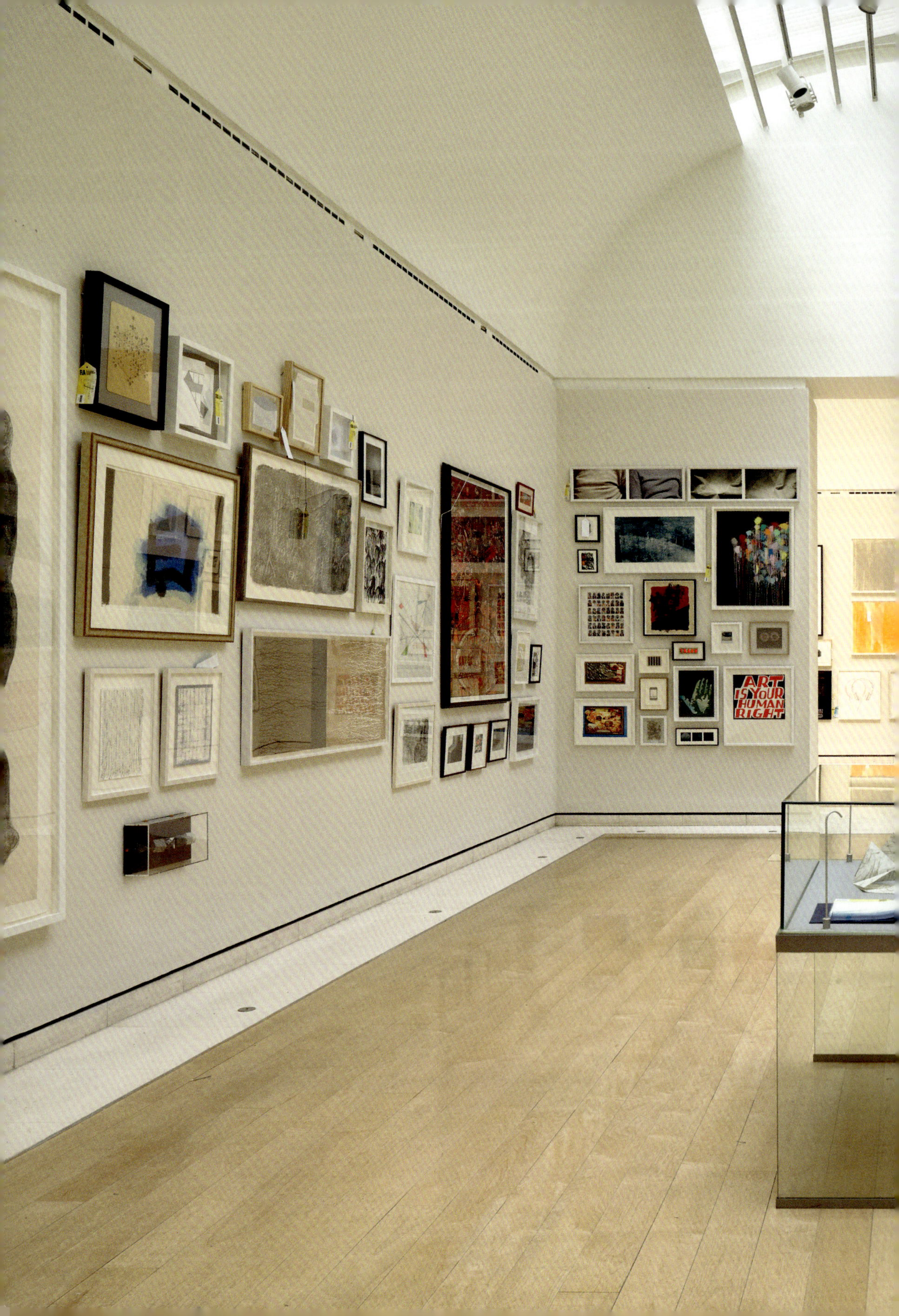
ART IS YOUR HUMAN RIGHT

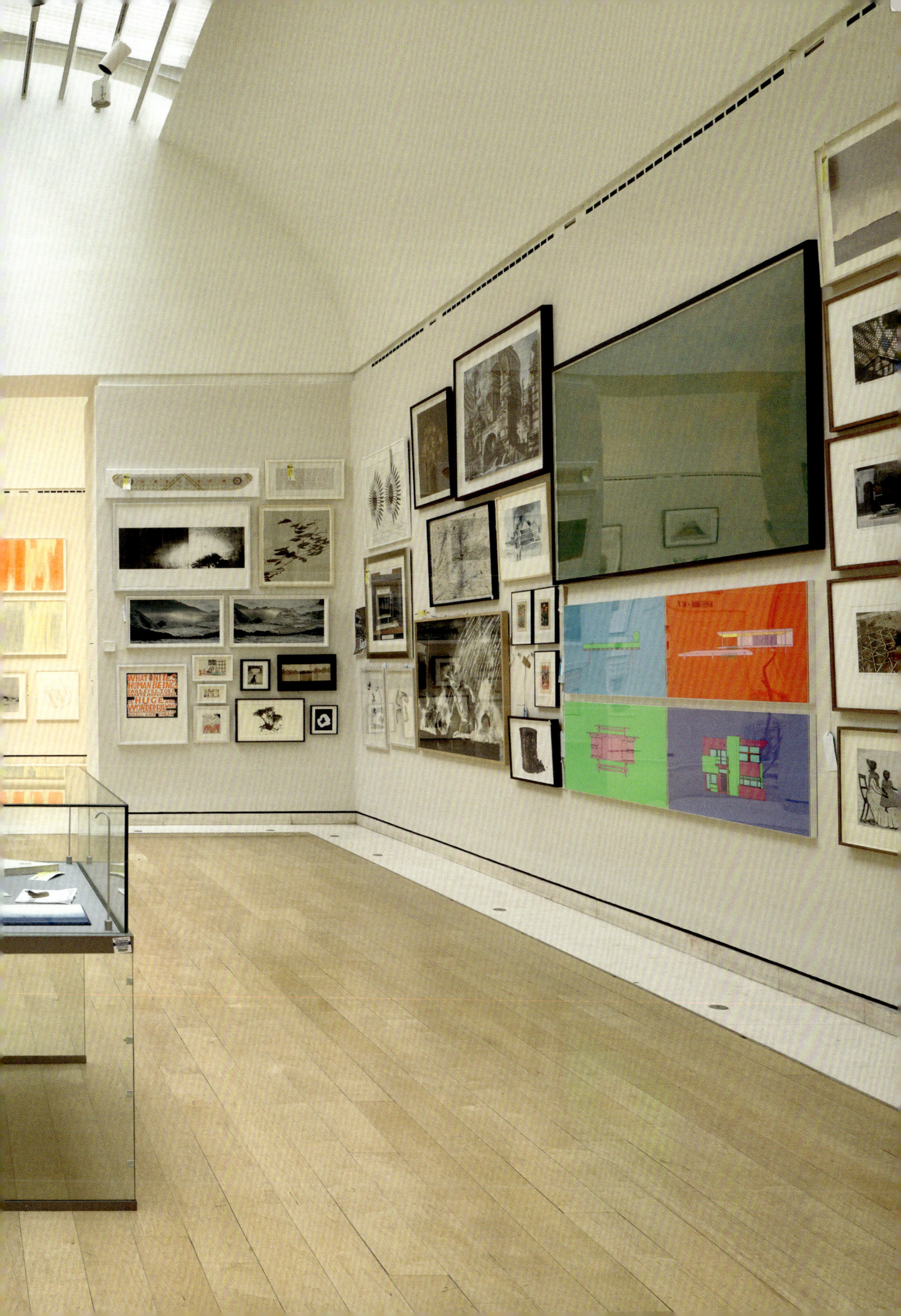
WHAT UNITES
HUMAN BEINGS
EARS EYES TOES
IS HUGE AND
WONDERFUL WHAT
SMALL AND MEAN

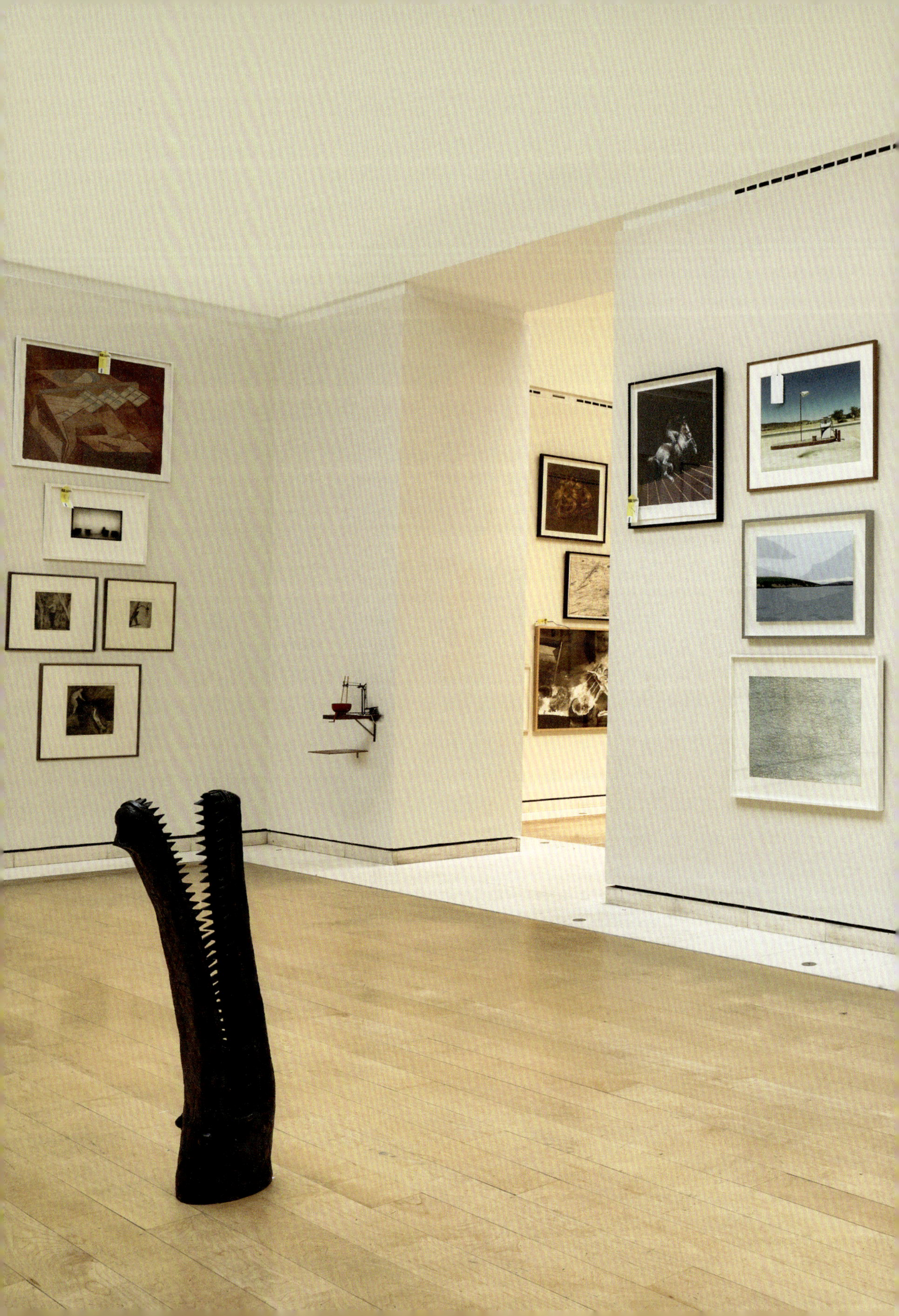

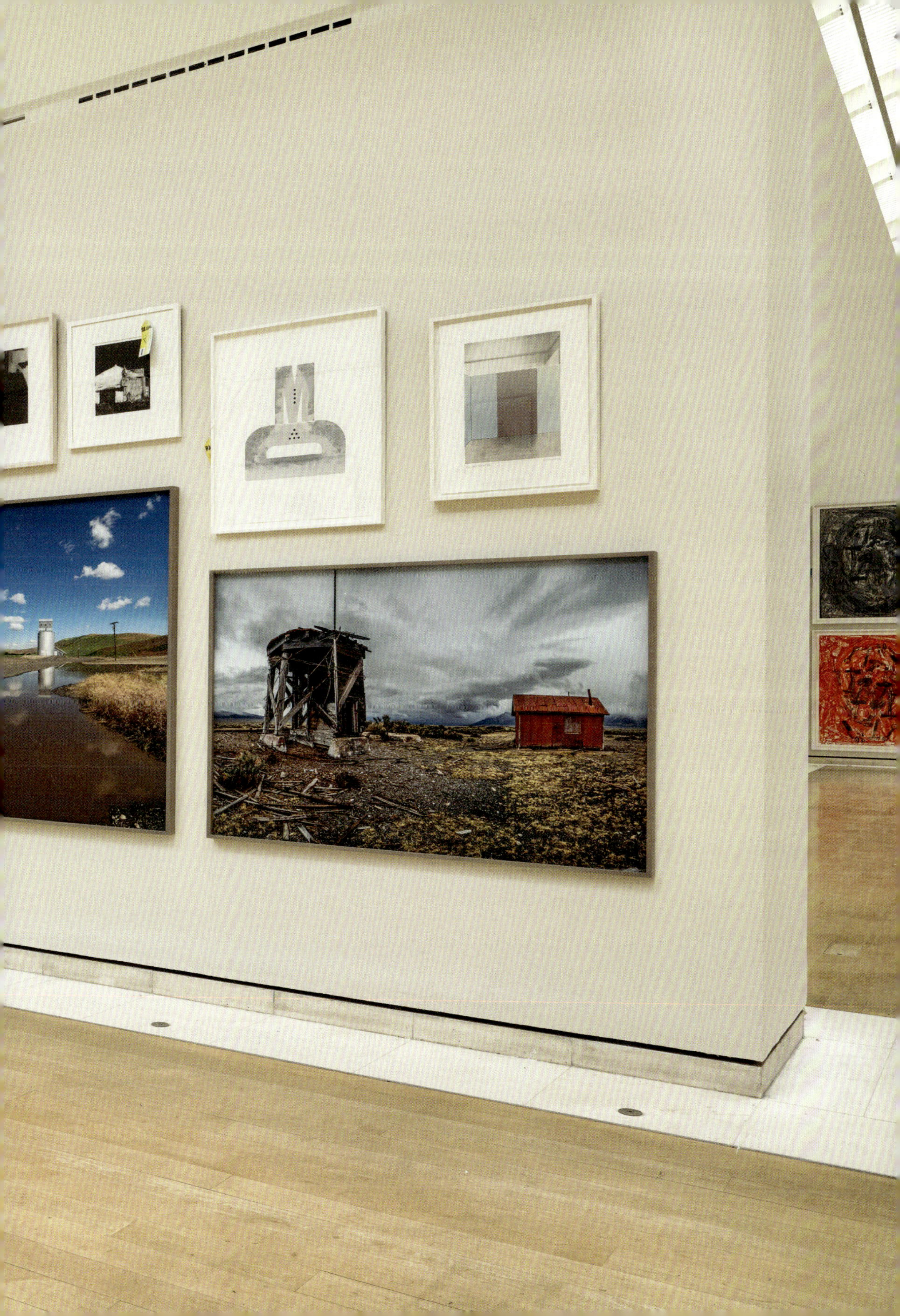

Freja Lijia Bao
Splendour: A Dream of the Eastern Capital (Plum Blossom Season)
Digital and hand drawing
137 × 87 cm

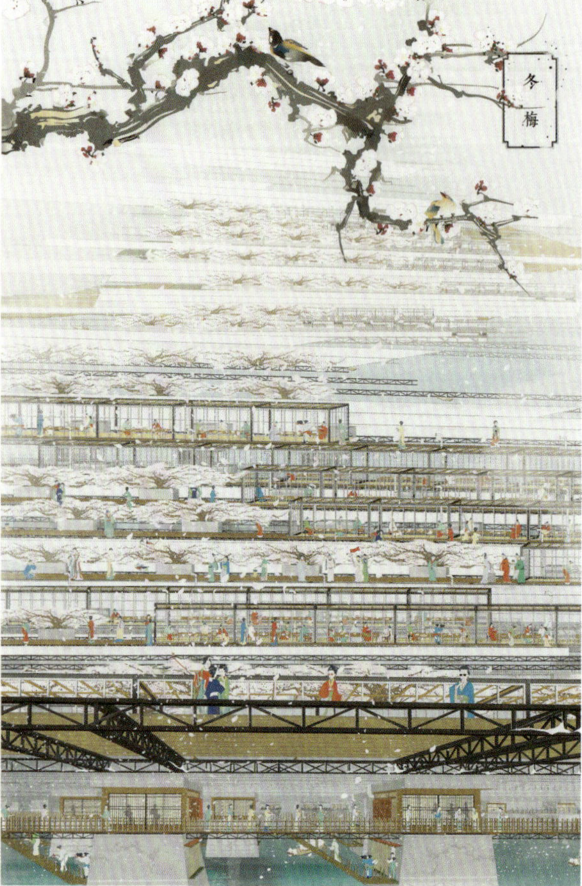

Anselmo Swan
Home
Graphite and conté pencil
38 × 29 cm

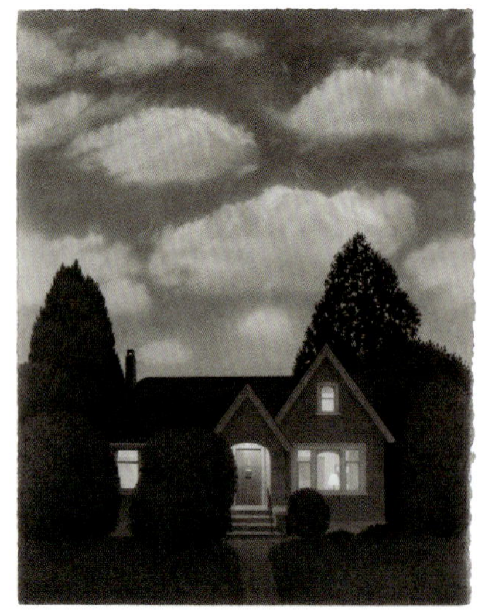

Prof David Mach RA
Under Siege
Mixed media
60 × 84 cm

Mark Beesley
Mock Tudor
Pen and crayon
65 × 65 cm

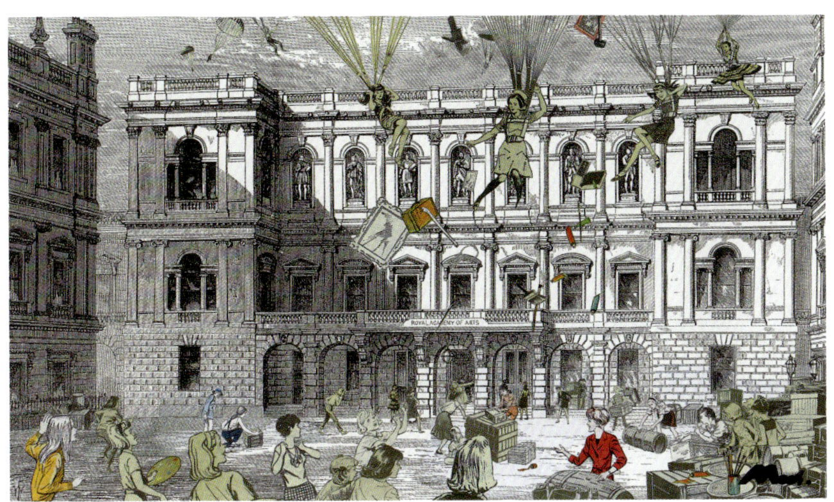

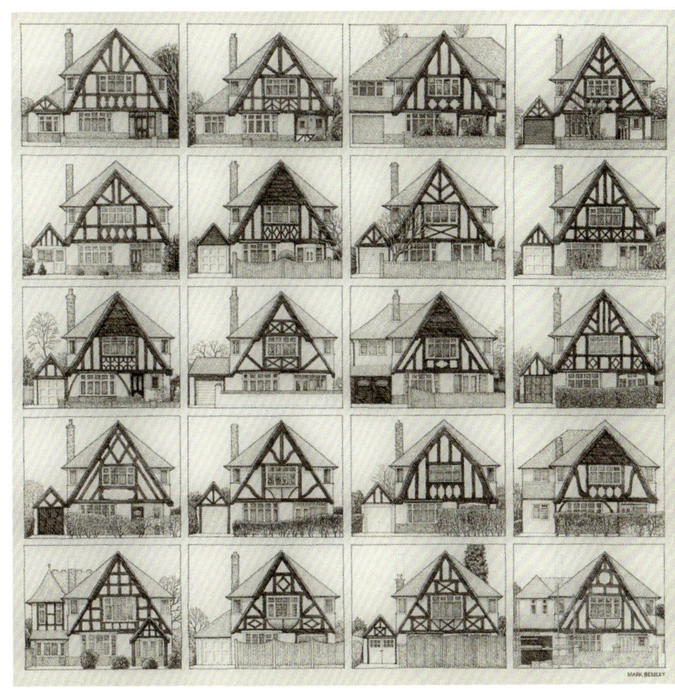

Hugh Hamshaw-Thomas
Swan (Blue)
Archival giclée print
140 × 105 cm

Jane Ward
In the Mountains 2
Archival digital print
70 × 90 cm

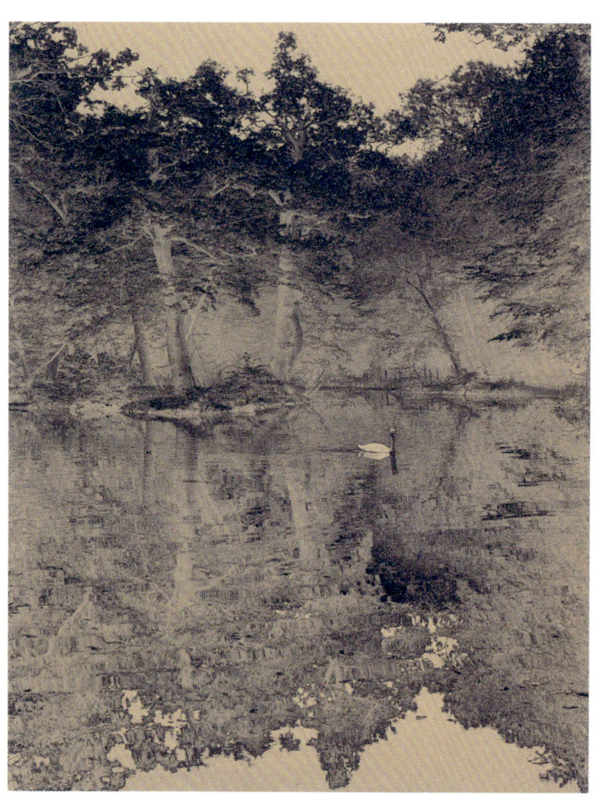

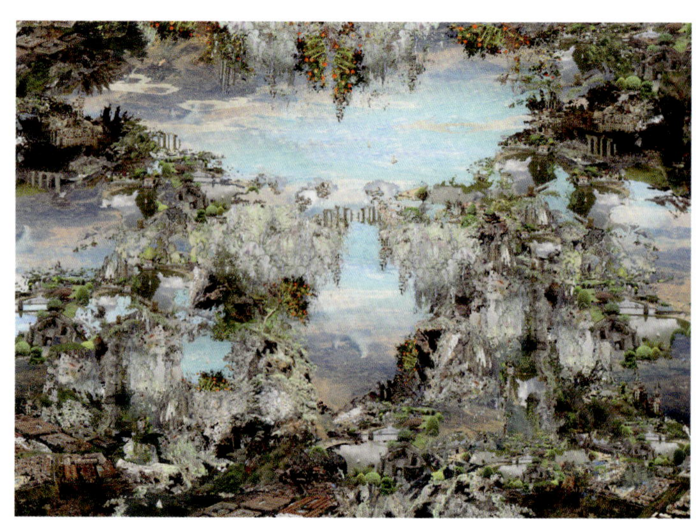

Andrew Carter
Here and There Overlap
Linocut
92 × 184 cm

G. W. Bot
Bent Glyph – Homage to Corot
Linocut
65 × 98 cm

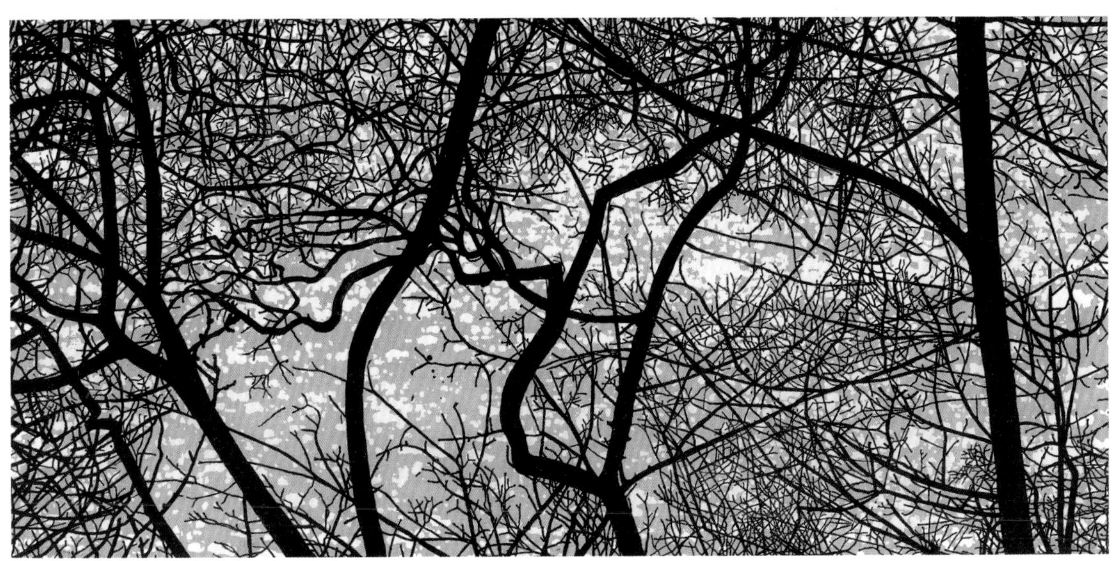

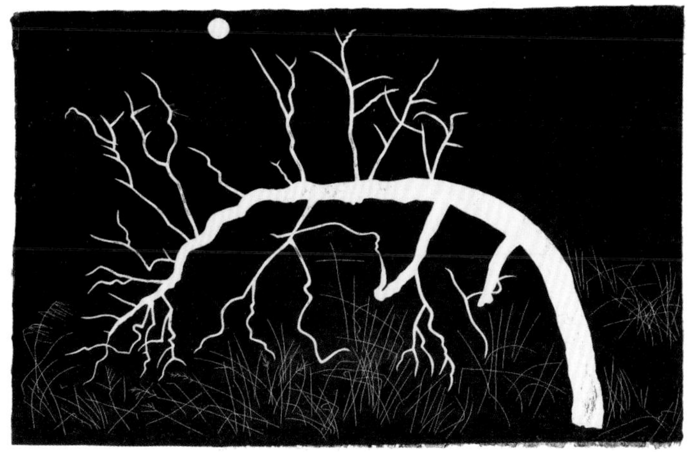

Jane Harris
Orbiters 6
Pencil
56 × 76 cm

Paul Noble
Man with Mirror
Mixed media
67 × 53 cm

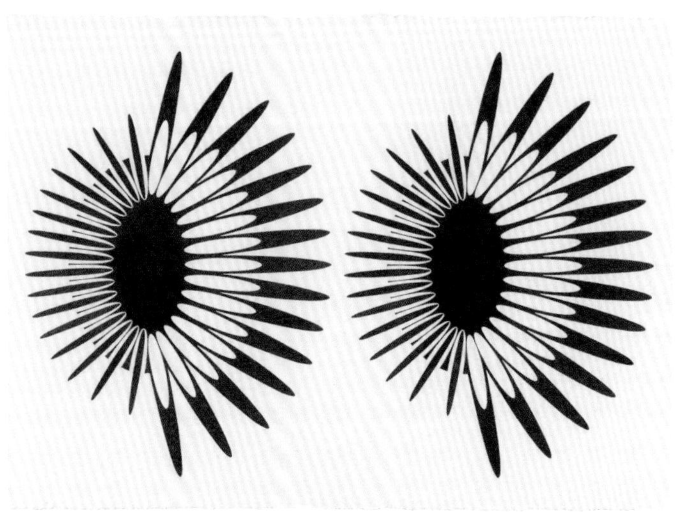

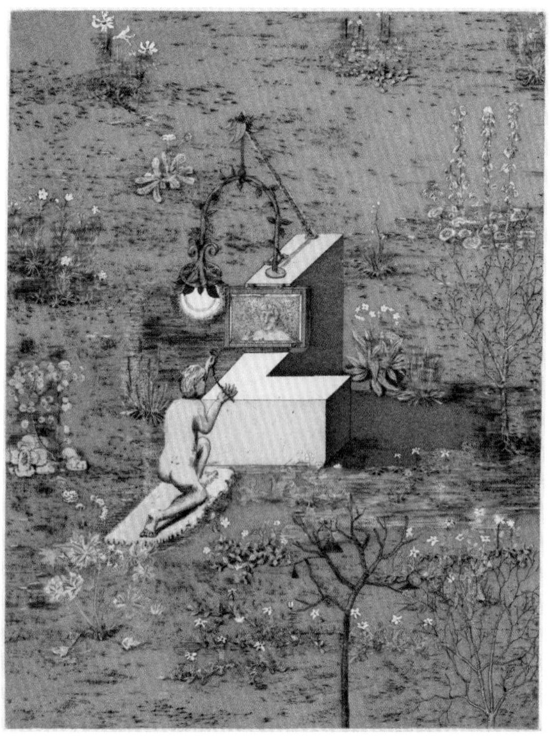

Sioban Piercy
Object Lesson (One)
Inkjet print
43 × 57 cm

Hector Geoffrey Hamilton
Brutally Untitled
Engraving, monoprint and torn paper
21 × 14 cm

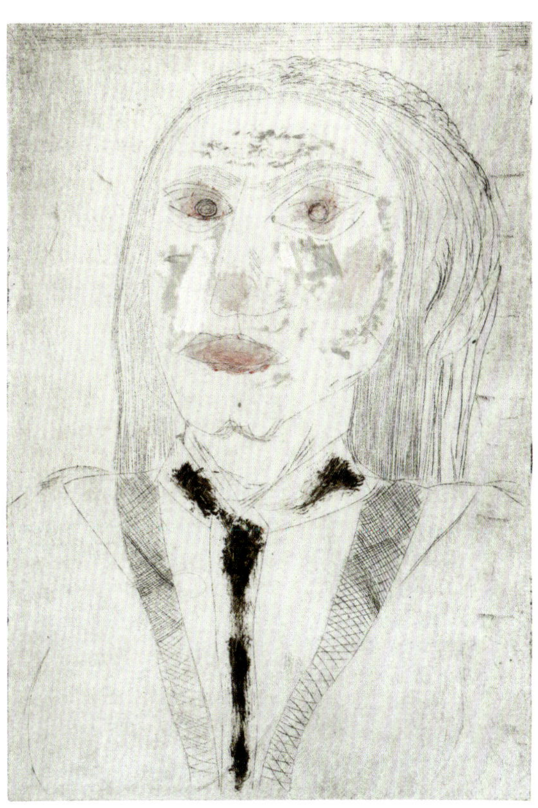

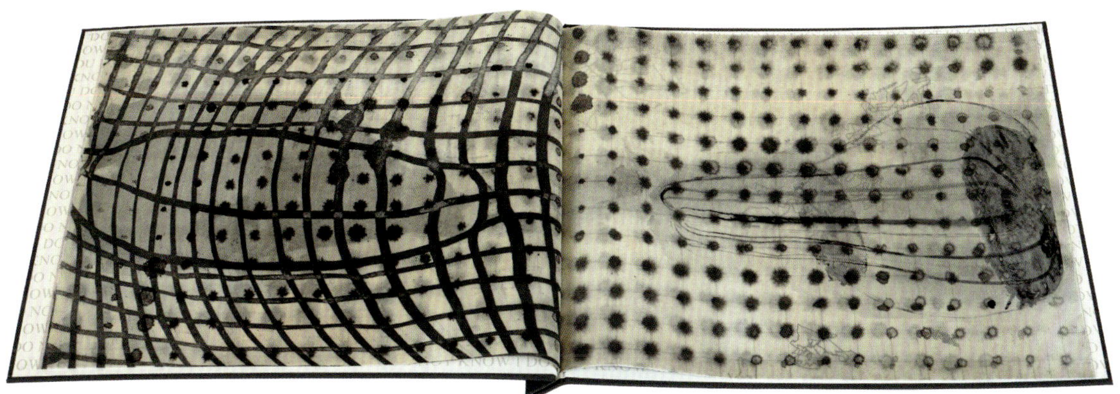

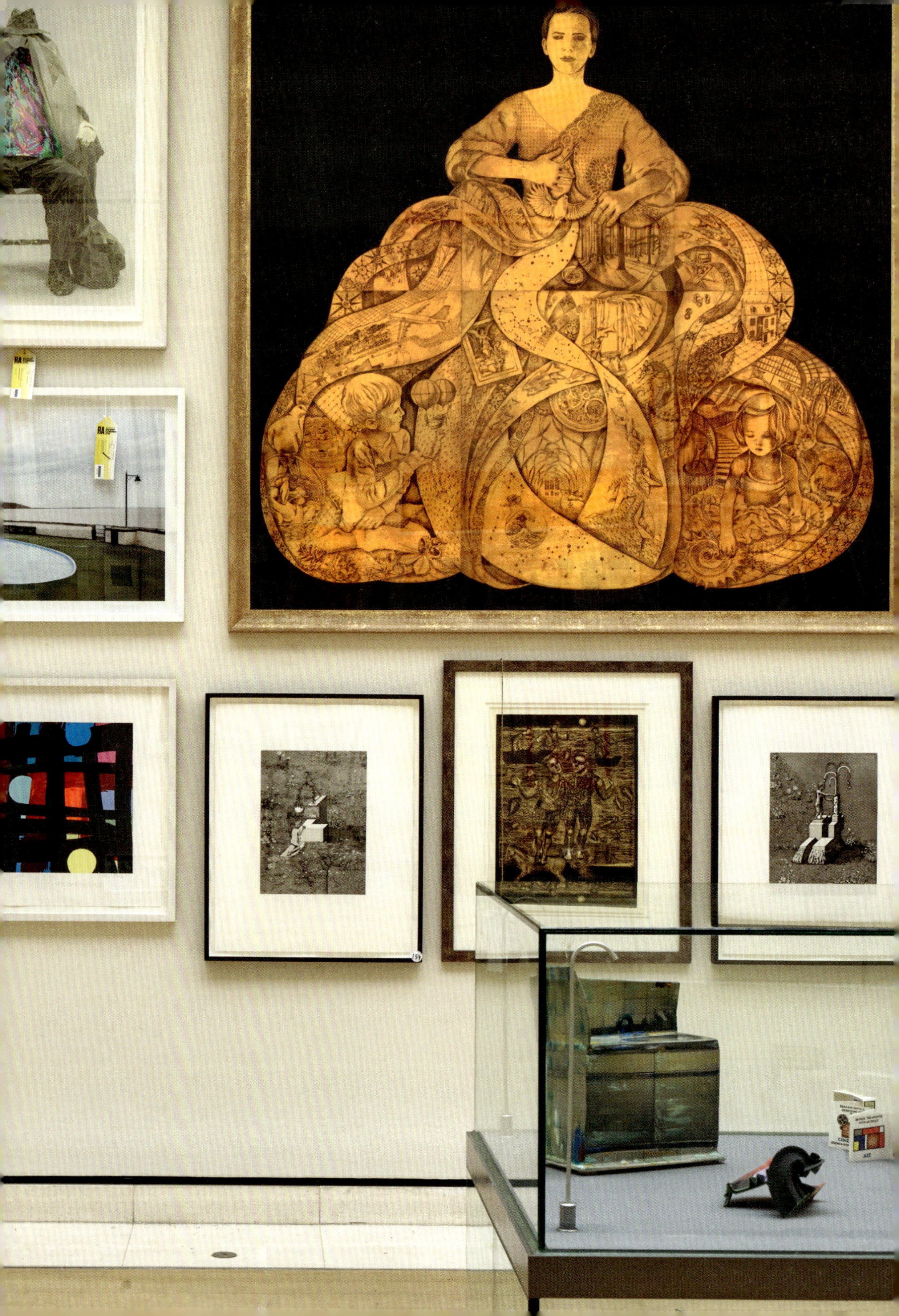

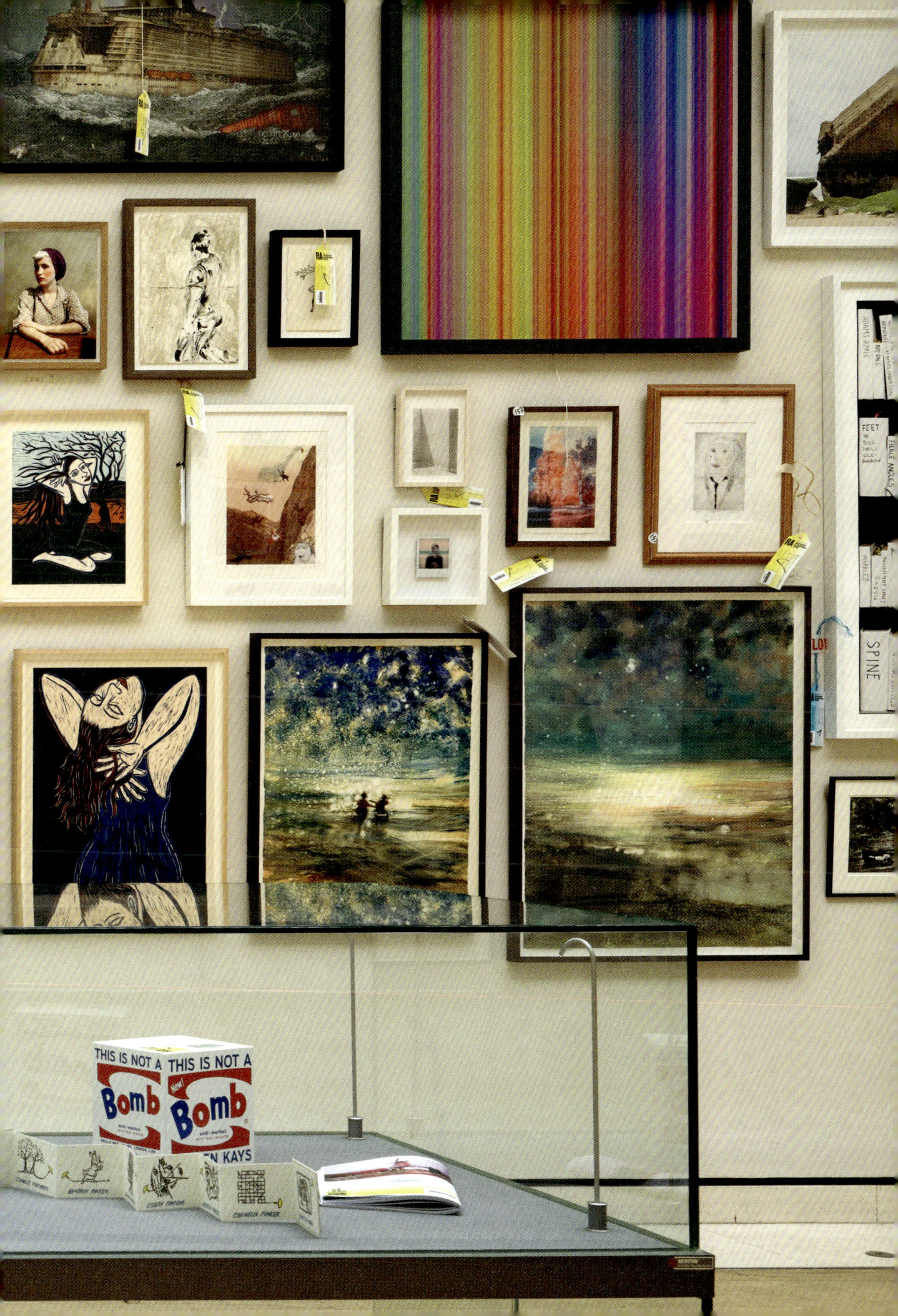
THIS IS NOT A
Bomb
THIS IS NOT A
New!
Bomb
SPINE

Victoria Ahrens
Allí (Over There)
Transfer print
30 × 22 cm

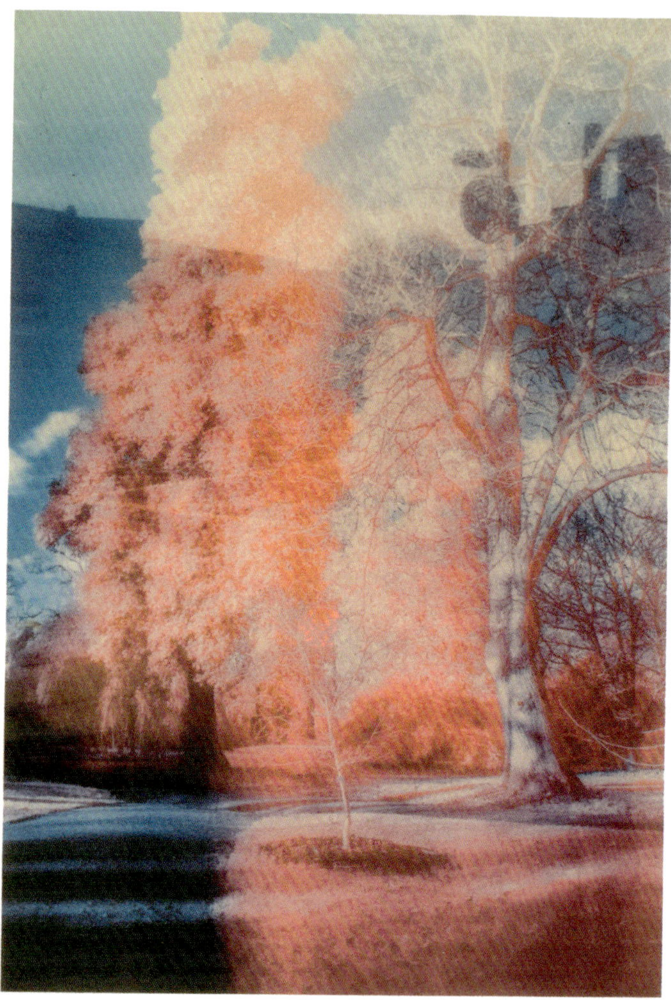

Katherine Jones
No Clear Space
Intaglio and block print
52 × 42 cm

Sadie Tierney
Fjord Draumr
Woodcut
56 × 76 cm

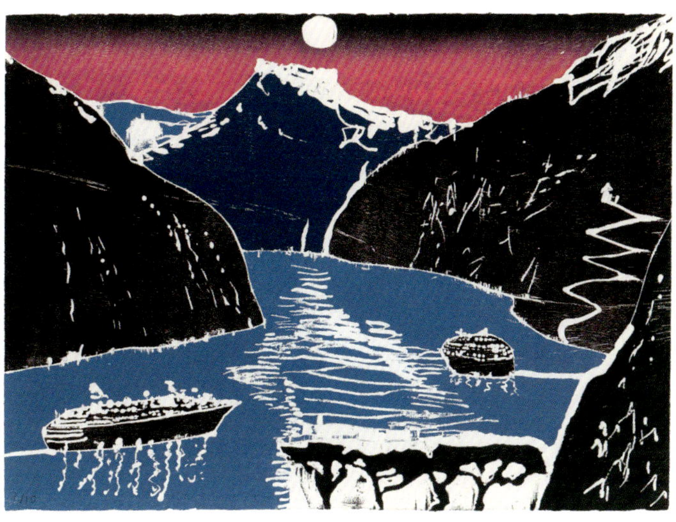

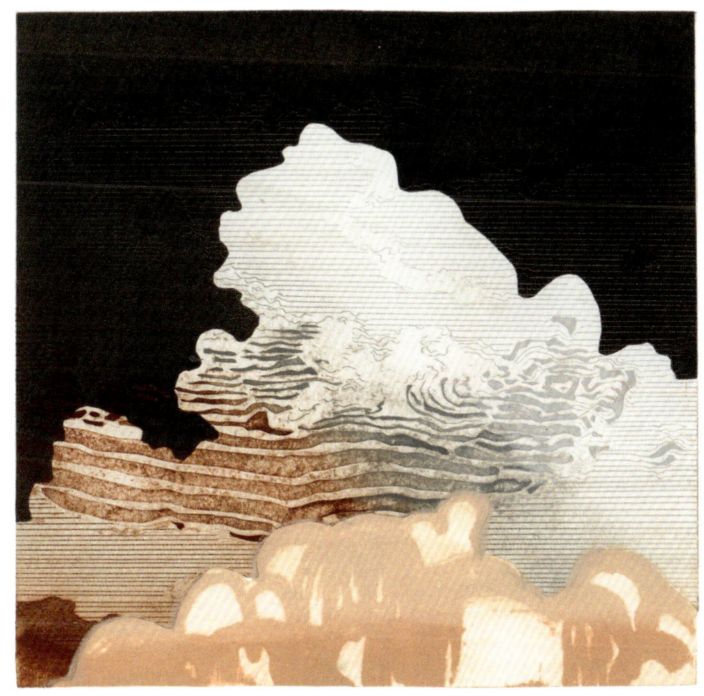

Mat Collishaw
Gasconade, Burnslow
Digital print
45 × 37 cm

Ackroyd & Harvey
Ash to Ash (Study)
Archival digital print
55 × 38 cm

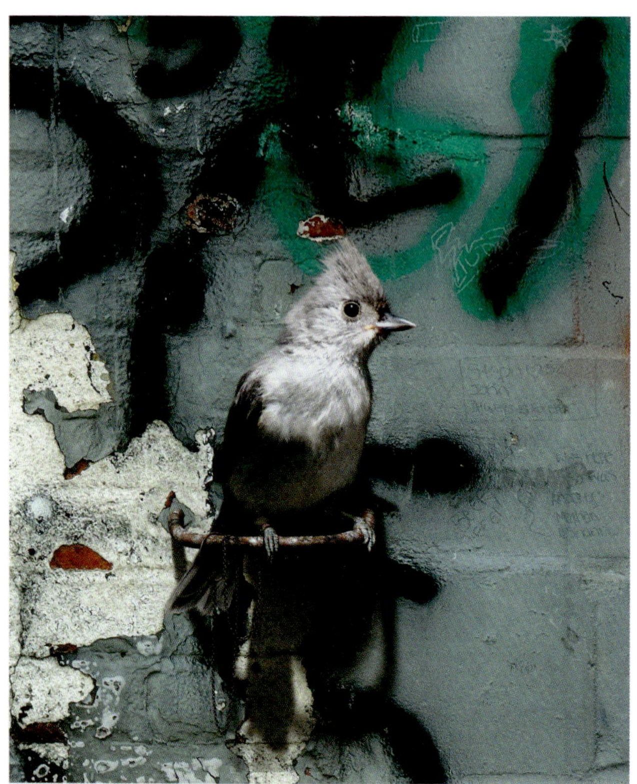

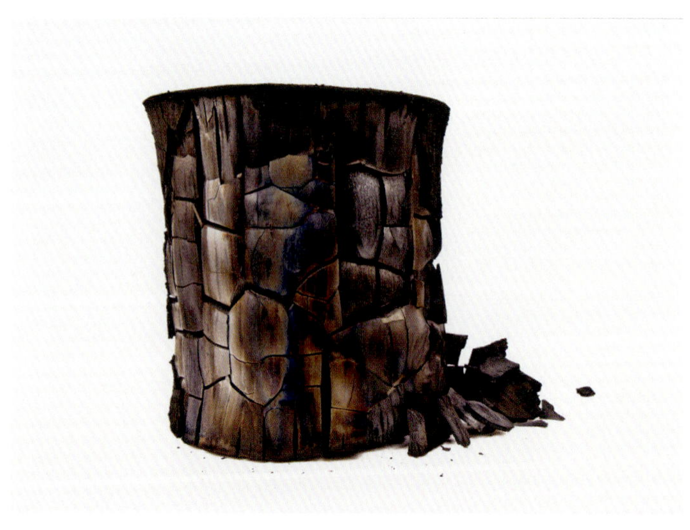

Peter Matthews
Twelve Hours in and with the Atlantic Ocean (England)
Mixed media
56 × 94 cm

Emma Stibbon RA
Lotto, Guns, Ammo
Intaglio
43 × 67 cm

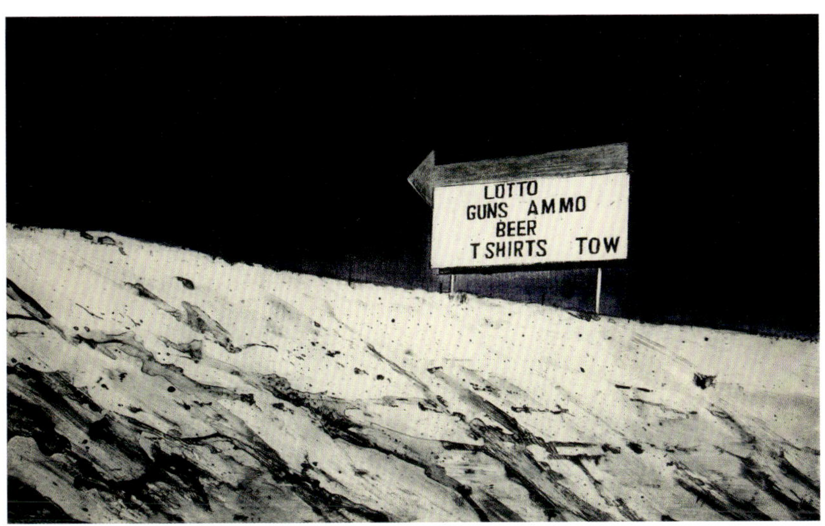

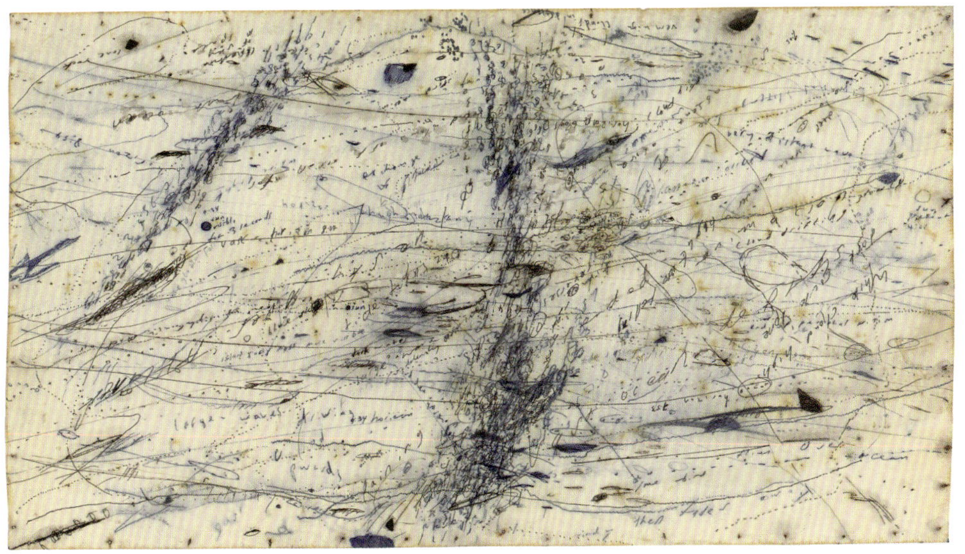

Grayson Perry CBE RA
Selfie with Political Causes
Woodcut
200 × 300 cm

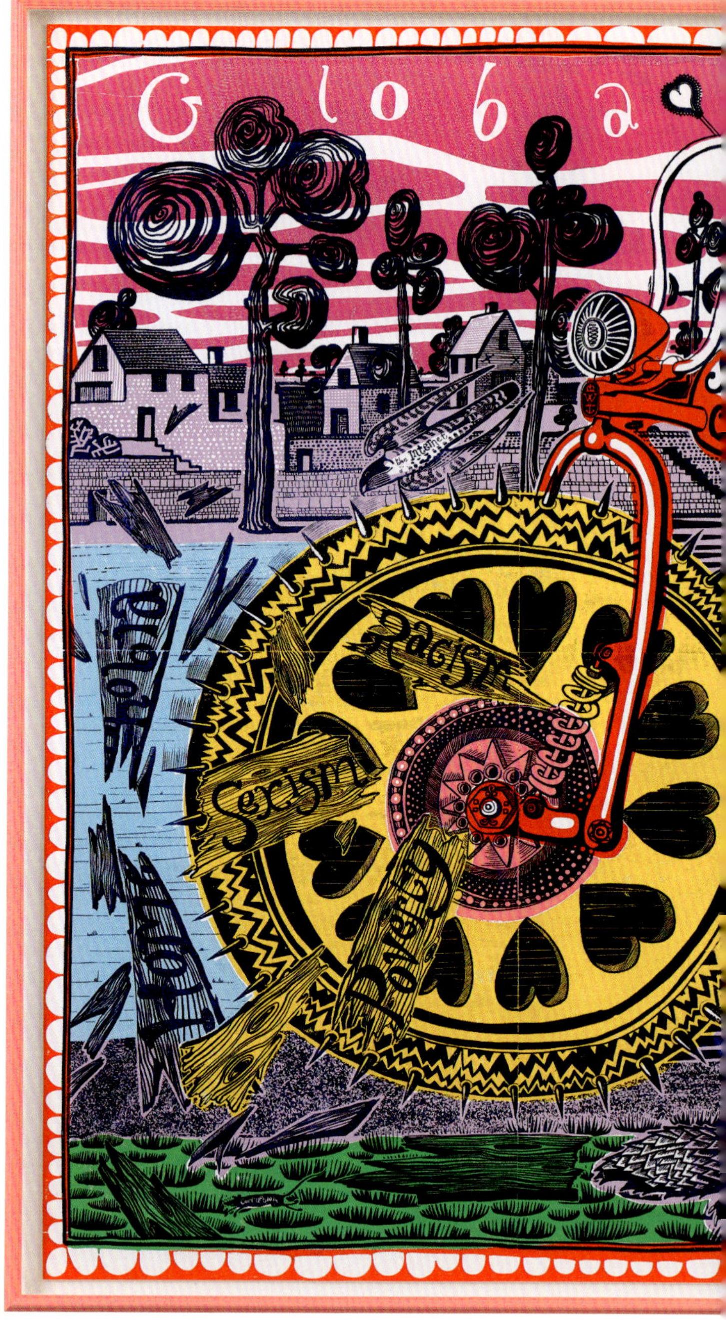

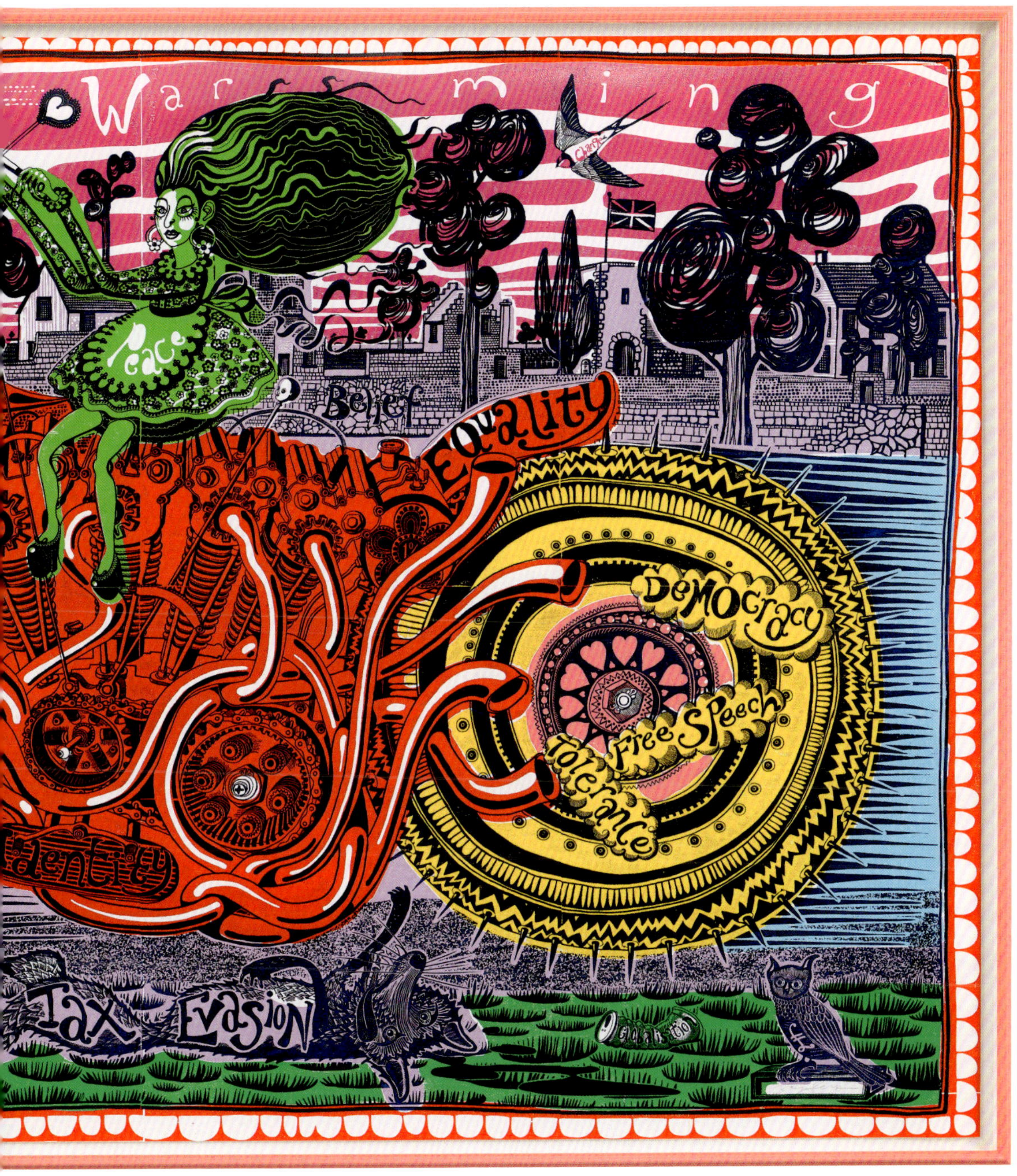
Warming
Peace
Belief
Equality
Democracy
Free Speech
Tolerance
Tax Evasion

Index

Royal Academy of Arts, 2018

Registered charity number 1125383

Supporting the Royal Academy of Arts

The Royal Academy of Arts has a unique position as an independent institution led by eminent artists and architects whose purpose is to promote the creation, enjoyment and appreciation of the visual arts through exhibitions, education and debate. The Royal Academy receives no annual funding via government, and is entirely reliant on self-generated income and charitable support.

You and/or your company can support the Royal Academy of Arts in a number of different ways:

- Donations from individuals, trusts, companies and foundations help support the Academy's internationally renowned exhibition programme, the conservation of the Collections and education projects for schools, families and people with special needs; as well as providing scholarships and bursaries for postgraduate art students in the Royal Academy Schools.
- As a company, you can invest in the Royal Academy through arts sponsorship, corporate membership and corporate entertaining, with specific opportunities that relate to your budgets and marketing or entertaining objectives. In celebration of the RA's 250th anniversary, twenty companies will be able to hold events in our new Benjamin West Lecture Theatre by becoming Corporate Founding Benefactors.
- By including a gift to the Royal Academy in your will, you could help to protect all that we stand for, and ensure we are there as a voice for art and for artists, whatever the future may hold. Your gift can be a sum of money, a specific item or a share of what is left after you have provided for your family and friends. Any gift, regardless of the size, can have an impact, and will allow art lovers to enjoy the Royal Academy in the years to come.

To find out ways in which individuals can support this work, or a specific aspect of it, please contact Karin Grundy, Head of Patrons, on 020 7300 5671.

To explore ways in which companies, trusts and foundations can become involved in the work of the Academy, please contact the Sponsorship and Partnership Team on 020 7300 5706/5813.

For more information on remembering the Academy in your will, please contact Frances Griffiths on 020 7300 5677, or email legacies@royalacademy.org.uk.

Friends of the RA membership

There's never been a better time to become a Friend of the Royal Academy. Join us in our 250th anniversary year to enjoy the very best of the RA's expanded campus and artistic programme, and help us to continue our work as an independent home for art, education and debate.

As a Friend you enjoy free entry to every RA exhibition and much more...

- Free entry to exhibitions for you and a family guest
- Previews to our exhibitions before they open to the public
- Private views and exclusive Friends events
- Priority booking to all RA events, including in our new Lecture Theatre
- All-day access to the Keeper's House
- RA Magazine and a weekly email newsletter
- 10% discount in the RA shop

Why not join today?

- At the Friends desk in Burlington House or in Burlington Gardens
- Online at roy.ac/friends
- By phone 020 7300 8090
- By email friends@royalacademy.org.uk

Head of Summer Exhibition and Curator (Contemporary Projects)
Edith Devaney

Summer Exhibition Organisers
Arzu Altin
Sinta Berry
Catherine Coates
Bronte Earl
Paul Sirr
Victoria Wells

Royal Academy Publications
Florence Dassonville
Alison Hissey
Rosie Hore
Carola Krueger
Peter Sawbridge
Nick Tite

Rights and Reproductions
Susana Vázquez Fernández

Editor's note: All given dimensions are unframed, height before width.

Book design: Adam Brown_01.02
Photography: John Bodkin, DawkinsColour (unless otherwise stated)
Colour reproduction: DawkinsColour
Printed in Wales by Gomer Press

British Library Cataloguing-in-publication Data
A catalogue record for this book is available in the British Library

ISBN 978-1-910350-84-3

Illustrations

Page 2: Grayson Perry RA at the beginning of the hang in Gallery III.
Page 4: Grayson Perry RA in Gallery VII.
Page 6: Detail of *The Fauves Picnic* by Chris Orr RA.
Page 9: Detail of *Map Mundi I* by Renata Adela.
Page 10: Installing *It Would Be Funny if it Wasn't True* by James Joyce in Gallery V.
Pages 12–13: Grayson Perry RA and David Mach RA in Gallery V.
Page 14: (top image) Emma Stibbon RA in the Sackler Galleries; (bottom image) Conrad Shawcross RA in the Lecture Room.
Page 15: (top left image) Piers Gough RA in Gallery VI; (top right image) Allen Jones RA and Tom Phillips RA in the Lecture Room; (bottom left image) Phyllida Barlow RA with Grayson Perry RA in Gallery VII; (bottom right image) Chris Orr RA in the Sackler Galleries.
Page 16: Installing Gallery III. Visible on the wall are *After Tacitus C. 100AD* by Tom Phillips RA, *School Run Mum* by Georgina Wedderburn and *The Stones of Venice San Cristofero* by Joe Tilson RA.
Page 17: Grayson Perry RA, Allen Jones RA and curator Edith Devaney in Gallery III.
Page 18: Emma Stibbon RA selecting works in the Sackler Galleries.
Page 19: Christopher Le Brun PRA with David Mach RA during the hang.
Pages 20–21: Installing *Tools in a Puzzled Vessel (One – Eight)* by Jim Dine Hon RA in the South Sackler Gallery.
Pages 22–23: Works ready to be hung in Gallery III. In the foreground are *The Bristol 2 Litre Engine* by Julie Heaton and *African Barber Shop Sign* by Rose Wylie RA.
Pages 24–25: *Closing Down Sale* by Michael Landy RA in the McAulay Gallery. On the right are visible six of a series of twenty works by David Shrigley.
Page 26: Conrad Shawcross RA positioning *House of Redlines* by Dong-Hwan Ko and *The Greenhouse* by Claas Gutsche in Gallery IX.
Page 27: Humphrey Ocean RA in front of *Memory* by Lisa Milroy RA.
Page 28: David Mach RA with *Rinse Relax Revive* by Camilla Bliss.
Pages 30–31: Installing *Learning to Draw* by Andreas Papanastasiu in Gallery IX. *Square Dance* by Nigel Hall RA is in the foreground.
Pages 34–35: Grayson Perry RA in Gallery III. In the background is *Tree No. 2* by Tony Bevan RA.
Pages 44–45: The installation of the end wall in Gallery III.
Pages 46–47: Gallery III, showing the sculpture *Infinity* by Olga Lomaka.
Pages 62–63: Gallery IV, showing *Wrestling with Angels* by Mark Alexander and *The Gaper* by Annie Whiles.
Pages 64–65: Gallery IV, showing the sculptures *Untitled* by Jo Kitchen and *Welcome Home, Come on In and Close the Door* by Harry Hill. On the wall behind, *Dome of the Rock, Façade* by Ben Johnson sits above *Water* by Gary Hume RA.
Pages 80–81: Gallery V, showing, in the foreground, *Full Metal Jacket* by David Mach RA. On the wall behind is *Red Bear* by Debbie Lawson.
Pages 82–83: Gallery V, showing, in the foreground, *W G Grace* by James Butler RA. On the left wall hangs *Not Fit For Purpose* by Michael Landy RA.
Pages 94–95: Gallery VII, showing, in the foreground, *The Other Grove* by Mike Ballard. Behind, the three floor-based works are, from left to right: *Bronze Tree Stump after Jacob de Gheyn II* by Rob and Nick Carter, *Untitled: Female; 2018* by Phyllida Barlow RA and *The Rock and the Arch* by Eva Rothschild RA.
Page 96: Gallery VII, showing, in the foreground, *Untitled: Female; 2018* by Phyllida Barlow RA. To the left is *Red Holed Column* by David Nash RA.
Pages 152–53: Gallery IX, showing, in the foreground, *Square Dance* by Nigel Hall RA. Behind is visible *Temporary Fence* by Graham Guy-Robinson.
Pages 160–61: The Lecture Room, showing, in the foreground, *Playing God I* and *Playing God II* by Peter Randall-Page RA.
Page 163: The Lecture Room, showing, in the foreground, *Stepping Out* by Allen Jones RA. On the wall behind are *Untitled* by Mimmo Paladino Hon RA and *House 44* by Tal R.
Pages 170–71: The North Sackler Gallery. Visible through the door into the West Sackler Gallery are four woodcuts by Christopher Le Brun PRA.
Pages 172–73: The West Sackler Gallery. On the left is *Crocodile Head* by James Mortimer. On the wall behind are *Tower, Cherry Creek NV* and *Tower, Dayton WA* by Boyd & Evans.
Pages 180–81: The installation of the South Sackler Gallery.

Photographic Acknowledgements

Front cover and page 70: Courtesy of the artist and Thomas Dane Gallery. © Michael Landy
Pages 2, 4, 10, 12–13, 14, 15, 16, 17, 18, 19, 20–21, 22–23, 26, 27, 28, 30–31, 34–35: Phil Sayer
Page 32: Courtesy of the artist and Chris Beetles Gallery
Page 37: (top image) Photo Tim Shaw
Pages 38–39: © the artist. Courtesy of Marlborough Fine Art, London
Page 39: (bottom image) Photo Perou
Page 40: Photo Luís Vasconcelos / Courtesy Unidade Infinita Projectos | Château de Versailles, 2012
Page 41: Photo Nelson Huxley
Page 48: © Anselm Kiefer. Photo © Anselm Kiefer (Georges Poncet). Courtesy of White Cube
Page 49: (top image) © the artist. Courtesy of Ben Brown Fine Arts, London; (bottom image) Photo courtesy of the artist and Harlan & Weaver, Inc. New York, NY. Photo Jason Mandella. © Kiki Smith 2018
Page 50: © the artist. Courtesy of Marlborough Fine Art, London
Page 51: Courtesy of the artist
Pages 52–53: Courtesy of the artist, David Zwirner, London, and Choi&Lager, Cologne / Seoul. Photo Soon-Hak Kwon
Page 55: Photo Thomas Jenkins
Page 56: Courtesy of the artist and Portland Gallery, London
Page 57: © the artist. Courtesy of Marlborough Fine Art, London
Page 58: (top image) Courtesy of the artist
Page 59: Photo Marcus Leith
Page 61: (top image) Courtesy of Chris Beetles Gallery
Page 66: Photo Stephen White
Page 67: Courtesy of the artist
Page 69: Courtesy of the artist
Page 71: © the artist. Courtesy of White Cube. Photo White Cube (Ollie Hammick)
Page 73: (top image) Courtesy of the artist; (bottom image) Photo Jaz Allen-Sutton
Page 74: (top image) Photo Sarah Eyton; (bottom image) © David Tindle RA. Courtesy of The Redfern Gallery
Page 76: Photo Colin Mills
Page 84: Photo Lucid Plane
Page 86: (top image) Courtesy of the artist and Chris Beetles Gallery, London; (bottom image) Courtesy of Ron Arad studio
Page 87: Courtesy of the artist
Page 88: (top image) Courtesy of the artist; (bottom image) Courtesy of Richard Long and Alan Cristea Gallery, London
Page 89: © Ian McKeever. All Rights Reserved, DACS / Artimage. Photo Jonathan Bassett
Page 90: © the artist. Image courtesy of the artist and Hales, London, New York. Photo Jess Littlewood
Page 91: (top image) © Jock McFadyen. Photo Peter Abrahams
Page 92: (top image) © Chantal Joffe. Courtesy of the artist and Victoria Miro, London / Venice; (bottom image) Photo Sumeru Mistry
Page 93: Photo Justin Piperger
Page 97: Courtesy of the artist
Page 98: © Michael Craig-Martin. Photo Mike Bruce. Courtesy of the artist and Gagosian
Page 99: © the artist. Photo courtesy of the artist. Photo Colin Mills
Page 100: (bottom image) © Anne Desmet
Pages 102–03: Photo Roz Woodward
Page 106: Photo Noah da Costa
Page 107: Courtesy of the artist and White Cube. Photo Stephen White, London
Page 108: (top image) Courtesy of Thomas Dane Gallery. © Phillip King
Pages 108–09: Photo Steve White
Page 110: (top image) Courtesy of the artist and Blain | Southern; (bottom image) Courtesy of the artist and Pangolin London
Page 112: (bottom image) Courtesy of the artist and Chris Beetles Gallery, London
Page 114: (top image) Courtesy of AI – DESIGN, s. r. o.; (centre image) Courtesy of Hopkins Architects
Page 115: (top image) © Sauerbruch Hutton
Page 117: (top image) Courtesy of the artist; (bottom image) Photo Jane Frere
Page 118: (top image) Courtesy of Rogers Stirk Harbour + Partners; (bottom image) Courtesy of WilkinsonEyre
Page 119: (top image) Courtesy of Heatherwick Studio and BIG; (bottom image) Courtesy of Cook Robotham Architectural Bureau
Page 120: (bottom image) Courtesy of Cullinan Studio
Page 121: (top image) Brady Mallalieu Architects; (bottom image) Courtesy of Kohn Pedersen Fox Associates PC
Page 123: (bottom image) Courtesy of Foster + Partners
Page 125: Courtesy of the artist
Page 127: (bottom image) © Martin Parr / Magnum Photos / Rocket Gallery
Page 128: (bottom image) Courtesy of the artist
Page 129: (top image) Courtesy of Gavin Turk / Live Stock Market; (bottom image) Courtesy of the artist
Page 131: (top image) © Isaac Julien. Courtesy of the artist and Victoria Miro, London
Pages 132–33: Courtesy of James Prosek and Singer | Wajahat, New York
Page 133: (bottom image) © Tal R. Courtesy of the artist and Victoria Miro, London / Venice
Page 134: (top image) Courtesy of the artist
Page 136: Courtesy of the artist
Page 138: © Conrad Shawcross. Courtesy of the artist and Victoria Miro, London / Venice. Photo Richard Ivey
Page 139: (top image) © Ryan Gander; Courtesy of Lisson Gallery. Photo Jack Hems; (bottom image) Courtesy of the artist
Page 140: Courtesy of October Gallery. Photo © Jonathan Greet, 2018
Page 141: (top image) Photo Jan Haug, The Royal Collection, Norway
Page 142: Courtesy of the artist and Maureen Paley, London
Page 143: (top image) © Jane & Louise Wilson. All Rights Reserved, DACS 2018; (bottom image) POP Magazine, Issue 38, Spring/Summer 2018, London 2018. © Juergen Teller, All Rights Reserved
Page 144: Courtesy of the artist and Blain Southern. Photo Kira Perov
Page 145: (top image) © Marina Abramović. Courtesy of Lisson Gallery. Photo Dave Morgan
Page 146: (top image) © Jennifer Dickson RA, 2018; (bottom image) Courtesy of the artist and Sperone Westwater
Page 147: Courtesy of Jim Dine and Alan Cristea Gallery, London
Page 149: (top image) Courtesy of the artist
Page 154: (top image) Courtesy of the artist
Page 158: (both images) © David Hockney. Photo David Hockney and Jonathan Wilkinson
Page 162: © Ed Ruscha. Courtesy of the artist and Gagosian
Page 164: (top image) Courtesy of the artist; (bottom image) Courtesy of the artist. Photo Stephen White
Page 166: Courtesy of the artist
Page 168: (top image) Courtesy of the artist
Page 169: Courtesy of Cornelia Parker and Alan Cristea Gallery, London
Page 175: (top image) Photo Richard Riddick, thedpc.com
Page 184: (bottom image) © Ackroyd & Harvey
Page 185: (top image) Photo Stuart Bunce
Pages 186–87: Courtesy of the artist and Paragon | Contemporary Editions Ltd